THE SCHIZOPHRENIAS

DIRECTIONS IN PSYCHIATRY
MONOGRAPH SERIES

A NORTON PROFESSIONAL BOOK

DIRECTIONS IN PSYCHIATRY
MONOGRAPH SERIES

THE
SCHIZOPHRENIAS

NUMBER 4

EDITED BY

Frederic Flach, M.D.

W·W· Norton & Company • New York • London

Published simultaneously in Canada by Penguin Books Canada Ltd., 2801 John Street, Markham, Ontario L3R 1B4.

Printed in the United States of America.

First Edition

Library of Congress Cataloging-in-Publication Data

The Schizophrenias.

   (Directions in psychiatry monograph series ; no. 4)
   "A Norton professional book."
   1. Schizophrenia. I. Flach, Frederic F. II. Series.
[DNLM: 1. Schizophrenia. WM 203 S3398]
RC514.S3367   1988   616.89′82   88-15245

ISBN 0-393-70062-3

W. W. Norton & Company, Inc., 500 Fifth Avenue, New York, N.Y. 10110
W. W. Norton & Company Ltd., 37 Great Russell Street, London WC1B 3NU

1 2 3 4 5 6 7 8 9 0

Contributors

Nancy C. Andreasen, M.D.
Professor of Psychiatry, The University of Iowa, Iowa City.
Manfred Bleuler, M.D., M.D.h.c.
Professor, University of Zurich, Switzerland.
Robert Cancro, M.D.
Professor and Chairman, Department of Psychiatry, New York University Medical Center; Director, Nathan S. Klein Institute for Psychiatric Research
Bruce L. Danto, M.D.
Member of the Consultant Staff, Patton State Hospital Forensic Center, Patton, Calif.
John M. Davis, M.D.
Director of Research, Illinois State Psychiatric Institute, Chicago.
Ian R. H. Falloon, M.D.
Consultant Physician (Mental Health), Buckingham Mental Health Service; Senior Clinical Research Fellow, Oxford University, Department of Psychiatry, Oxford, England.
John G. Howells, M.D., F.R.C.Psych., D.F. A.P.A.
Former Director of the Institute of Family Psychiatry, Ipswich, England; Editor, *International Journal of Family Psychiatry*.
Julian Leff, M.D.
Professor of Social and Cultural Psychiatry, Institute of Psychiatry, London, England.
Robert Linden, M.D.
Research Psychiatrist, University of Chicago.
Louis Linn, M.D.
Clinical Professor of Psychiatry Emeritus, Mount Sinai School of Medicine, City University of New York; Consulting Psychiatrist, Mount Sinai Hospital, New York City.
John R. Lion, M.D.
Clinical Professor of Psychiatry, University of Maryland School of Medicine, Baltimore.

Don R. Lipsitt, M.D.
Associate Professor, Harvard Medical School; Chairman, Department of Psychiatry, Mount Auburn Hospital, Cambridge, Mass.

Terry Patterson, Ph.D.
Principal Investigator, Menninger Foundation Research Department, Topeka, Kansas.

Michael L. Perlin, Esq.
Associate Professor of Law, and Director, Federal Litigation Clinic, New York Law School, New York City.

Joan Rubinstein, M.D.
Fellow in Clinical Pharmacology, Pharmaceutical Manufacturers Association.

Robert L. Sadoff, M.D.
Clinical Professor of Psychiatry, University of Pennsylvania School of Medicine; Director, Center for Studies in Social-Legal Psychiatry, University of Pennsylvania.

Herbert E. Spohn, Ph.D.
Director of Research, Menninger Foundation Research Department, Topeka, Kansas.

Contents

Introduction

After many years of psychiatric practice, one of the most disturbing feelings I experience is a special sense of regret. I cannot escape the haunting notion that I could have done so much more for many patients had I known then what I know now. This is particularly true for those who carried the diagnosis of schizophrenia.

Some I remember with special sadness. In particular, I recall one young woman whom I shall give the name Melody. She was then 23 years old, a graduate of a fine college, charming, well-mannered, literate, gentle, and soft-spoken. Her illness was reflected in a vagueness of thought which seemed innocent enough and a curious indifference to the numerous opportunities which her socioeconomic status offered her. When my experienced supervisor explained her diagnosis to me, I found it hard to believe. When, after six months of private hospitalization, she was transferred to a sanatorium for the chronically ill, I felt a terrible sense of personal failure and confusion.

Thirty years ago, we all believed in the immense power of analytically oriented individual psychotherapy. The major tranquilizers, which have come to play such a significant role in the management of schizophrenic patients, were just being introduced. Such obviously relevant measures as family therapy, the creation of social support groups, and training in skills of everyday living were often given low priority as we struggled to analyze away an illness which, it has become clear, cannot be understood without due attention to its biological and environmental dimensions.

We even believed in the reality of the diagnosis itself. Schizophrenia was a frightening term. As medical students, we had routinely been exposed to chronically ill hospitalized patients, listening carefully, making prolific notes as they rambled on about their delusions, shifting uncomfortably in our chairs as our questions went unanswered, our interest met only with silent apathy. To be schizophrenic meant to be hopeless (even though we seldom put that idea into words). The schizophrenic who recovered had probably been misdiagnosed in the first place.

With such an outlook, it is amazing that any of the schizophrenic patients under our care got better. But a significant number did. Looking back, I can now see that my naïveté contributed to my therapeutic enthusiasm. The determination with which I approached their treatment must have conveyed a measure of hope, which, in turn, fueled their own efforts to get well. Then, too, we were aware of the concept of spontaneous remission, a mysterious phenomenon not unlike that which we had been taught to anticipate in other medical conditions, such as various blood dyscrasias; thus, when a schizophrenic improved, we often viewed that change as part of the ebb and flow of the condition itself, assuming, of course, that full recovery was not in the realm of possibility.

Few things have excited me in recent years as much as the studies of Professor Manfred Bleuler, whose father originally coined the term "the schizophrenias." A lifetime of research has led him to conclude that a significant number of patients suffering with schizophrenia *do recover*. They not only become better symptomatically but *lead effective lives*. And of these, an equally significant number *do so without maintenance antipsychotic medication*.

The ongoing search into the nature of the schizophrenias has legitimately focused on biological factors where it clearly belongs. Careful investigations have allowed us to distinguish between schizophrenic patients with so-called negative symptoms and those with positive ones, the former having poor prognoses but also possessing a high incidence of physical changes suggestive of cerebral disease. Other studies have helped clarify the role of genetics in the etiology of the schizophrenias. As Dr. Robert Cancro points out, whatever is transmitted genetically is not the disease itself; rather it is a vulnerability to the development of schizophrenic symptoms, which may or may not be activated by various life experiences.

But, at the same time, the difference between health and invalidism in this group of patients often depends critically on the attitudes of family members and others close to the patient. Hence family therapy has become a routine part of rehabilitation. So too has a commonsense approach to providing the patient with the skills he or she requires to work and meet the demands of everyday life outside institutions.

Although still crippled by the tendency of professionals to bicker over territorial privileges, the effort to treat and rehabilitate schizophrenic patients has increasingly become a group enterprise, involving physicians, psychiatrists, psychologists, nurses, social workers, occupational and recreational therapists, rehabilitation counselors, teachers, and families. Nowhere in the field of mental health is such collaboration more vital to therapeutic success.

Nowhere is the need for innovation in research and treatment approaches more vital too. Resistance to creative solutions has not served the schizo-phrenic patient well. Some years ago, I was chairman of a regional Commit-tee on Biological Therapy of the American Psychiatric Association. The members of that committee were well-intentioned, capable, knowledgeable and concerned professionals. But if I wanted to stimulate intense controver-sy, all I had to do was bring up the subject of nutritional treatment. I had studied calcium metabolism in depression for years and believed that this was a line of investigation that should not be so extensively ignored. To listen to their outburst of criticism (friendly, respectful, but skeptical of my good sense) one would have thought I had questioned the legitimacy of the democratic form of government or some equally cherished value. To be sure, nutritional therapy has never been established in double-blind control stud-ies; a few unimpressively structured investigations have failed to substantiate the claims of nutritional therapy advocates. Nonetheless, I was, and contin-ue to be, surprised by the opposition I encountered to *imaginative possibili-ties* in appraising and managing a condition for which no final explanation or sure treatment approach has been established.

What can we look forward to?

Walking the streets of city on the way to and from work, none of us can avoid the homeless, many of whom have been diagnosed as schizophrenic. They are visible testimony to the emotional, social and economic plight of the mentally ill. Caught between pressures to assure civil liberties for all on the one hand and public and governmental indifference on the other, the schizophrenic has traditionally possessed little political power. This has probably been the result of the stigma which the mentally ill have historical-ly endured. It is certainly a reflection of the disorganization and isolation so characteristic of such patients, a force that has prevented them from mobi-lizing themselves as a bloc to influence votes and demand and receive the attention they deserve. Now, at last, as in the efforts of such groups as the National Alliance for the Mentally Ill, tens of thousands of their fathers, mothers, brothers, sisters, and children are standing up on their behalf and making up for centuries of silence.

Hopefully, in doing so, they will insist on: widespread reconsideration of what schizophrenia really is; well-organized programs of rehabilitation; *tru-ly creative* biological research efforts; greater public understanding and ac-ceptance of those who suffer with the "condition"; and, even with the limit-ed knowledge we now have, serious, intelligent efforts at prevention.

Compiling this volume and writing this introduction have made me won-der whether Melody is still alive somewhere. Maybe I'll accidentally come across her at some hospital where I am lecturing, or see her lying on a bench in Grand Central Station on my way to catch a train. Or, perhaps, Melody was one of the lucky ones, one of Professor Bleuler's group of people who defied prognosis, middle-aged now, living and well somewhere, Arizona maybe, the nightmare of her past no more real than a distant dream, married, working in a local nursery (she had a special touch with plants), looking ahead to a visit from her children and grandchildren.

—Frederic Flach, M.D.

THE SCHIZOPHRENIAS

1

Prognosis of Schizophrenic Psychoses:

A Summary of Personal Research

Manfred Bleuler

EDITOR'S NOTE

Manfred Bleuler has devoted much of his professional life to studying the long-term course of schizophrenia, the psychiatric disorder originally described and formulated by his late father, Eugen Bleuler. His observations have profound clinical significance; they offer us an important, contemporary perspective on a condition once thought to be diagnosed on the basis of its irreversibility. Even Emil Kraepelin, who coined the term dementia praecox, observed later in his career that a certain number of such patients did eventually attain symptom-free states of stability and successful adaptation to life.

Reviewing a number of studies and taking his own experience into consideration, Bleuler concludes that, if one evaluates schizophrenic patients at a point in time five or more years after the onset of the disorder, about 40% have recovered; about 50% remain psychotic, but not severely so; and about 10% are still very seriously psychotic. If one takes a more linear viewpoint, considering the evolution of the patients' lives on a continuum, he notes that about one-third of them never reach a stable condition, but about two-thirds do, and of these two-thirds 25% have recovered for good, 60% show mild psychotic symptoms and 10% are severely ill. In other words, a significant number of schizophrenic patients can go on to make more or less normal life adjustments, those with a phasic course development having a much better chance of doing so than those with insidious, chronic onsets.

Although the general symptoms of schizophrenia characterize recurrences of illness, specific symptoms — such as catatonia, affective components, hallucinations — may vary from one episode to another.

For the individual patient, one can estimate prognosis according to certain key factors. A better outlook seems to exist for schizophrenic patients with an acute onset, prominent mood factors such as elation or depression, stable social prepsychotic personalities, a supportive family network, relatively non-traumatic childhoods and good medical care. Surprisingly, patients with a family history of schizophrenia, particularly if the relatives' illnesses were relatively benign, seem to have a better prognosis than those without such a family history, although this point has not been conclusively established.

Historical Introduction

Research on the long-term course of schizophrenic psychoses has now lasted nearly a century. The need for this research and the appreciation of its importance became evident in the late part of the last century when Emil Kraepelin, in the 1880s, started to define the concept of "dementia praecox." At this time, he became aware that a large number of the psychotics in the clinics he worked in had in common a particular psychopathology which distinguished them from other psychotics, namely the psychopathology which today we usually call schizophrenic. He hoped to succeed in describing a particular disease with specific cause, specific symptomatology and specific outcome. As physician of psychiatric university clinics in Germany, Kraepelin mainly became acquainted with selected severely psychotic patients and he therefore had the impression that, as a rule, the disease progressed to severe deterioration (to dementia). He made a distinction, however, between the "dementia" of these patients and the most common "dementia" of older people (dementia senilis). He therefore introduced the designation of "dementia praecox" in his textbook for psychiatry in 1893. It suggests poor prognosis and early onset. Kraepelin, however, was a very critical and very realistic clinician. He did not overlook clinical facts which were contradictory to his former experience and to his theories. He thus did not overlook the fact that, later in life, he met recovered patients with the former diagnosis of dementia praecox. He acknowledged and published his observations of the recovery of some patients he had considered as suffering from dementia praecox, even though they did not correspond to his first hypotheses and to the denomination "dementia praecox."

At the same time, Eugen Bleuler was impressed by his observations of the recovery of patients with dementia praecox. He had also seen the beginning of the same psychosis in many older patients. He therefore proposed a designation which pointed neither to incurability nor to an early onset. He started to speak of the "group of schizophrenic psychoses" instead of dementia praecox. The expression "schizophrenic" pointed to the most typical psychopathology of these patients, namely to their dissociation, their split personality, their disharmony with regard to thought, feeling, emotion and will.

Both Kraepelin and Bleuler realized that their own research and the research of their pupils into the long-term course of schizophrenic psychoses were not sufficient as yet. They urged younger clinicians to continue their studies in this respect. It took, however, more than half a century before we obtained much more reliable and more detailed knowledge of the long-term course of these psychoses—and of the story of the whole life of schizophrenics. The difficulties as regards this research have been unexpected and tremendous. They start with the definitions of the designation "schizophrenia," of the term "full recovery" and of many other terms. The question also arose: Is schizophrenia a disease which can attack a healthy man like many other diseases, or is it, rather, the result of personal development? (Does one become schizophrenic—or does one's own nature develop into what we call schizophrenia?) It seems simple to work out statistics of a disease which takes possession of anyone, but more problematic to make statistics with regard to life histories. Great and manifold are also such mere statistical difficulties: How can we find an unselected group of patients? As schizophrenic psychoses can last for decades and for the whole of life, the question arises: Who can follow their destinies? As a rule, only a clinician who decides at the beginning of his professional career that he will devote a good part of his life's work to the great task can hope to do so.

I shall start my chapter with its most important part—a summary of our present-day knowledge of course and prognosis. I shall add a survey of the theoretical difficulties which had to be overcome in order to obtain this knowledge. Later I shall discuss the statistical problems of the research. Finally, I shall mention the most important research experience on the basis of present knowledge.

Essential Results of Recent Decades' Research

Various studies indicate the patients with schizophrenic psychoses show the following outcome five or more years after the onset of illness at a given moment in time:

- about 40% of the patients have recovered;
- about half are still psychotic, but not in a severe psychotic condition, many

of them living with their families, others living in open wards of hospitals or open homes;

- about 10% are very severely psychotic and need urgent care in particular wards of psychiatric hospitals.

Considering the fate of schizophrenics constantly over decades (and not only at one given moment), one finds that about one-third of them never reach a somewhat stable condition. Many of them have temporarily recovered or almost recovered but have again and again relapsed into a severe psychosis. Two-thirds of the patients, however, reach a fairly stable condition after some years. It is never quite stable but remains without marked variation. Experience demonstrates that most of these two-thirds of all patients whose condition has been fairly stable for more than five years will remain in a similar condition for the rest of their lives.

What is their clinical condition?

- about 25% of them have recovered for good;
- more than 60% of them show significant but rather mild signs of a psychosis and can be cared for either at home or in open wards;
- about 10% are severely psychotic and need intensive hospital care.

If we consider both groups together (those with fairly stable conditions after some years and those with unstable conditions after an observation of more than 20 years), we can summarize as follows:

- more than 20% have recovered well and their recovery is stable;
- about 33% have either recovered or are mildly psychotic but in danger of temporary acute new psychotic episodes;
- 33% are chronically mildly psychotic;
- 10% are chronically severe psychotics.

Comments regarding the preceding statements are necessary. The percentages given are not exact. They vary somewhat in different statistics depending on the selection of the patients, the decade of this century the research was started, the length of observation, etc. If I mentioned, for instance, that "40%" of the patients have recovered, the result of different statistics might well be between 35% and 45%. If one compares superficially the numbers given in the "point in time" evaluation versus the "continuing" evaluation, one might·be shocked, as they seem to be somewhat contradictory. The reason for the lack of conformity, however, is clear: Under the first, the condition is only considered at a given moment; under the second, the condition is considered as it evolves over years. In the former, the number of recovered patients is 40%; in the latter it is stated as over 20%. However, among the 40% there are many who will have relapsed, whereas in the continuing evaluation only those patients whose recovery is stable are considered recovered (over 20%). Neither is it a contradiction if it is mentioned first that 10% of all patients at a given moment are most severely psychotic, and it is mentioned later that 10% of the two-thirds of patients with stable conditions are severely psychotic. Of the 10% severely ill psychotics at a point in time several will improve or recover later on, while of the 10% severely ill psychotics among the patients with stable condition none or very few will recover.

Having considered the general outcome of schizophrenic psychoses, we have still to consider the whole course over decades. It is very different from patient to patient. More than half of schizophrenic psychoses take a phasic course, whereas only about a third of them develop chronically. The majority of the patients with phasic course reach temporary periods of stable recovery. Of the patients with chronic onset, on the other hand, only few recover again. Chronic conditions can occur after acute onset, but not frequently.

Tables 1 and 2 give a survey of the variability of the course of schizophrenic psychoses. They represent only a rough schematization of the great variability of courses. The number of intermediate courses between those schematized groups in the figures is considerable.

Variations in Psychopathologic Features

How much does the symptomatology of schizophrenic psychoses vary during the course of the psychosis? The general picture usually remains the same insofar as it remains mainly "schizophrenic" and does not go over into an acute or chronic brain syndrome (if schizophrenia is not complicated by quite another disease such as, for instance, arteriosclerosis of the cerebral vessels). Most stable are the paranoid subtypes of schizophrenia, starting slowly in the forties or later. There are also phasic cases in which the acute symptomatology is nearly the same in each phase.

However, the specific schizophrenic symptomatology may also change very much through the years. Catatonic symptomatology in an acute phase, for instance, may disappear in later phases and be replaced by a schizoaffec-

TABLE 1
Types of Course Among Schizophrenic Patients Without Acute Transitory Phases

1. Acute onset followed by lifelong severe chronic psychosis	no longer seen
2. Slow onset followed by lifelong severe chronic psychosis	less than 10%
3. Acute onset followed by lifelong mild chronic psychoses	circa 5%
4. Slow onset followed by lifelong mild chronic psychosis	15–25%

TABLE 2
Types of Course with Acute Transitory Phases

1. After acute phases, lifelong severe chronic psychosis	less than 5%
2. After acute phases, mild chronic psychosis	20–25%
3. After one or several acute phases, recovery (new phases possible)	35–40%

tive syndrome. If schizophrenic psychoses take a chronic course, "positive" symptoms often become rarer and "negative" symptoms are more and more in the foreground. ("Positive" symptoms include dissociation of thoughts, agitation, mood swings, hallucinations, delusional thinking. "Negative" symptomatology is characterized by withdrawal into autism, inactivity, mutism.)

If a schizophrenic psychosis ends in deterioration, it is a different deterioration from that due to diffuse cerebral atrophy. (There are, however, some clinicians who do not entirely agree with this statement; they point out that the inactivity, the lack of initiative, in some chronic schizophrenics cannot be easily distinguished from some sequelae of mild cerebral atrophy.) One of the most characteristic syndromes for deterioration due to diffuse cerebral damage, the amnesic syndrome, is foreign to schizophrenic psychoses.

Suicide and Physical Illness

The schizophrenic psychoses might indirectly – although never directly – threaten the physical health and even threaten life. Suicide among acute and chronic schizophrenics is somewhat more frequent than among the average population. Furthermore, some schizophrenics refuse food and are, if not cared for, threatened by starvation. Highly excited schizophrenics in acute delirious condition are threatened by desiccation and cardiovascular exhaustion or by pneumonia resulting from swallowing the wrong way, stressed respiration and lack of expectoration. The psychotic behavior is frequently a dangerous difficulty in the diagnosis and therapy of physical complications of the psychosis. In other cases, the general neglect of personal hygiene may threaten the physical health; many schizophrenics have periods, for instance, during which they lie motionless in soiled beds and have decubitus if they are not well cared for.

All these physical complications of schizophrenic psychoses are due to the psychotic behavior and are not a symptom of the psychotic process in itself. Schizophrenics who do not threaten their physical health by morbid behavior and who are well cared for frequently become very old and do not die on an average earlier than healthy people, nor do they develop, even in the final stages, neurological, endocrinological or other physical disabilities more frequently than other people.

Prognosis for the Individual Patient

I shall now enumerate the factors known to influence the prognosis; first the most important ones and, at the end of the list, those of least significance.

1. Acute onset is a good prognostic sign.
2. Symptomatology: agitation, exaltation, elated or depressed mood, great dissociation versus hallucinations and delusional thinking or catatonic symptoms in calm, seemingly indifferent patients. Most decisive for the prognosis is the question of whether the psychosis has begun suddenly with agitation, exaltation, an elated or depressed mood or, on the contrary, if the psychosis had a slow, insidious onset and schizophrenic symptoms (mostly negative symptoms) develop in a calm and hardly moved patient. On an average, the prognosis is so greatly different in the two cases that one is tempted to think that benign acute psychoses with positive symptomatology are a different disease from malignant chronic psychoses with mostly negative symptomatology. Langfeldt and other authors have tried to make this distinction. There are, however, many clinical observations which do not allow a strict separation of two kinds of schizophrenic psychoses, inasmuch as (a) there are many intermediate cases; (b) it frequently happens that in the course of many years a psychosis changes its type; (c) among the schizophrenic family members of each type are also schizophrenic family members of the other type.
3. Stable, social prepsychotic personality versus difficult personality with rare and difficult contacts with others. The kind of prepsychotic personality has a moderate but statistically significant influence on the prognosis, which, however, is not as decisive as the acute or chronic onset. The prognosis is better for healthy than for reclusive and difficult characters.
4. Appropriate treatment versus neglect of care and treatment. Experience has clearly shown that poor hospital care with isolation of the patient favors chronicity and bad outcome. The improvement in the organization of clinical therapeutic communities in psychotherapy and in pharmacotherapy has not increased as yet the percentage of full recoveries to a statistically significant degree, but it has improved the psychotic condition in most patients.
5. Favorable attitude of the family members and other people to the patient versus rejection or unfavorable attitudes. As Wing has statistically

demonstrated and as is evident from clinical experience, the attitude of relatives to the patient plays a prognostic role. It is favorable if they accept the patient, have warm and steady feelings for him and want to help him but are not overcritical of him and not overanxious. It is very unfavorable if they are too anxious about him, if they react with exaggerated emotions to his behavior and try to overprotect him or, on the contrary, if they exclude him from the family and become indifferent to him.

6. Healthy childhood versus childhood in a broken home and under other terrible conditions. A broken home in the childhood of the patient or disastrous childhood conditions of any kind have a statistically significant influence on the development of schizoid prepsychotic personality traits and have an unfavorable influence on the prognosis.

7. The occurrence of other schizophrenic psychoses in the family versus lack of schizophrenic psychoses in the family. In the old days it was believed that the occurrence of other psychoses in the family was a bad prognostic sign. This belief had its origin in the degeneration hypothesis of the early 19th century; according to this hypothesis, the psychoses we today call schizophrenias were one of the consequences of progressive degeneration from one generation to the other. Today it has become clear that the occurrence of schizophrenic psychoses among the relatives of a schizophrenic patient does not impair the prognosis. Quite the contrary, it seems probable that it improves it. (In particular it improves the prognosis if the schizophrenic psychosis of the relative is benign.) Such a correlation, however, is not statistically proven.

In spite of all these factors which have an influence on prognosis, however, the individual prognosis is never certain; it always remains a guess. We must be modest with regard to our possibility to make long-term prognoses for a schizophrenic patient. Frequently course and outcome do not correspond to the prognostic rules. Unexpected ameliorations and recoveries do occur. We should never think and maintain that there is absolutely no hope of improvement. This could prove to be wrong, and it diminishes therapeutic enthusiasm and hurts the feelings of the relatives.

Additional Reading

Bland RC, Parker JH: Prognosis in schizophrenia. *Arch. Gen. Psychiatry* 33:949, 1976.

Bleuler, E: Dementia praecox oder Gruppe der Schizophrenien. In Aschaffenburg, G (Ed.): *Handbuch der Psychiatrie*, Deuticke, Leipzig, 1911.

Bleuler E: Die Prognose der Dementia praecox (Schizophreniegruppe). *Allg. Z. Psychiat.* 65:436, 1908.

Bleuler M: *Krankheitsverlauf, Persönlichkeit und Verwandschaft Schizophrener und ihre gegenseitigen Beziehugen,* Thieme, Leipzig, 1941.

Bleuler M: *Die schizophrenen Geistesstörungen im Lichte langjähriger Kranken- und Familien-Geschichten,* Thieme, Stuttgart, 1972.

Bleuler M: Das Wesen der Schizophrenieremission nach Schockbehandlung. *Z. gesamte Neurol. Psychiatr.* 183:553. 1941.

Bleuler M, Huber G, Gross G, Schuettler R: Der langfristige Verlauf schizophrener Psychosen. Gemeinsame Ergebnisse zweier Untersuchungen. *Nervenarzt.* 47:477, 1976.

Ciompi L: Catamnestic long-term studies on the course of life of schizophrenics. *Schizophrenia Bull.* 6:606, 1980.

Ciompi L: Review of follow-up studies on long-term evolution and aging in schizophrenia. Paper presented at the International Conference on Schizophrenia and Aging, NIMH, Washington, DC, June 7–9, 1982.

Ciompi L, Mueller C: *Lebensweg und Alter der Schizophrenen. Eine katamnestische Langzeitstudie bis ins Senium.* Springer, Berlin, Heidelberg, New York, 1976.

Engelhardt DM, Rosen B, Feldman J, Engelhardt JZ, Cohen P: A 15-year follow-up of 646 schizophrenic outpatients. *Schizophrenia Bull.* 8:493, 1982.

Ey H: *Manuel de Psychiatrie,* 4th Ed., Masson, Paris, 1974.

Gross G, Huber G, Schuettler R: Verlaufsuntersuchungen bei Schizophrenen. In *Verlauf und Ausgang Schizophrener Erkrankungen,* 2. Weissenauer Schizophrenie Symposion, Schattauer Verlag, Stuttgart, New York, 1973, p. 101.

Huber G: *Psychiatrie, Systematischer Lehrtext für Studenten und Aerzte,* Schattauer, Stuttgart, New York, 1974.

Huber G: Zum Stand der Verlaufsforschung bei den Schizophrenen (Schlussbemerkungen), 2. Weissenauer Schizophrenie Symposion, Schattauer Verlag, Stuttgart, New York, 1973, p. 259.

Huber G, Gross G, Schuettler R: Course and long-term prognosis of schizophrenic illness. In *Biological Mechanisms of Schizophrenia and Schizophrenia-like Psychoses,* Mitsuda and Fukuda, Tokyo, 1974.

Kraepelin E: *Einführung in die psychiatrische Klinik,* 3rd Ed., Barth, Leipzig, 1916.

Kraepelin E: *Psychiatrie,* 8th Ed., Barth, Leipzig. 1910.

Langfeldt, G., La Portée d'une Dichotomie du Groupe des Schizophrénies Evolution Psychiatrique 1966, No. 2, p. 321.

Marinow A: Klinisch-statistische und katamknestische Untersuchungen an chronisch Schizophrenen. *Arch. Psychiatr. Nervenkr.* 218:115, 1974.

Marinow A: Ueber Verlauf, Ausgang und Prognose bei Schizophrenien, 4. Weissenauer Schizophrenie Symposium, Schattauer, Stuttgart, New York, 1981.

Mueller, C: *Psychische Erkrankungen,* Huber, Bern, Stuttgart, Vienna, 1981.

Mueller C: Schizophrenia in advanced age. *Br. J. Psychiatry* 118:347, 1971.

Mueller C: *Psychische Erkrankungen,* Huber, Bern, Stuttgart, Wien, 1981.

Mueller, C: *Ueber das senium Schizophrener,* Karger, Basel, 1959.

Stephens JH: Long-term prognosis and follow-up in schizophrenia. *Schizophrenia Bull.* 4:25, 1978.

Sternberg E: Verlaufsgesetzlichkeiten der Schizophrenie im Lichte von Langzeituntersuchung en bis zum Senium, 4. Weissenauer Schizophrenie Symposion, Schattauer, Stuttgart, New York, 1981.

Stroemgren E: Verlauf der Schizophrenien, 2. Weissenauer Schizophrenie Symposion, Schattauer, Stuttgart, New York, 1973.

Wing, J K: Eine praktische Grundlage für die Sozialtherapie bei Schizophrenie. In Huber, G (Ed.): *Therapie, Rehabilitation und & Prävention schizophrener Erkrankungen*, Schattauer Verlag, Stuttgart, 1976.

2

The Course, Outcome, and Prognosis of Schizophrenic Psychoses

Manfred Bleuler

EDITOR'S NOTE

In this chapter, Professor Bleuler explores the background for his observations on the course of schizophrenic illnesses, noting, to begin with, that there is no generally acknowledged opinion on the genesis and nature of the condition. He feels that this diagnosis should be reserved for patients who have experienced a true psychosis; he outlines the essential ingredients in the concept of psychosis. Some forms of psychosis are schizophrenic, so determined by meeting certain criteria.

In his experience and that of others the prognosis for schizophrenia has improved during this century; he attributes this to better care and treatment. He states, however, that "none of the patients included in my statistics who recovered permanently has long been under the influence of neuroleptic drugs." While not denying the value of such drugs in acute episodes of illness or in reducing the risk of relapse in improved patients with phasic courses, he feels that it has not been proved that stable, long-standing, full recoveries are due to them.

He concludes with a personal statement about his own interest in the problem of schizophrenia — over a lifetime — and compares his own findings with those of others who, following somewhat different methodologies, have arrived at similar conclusions.

The Meaning of the Term Schizophrenia

Every statement on the course, outcome and prognosis of schizophrenic
psychoses depends on the question: What do we mean by the term schizophrenia? Research work in this respect cannot be started before the question
has been answered, and it is not too easy to find the answer.

It would be easy, however, if we could say what schizophrenia is in the
same way we can say that general paresis is the consequence of cerebral
damage by a cerebral infection with *Treponema pallidum*, or that Down's
syndrome is the consequence of trisomy 21. We are, however, confronted
with a hard fact — no generally acknowledged opinion on the genesis and
nature of schizophrenic psychoses exists. There is no definite answer to the
important question, "What is schizophrenia?" There are many personal
opinions — and I have my own — but none of these opinions is generally
acknowledged and sufficiently certain. A tremendous amount of research
work has been done with the aim of finding a biological "marker" of schizophrenic psychoses or of the disposition to them, up to now without result.
Many and varying peculiarities have been found in certain schizophrenics,
but none which characterizes all schizophrenics and which is not also found
in many other patients or in healthy persons. A couple of years ago it was
hoped that the action of neuroleptics on the neurotransmitters of particular
synapses of nerve cells would become the clue to the discovery of a particular neuroendocrine marker for schizophrenia. The hope has remained unful-
filled. As the question "What is schizophrenia?" cannot be answered as yet,
we have to ask a more modest question: What do we designate with this
expression? Our problem becomes much easier as soon as we have, in all
modesty, introduced this question.

An initial statement is important. The designation schizophrenia is reserved for a real psychosis with a particular symptomatology. No morbid
psychological condition should be labeled as schizophrenic if it has never
been characterized as a real psychosis. The expression "psychosis" only
became common after the year 1859, but in all cultures and in all times we
have had knowledge of expressions for the same conception. Some of the
outstanding signs of a psychosis are:

- Psychotics speak the same language as before the beginning of their ail-
  ments, but they speak in a way in which they are no longer or only partially
  understood; their thought impresses one as confused, dissociated.
- They may not distinguish between perceptions and imaginary ideas; they
  have hallucinations.
- They have delusional ideas which seem absurd to the healthy.
- Their moods and emotions are foreign and enigmatic to the healthy; empa-
  thy, the power of sharing feelings with them, is extremely difficult.
- What they do and what they neglect has become inconceivable and mysteri-

ous to others. They may do what hurts and threatens themselves and those they have loved; they can do what threatens their existence or even their lives, and they may neglect what is urgent for their existence and even their lives.

- They frequently give the definite impression that they do not know who they are, and frequently they may complain of their ignorance with regard to who they are or in what time or what surroundings they live.
- To those who knew them before the outbreak of the psychoses they seem entirely altered, not the same person as before; frequently they seem this way to themselves as well.

Research on the course of schizophrenic psychoses must restrict the diagnosis to patients who are or have once been in a really psychotic condition, marked by several of the signs mentioned. Mental disorders which could also be called pseudo-neurosis, severe schizoid psychopathy, borderline cases, for instance, are not truly schizophrenic psychoses. If one does not constantly bear in mind that one means a psychosis when one diagnoses schizophrenia, statistical work on the course of schizophrenia becomes confused and worthless. All the researchers whose work is considered in this article consider schizophrenia as a psychosis.

What psychoses, then, do we call schizophrenic psychoses? It is neither possible nor necessary to describe the essentials of the psychopathology we describe as schizophrenic in this article. We are, however, internationally very close to a mutual opinion in this respect. It was already formulated by Emil Kraepelin and by Eugen Bleuler; it corresponds widely to the definitions of Kurt Schneider and to the latest edition of the ICD key. It cannot be denied that all these characterizations of a schizophrenic psychosis do not always delimit them sharply from other psychoses, for instance from manic-depressive psychoses. In accordance with these characterizations, however, uncertain diagnoses are very rare compared with the certain ones.

The Role of Irreversibility as Part of Diagnosis

Since the beginning of this century it has been proposed from time to time that only psychoses that have a chronic course towards deterioration and never recover should be considered as schizophrenic or as dementia praecox. If one accepts such a definition, research on outcome becomes senseless; in this case, the outcome is decisive for the diagnosis.

What arguments are presented in favor of the inclusion of hopelessness as regards recovery in the definition of dementia praecox and schizophrenic psychoses?

Some authors refer to Kraepelin as the authority. This argument, however, is erroneous. As I have mentioned before, Kraepelin's designation "dementia" suggests incurability, but Kraepelin himself reported on patients he diagnosed as suffering from dementia praecox and who recovered.

The other unacceptable argument is the consequence of the belief that dementia praecox or a schizophrenic psychosis must be in accordance with the old conception of a "morbid entity." The conception stems originally from the ingenious ideas of Linné on the *systema naturae* developed in the middle of the 18th century; it suggested that the tremendous variety of morbid conditions consisted of a sum of disease entities, just as the variety of plants and animals can be subdivided into clearly defined species. The tendency to discover "disease entities" in medicine has proved to be very useful in many respects with regard to psychiatry and particularly useful with respect to infections by a definite microbe or to hereditary diseases due to a definite gene in a chromosome. If one wishes to describe disease entities with definite symptomatology, definite cause and definitive course and outcome, it is very disappointing that, under the same name of schizophrenic psychoses or dementia praecox, benign and malign psychoses should both be included. To acknowledge that psychoses with the same or similar psychopathology may be benign or malign is in sharp contrast with the endeavor to achieve a clear nosological system.

What speaks against the definition of dementia praecox or schizophrenic psychosis as an incurable psychosis? To begin with, we do not have the possibility of making a certain prognosis when we are confronted with a patient with schizophrenic symptomatology. As I mentioned before, there are circumstances which allow the statement that benign or malign outcome is probable, but this is never certain. In many cases we do not know for years if a patient with the schizophrenic symptomatology will finally recover or never recover. Late, unexpected improvements are frequent; late recoveries do occur. It would be impossible to make a diagnosis in a case with schizophrenic psychopathology if we were forced to include in this term a malign prognosis.

Furthermore, cause and outcome of schizophrenic psychoses are certainly dependent, to a high degree, on living conditions, on the kind of care and therapy and on many other circumstances independent of the real disease process. If a schizophrenic never recovers, we are never certain if the malign course is due to the disease process or to poor conditions of care and treatment. In other words, we do not know if a deteriorated schizophrenic has suffered from an incurable dementia praecox or from a curable schizophrenic psychosis which has not been properly treated.

Finally, the schizophrenic psychoses of near relatives of schizophrenics frequently take a different course and frequently have a difficult outcome.

In our times we hear of another confusing objection regarding statistics on schizophrenia: "You can make statistics on diseases but not on the attitude of a man who has himself chosen the way he wants to live or into which he has been pushed by society." There is a modest and simple answer to this objection. Schizophrenia might be a disease or not; in either case, it is important and interesting to follow the evolution of the "psychological syndrome" called schizophrenia.

What Is Meant by Recovery?

The main facts which allow us to speak of a recovery are: (a) the patient can be fully employed in gainful work as far as outer circumstances allow; (b) he can reassume his former role in family and society as far as outer circumstances allow; (c) psychiatric examination does not demonstrate the existence of psychotic symptoms; and (d) the relatives and other persons who know him no longer consider him as psychotic.

However, in the definition of recovery we must not include personal traits which are normal consequences of having gone through the crisis of a psychotic. Even if he is fully recovered, a recovered psychotic is not able to judge everything he did during the psychosis in the same way as the objective observer. The normal need for ego defense forbids him to acknowledge all his strange behavior in the psychosis. He is inclined, for instance, to confuse cause and consequence. He may think that he became agitated on account of the hospitalization, whereas he was hospitalized on account of the agitation. As a healthy man after a long period of terrible physical sickness may become more withdrawn or less active than before, the recovered psychotic is not always exactly the same person as before.

Statistical Problems

A central issue is how we can find a random selection of patients to be studied. As a rule, patients are studied who have been hospitalized. Is the course of their psychoses very different from the course of schizophrenic psychoses of patients who have never been hospitalized? I have studied the question during research on the mental health of relatives of schizophrenics and of surgical and tuberculous patients, among whom were schizophrenics who had never been hospitalized. I also saw patients who were never hospitalized during the course of my general medical practice. From this experience I can conclude that in Switzerland (whence my patients mostly come) the number of schizophrenics among the whole population who are not or not as yet hospitalized is very small in comparison with the patients to whom our attention is drawn on account of hospitalization. Furthermore, the difference in the course of the psychosis is not as marked as one might expect. For these reasons the approximate percentages as regards course and outcome I have mentioned are not only representative for hospitalized schizophrenics but roughly for all schizophrenics.

Changes in Schizophrenic Prognosis in Recent Decades

My experience (and the experience of many other authors) clearly shows that the prognosis of schizophrenics in countries of Western culture has changed during this century. The main changes concern the condition of the chronic patients; it has become much better since the middle of the century than it was in the 1920s and 1930s. Very hopeful is the fact that schizophrenic psychoses with acute onset followed by lasting severe deterioration have almost disappeared. (They played a great role when Kraepelin formed the concept of dementia praecox.) On the other hand, the following two statements show how serious therapeutic needs still are: The percentage of long-standing full recoveries has not increased. The percentage of psychoses with chronic onset leading to lifelong duration has not diminished.

What, then, are the influences which have changed the prognosis of schizophrenic psychoses during our century? Considering all possibilities, one must come to the conclusion that improvement in care and treatment has had this happy influence. In the middle of the century hospital care for schizophrenics was essentially improved. Great interest was aroused by the introduction of somatic treatments (insulin, shock treatments, psychopharmacologic agents), which was connected with much more concern for the individual patient. At the same time, the transformation of old hospital life into therapeutic communities made great progress. After World War II the psychotherapy of schizophrenics (started at the beginning of the century) awoke to activity. And last, but not least, financial endowments to mental hospitals, which had mostly been meager, have improved; more nurses, more physicians and social workers can care for the patients than before. Statistical studies have not revealed which of all these steps towards better care for the patients has been decisive for the prognostic improvement. This question is still open to discussion. I personally think that all taken together were effective.

It is important to stress one fact: None of the patients included in my statistics who recovered permanently has long been under the influence of neuroleptic drugs. Some of them have taken such drugs during an acute stage of the psychosis, but not during the five and many more years during which they recovered. Other statistics and daily experience demonstrate that neuroleptics improve schizophrenic psychoses in many circumstances. Given for a long while, they diminish the danger of relapses in improved or recovered patients with phasic course. It has not been proved, however, that stable, long-standing, full recoveries are due to them.

Cultural Similarities and Differences

The statistics on which my statements on the prognosis are based are not representative for schizophrenics in all cultures. Many studies in African and some Asian countries show what also corresponds with my own limited experience in this respect. In many cultures of southern countries the number of acute schizophrenic psychoses and the number of benign outcomes is much greater than in Europe. Perhaps, however, the number of deaths in acute agitation and by starvation is also greater, but this is difficult to study.

As far as statistics show, however, there are no essential differences in the prognosis of schizophrenic patients within different countries of Western culture. My own statistics on patients coming mostly from an Alpine valley in Switzerland gave results similar to those on patients coming mostly from the cities of Zurich or Basel. Furthermore, these statistical results are similar to those I obtained from studies at the Westchester Division of the New York Hospital. Important statistics of other authors from the United States, Germany, France, Scandinavian countries and Bulgaria confirm the great similarity of the course of schizophrenic psychoses in different Western countries.

Other Research Problems

There are many other statistical problems in research on schizophrenia. These include: how cases are to be statistically handled in which observation ends with an early death; how need for hospital care on account of schizophrenic psychosis and of senility can be distinguished; and whether we statistically have to consider only schizophrenics who come for the first time to a psychiatric hospital or also those who are readmitted. There is only one manner of dealing with these questions—by drawing up different statistics, selecting the patients in each in some different way and comparing them. This I did for decades. The data on outcome, course and prognosis I mentioned in the first part of this lesson are rough averages of many statistics with somewhat varying selection of patients. The differences seen, however, are not as significant as one would suspect. For this reason, it was possible to summarize them only in rough numbers.

Evolution of the Author's
Experience and Study

As an intern at the Boston Psychopathic Hospital under the directorship of Macfie Campbell, I started to plan a lifelong research on course and outcome of schizophrenic psychoses in 1932. Ever since then I have systematically followed course and outcome of 566 schizophrenics. The main results of this study have been published. At the same time I studied as much as possible the destiny and the mental condition of their relatives and in particular of their schizophrenic relatives. As I grew up in the Psychiatric University Clinic in Zurich, the director of which was my father, who had the family apartment in the clinic, I was surrounded throughout my childhood and youth by schizophrenics. For 38 more years I was a physician in psychiatric hospitals where more than a third of the patients were schizophrenics, and during all these years I lived under the same roof as they did. The experience with the 566 schizophrenics I have studied for statistical purposes could be compared, therefore, during my daily medical experience, with the destiny of many other schizophrenics.

The first 100 schizophrenics whose psychotic development I followed were cared for in 1929–30 in the Westchester Division of the New York Hospital (at that time called Bloomingdale Hospital). Thanks to the studies of Dr. Cheney, I received catamneses of these patients eight years later when I was back in Switzerland. As a physician in a Swiss mountain village (Taminatal) I studied the evolution of the psychoses of 100 patients in the St. Pirminsberg Clinic. I could not get long catemneses of these patients, but I was able to obtain information concerning the fate and mental condition of 8776 relatives of these patients. This was possible because, up to that time, the population in the mountains had been very stable. The comparison of the schizophrenic psychoses in the same family is one basis of my conclusions. I published these studies from Taminatal in 1941. As head doctor at the Psychiatric University Clinic in Basel, I studied the evolution of the schizophrenic psychoses of 157 selected patients; one group was made up of schizophrenics who had responded well to insulin therapy and the other group was of schizophrenics with late onset of the psychosis.

The longest study I started was in 1942, when I took over the directorship of the Psychiatric University Burghölzli Clinic in Zurich. I planned to follow the fate of the first 208 schizophrenics admitted to the clinic together with the fate of their near relatives. I continued this study until I retired from the Clinic in 1969. I was able to follow the fate of all the 208 patients until their deaths or until at least 20 years after hospitalization. I obtained insight, on an average, into the course of over 30 years after the onset of the psychosis. This study was supplemented by the work of several other members of our Zurich team. It is essential, however, not to draw conclusions from one's personal research work alone. It has to be compared with the research results of other clinicians. There are in existence the studies of schizophrenic psychoses over decades by two teams of researchers which are particularly suitable for comparison with my research results — those of Gerd Huber together with Gisela Gross and Reinhold Schuettler, and of Christian Mueller and Luc Ciompi. The definitions of "schizophrenic psychosis," of "recovery" and of other important designations are practically identical in all three studies.

All three studies arrive at practically the same conclusions. This is even more astonishing as there were great differences both in the type of planning for the studies and in the choice of patients, as well as in some theoretical concepts. Huber and his team examined patients at some intervals after their hospitalization and had the chance to treat and to advise the patients described for long periods. Mueller and Ciompi selected their patients in quite a different way; they selected patients who had been hospitalized many years before the beginning of their research. They were over 65 years old at the beginning of the research. Their anamneses and their present conditions were studied. The patients of Huber and his team came from Western Germany; my patients came from cities and Alpine regions in the German-speaking part of Switzerland and from the United States; Mueller's and Ciompi's patients came from the French-speaking part of Switzerland. While Mueller and I had worked for a long time together, we had had a very different psychiatric education from Huber and his team. The research plans of Huber, on the one hand, and research of Mueller and Ciompi and me, on the other, were planned and carried out quite independently. Furthermore, Huber introduced new concepts regarding chronic schizophrenics with negative syndromes.

There are several other important statistics on the long-term course of schizophrenic psychoses. In some respects it is not possible to compare them with our statistics. It can be stated, however, that their essential results correspond astonishingly well with ours. Such research has been done in Denmark by Erik Stroemgren, in France by Henry Ey, in Bulgaria by A. Marinow, in the United States by D. M. Engelhardt, B. Rosen, Judith Feldman, JoAnn Engelhardt, Patricia Cohen, J. H. Stephens, R. C. Bland and J. H. Parker. The list could be continued, but I have only presented important examples. Two Russian authors, E. Sternberg and A. V. Sneznewsky, have also done great research work, subdividing schizophrenic psychoses into acute and chronic ones. In spite of their different theoretical conceptions, their results are not essentially contrary to ours. An important newer study from Kendler confirms again the results of the mentioned studies regarding the long-term course of schizophrenic psychoses.

Conclusions

The data on course and outcome of schizophrenic psychoses given in the first part of this lesson are not exact percentages. Exact percentages vary somewhat as the type of statistical evaluation varies. These data are rough indications. As such, however, they are reliable for schizophrenic psychoses in the middle of our century and in countries of Western culture. Hopefully they will serve as a basis for deepening our understanding of schizophrenia and stimulate an active, positive approach to patient treatment and care.

Additional Reading

Bland RC, Parker JH: Prognosis in schizophrenia. *Arch. Gen. Psychiatry* 33:949, 1976.

Bleuler E: Dementia Praecox oder Gruppe der Schizophrenien. In *Handbuch der Psychiatrie*, Aschaffenburg G (Ed.): Deuticke, Leipzig, 1911.

Bleuler E: Die Prognose der Dementia praecox (Schizophoreniegruppe) *Allg. Z. Psychiat.* 65:436, 1908.

Bleuler M: *Krankheitsverlauf, Persönlichkeit und Verwandschaft Schizophrener und ihre gegenseitigen Beziehungen*, Thieme, Leipzig, 1941.

Bleuler M: *Die schizophrenen Geistesstörungen im Lichte langjähriger Kranken- und Familien-Geschichten*, Thieme, Stuttgart, 1972.

Bleuler M: Das Wesen der Schizophrenieremission nach Schockbehandlung. *Z. gesamte Neurol. Psychiatr.* 173:553, 1941.

Bleuler M, Huber G, Gross G, Schuettler R: Der langfristige Verlauf schizophrener Psychosen. Gemeinsame Ergebnisse zweier Untersuchungen. *Nervenarzt* 47:477, 1976.

Ciompi L: Catamnestic long-term studies on the course of life of schizophrenics. *Schizophrenia Bull.* 6:606, 1980.

Ciompi L: Review of follow-up studies on long-term evolution and aging in schizophrenia. Paper presented at the International Conference on Schizophrenia and Aging, NIMH, Washington, DC, June 7–9, 1982.

Ciompi L, Mueller C: *Lebensweg und Alter der Schizophrenen. Eine katamnestische Langzeitstudie bis ins Senium*, Springer, Berlin, Heidelberg, New York, 1976.

Engelhardt DM, Rosen B, Feldman J, Engelhardt JZ, Cohen P: A 15-year follow-up of 646 schizophrenic outpatients. *Schizophrenia Bull.* 8:493, 1982.

Ey H: *Manuel de Psychiatrie*, 4th Ed., Masson, Paris, 1974.

Gross G, Huber G, Schuettler R: Verlaufsuntersuchungen bei Schizophrenen. In *Verlauf und Ausgang Schizophrener Erkrankungen,* 2. Weissenauer Schizophrenie Symposion, Schattauer Verlag, Stuttgart, New York, 1973, p. 101.

Huber G: *Psychiatrie. Systematischer Lehrtext für Studenten und Aerzte. Schattauer.* Stuttgart, New York, 1974.

Huber G: *Zum Stand der Verlaufsforschung bei den Schizophrenen (Schlussbe-*

merkungen), 2. *Weissenauer Schizophrenie Symposion,* Schattauer Verlag, Stuttgart, New York, 1973, p. 259.

Huber G, Gross G, Schuettler R: Course and long-term prognosis of schizophrenic illness. In *Biological Mechanisms of Schizophrenia and Schizophrenia-like Psychoses,* Mitsuda and Fukuda, Tokyo, 1974.

Kendler K, Gruenberg A, Tsuang M: Outcome of schizophrenic subtypes defined by four diagnostic systems. *Arch Gen Psychiatry* 41: 149, 1984.

Kraepelin E: *Einführung in die psychiatrische Klinik*, 3rd Ed., Barth, Leipzig, 1916.

Kraepelin E: *Psychiatrie*, 8th Ed., Barth, Leipzig, 1910.

Marinow A: Klinisch-statistische und katamnestische Unter-suchungen an chronisch Schizophrenen. *Arch Psychiatr. Nervenkr.* 218:115, 1974.

Marinow A: *Ueber Verlauf, Ausgang und Prognose bei Schizophrenien,* 4. Weissenauer Schizophrenie Symposium, Schattauer, Stuttgart, New York, 1981.

Mueller C: *Psychische Erkrankungen*, Huber, Bern, Stuttgart, Vienna, 1981.

Mueller C: Schizophrenia in advanced age. *Br. J. Psychiatry* 118:347, 1971.

Mueller C: Ueber das Senium Schizophrener, Karger, Basel, 1959.

Sneznewsky, AV: Symptomatology and Nosology. In *Schizophrenia, Sneznewsky Edition "Medicina"*, Moskau, 1969.

Stephens JH: Long-term prognosis and follow-up in schizophrenia. *Schizophrenia Bull.* 4:25, 1978.

Sternberg E: Verlaufsgesetzlichkeiten der Schizophrenie im Lichte von Langzeituntersuchung en bis zum Senium, 4. Weissenauer Schizophrenie Symposion, Schattauer, Stuttgart, New York, 1981.

Stroemgren E: Verlauf der Schizophrenien, 2, Weissenauer Schizophrenie Symposion, Schattauer, Stuttgart, New York, 1973.

3

Etiologic Concepts in the Schizophrenic Disorders

Robert Cancro

EDITOR'S NOTE

Both physiological and psychosocial factors have been considered in exploring the etiological factors that may contribute to schizophrenic illnesses. According to the author, the most compelling evidence for the existence of physiologic contributants comes from genetic studies, particularly those involving twins where there is an approximately threefold increase in the concordance rate of monozygotic versus dizygotic twins. In adoptive studies, the key factor influencing the incidence of schizophrenia was who bore the child, not who reared it.

The author does not consider the more psychodynamic and environmental factors well supported. There does not seem to be a predictable premorbid personality type. Some studies suggest a seasonal correlation of birth date, with a disproportionate number of people in the northern hemisphere who develop schizophrenic illnesses having been born between January and April. The high rates of schizophrenia among lower-status occupations does not solve the cause-or-effect controversy: Does poverty breed schizophrenia or does schizophrenia promote downward social drift? Interestingly, in cities under 100,000 people, the relationship between social class and the prevalence of schizophrenia noted in larger cities disappears.

There is some evidence that a cluster of stressful events seems to precede acute schizophrenic decompensation. Moreover, in other studies, the existence of a significant degree of hostility, criticism, and emotional overinvolvement in the parental home seems to set the stage for a higher relapse rate among single male schizophrenics.

In his conclusion, the author stresses the concept that schizophrenia itself is probably not an illness that is genetically transmitted as such, but rather a characteristic that is necessary — but not sufficient in itself — for the illness to develop at some point in life. Without such a vulnerability, the illness will not emerge. However, even with it, not everyone will necessarily become ill.

Introduction

The search for etiologic factors in the development of the schizophrenic disorders must at times have appeared to a neutral observer to be bizarre. There was remarkably little agreement as to the existence—let alone the definition—of the disorder, and yet intrepid investigators pursued its etiology. What is truly remarkable is not that the findings are ambiguous but that consistent findings do exist.

Schizophrenia has meant many things to different observers over time. It would not be practical to restrict this lesson to studies on the etiology of this disorder that have used only similar and specified diagnostic criteria. With the increasing utilization of *DSM-III*, however, such a restriction may be more possible in the future.

The studies to be reported are being arbitrarily divided into physiologic and environmental categories. This distinction has a noble tradition, but obviously it has severe limitations as well. The complexity of the human organism cannot be captured with arbitrary categories. It is apparent that environmental influences act on the organism through physiologic pathways, and it is equally apparent that the organism creates and modifies its environment to a real degree. A so-called response to an environmental stimulus can occur only if the physiologic capacity for that response is present in the organism. Obviously, in this illustration the outcome would not occur in the absence of either the physiologic or the environmental factor. The two are equally necessary for the event to take place.

Physiologic Factors

The most compelling evidence for the existence of so-called physiologic factors in the etiology of schizophrenic disorders lies in the area of genetics. The methods for demonstrating the presence of a genetic factor are three. The first is the consanguinity method. If an illness runs in families, it will by definition be more common in relatives of afflicted persons than in the general population. However, if genetic factors are operating, there will be a direct relationship between the strength of the genetic relationship and the incidence. In other words, the closer the relative is to an established case, the more likely the illness will also occur in that relative.

It has long been demonstrated that the schizophrenic disorders run in families. This was first reported in 1916 by Rüdin[1] and has been noted by a number of investigators since that time.[2,3] The consensus of the early investigations was that 10% to 15% of the first-degree relatives (i.e., parents, siblings, and offspring) of schizophrenic patients showed the disorder. The incidence among second-degree relatives was between that of the general population and that of the first-degree relatives.

There are obvious limitations to the consanguinity method. The demonstration that the disorder runs in families does not prove that it runs on a genetic basis. Families share much more than genes, and one can conclude from the consanguinity method only that the illness in question is familial.

A much more powerful method in genetic research is that of studying twins. Twins represent an interesting natural experiment because some twins are identical genetically while others are no more alike genetically than ordinary siblings. Dizygotic twins share the uterus at the same time; therefore, intrauterine differences between pregnancies that would be found in the study of ordinary siblings are eliminated. The genetically identical, or monozygotic, twins represent a unique resource for research, particularly when compared with fraternal, or dizygotic, twins. If a genetic factor is operating, it will be much more powerful in the genetically identical twin pair than it will be in the dizygotes, who are genetically no different from ordinary siblings.

By studying the concordance rate for an illness in monozygotic twins and comparing it to the concordance rate in dizygotic twins, one can demonstrate the presence but not the power of genetic factors. There are different ways of determining concordance rates, and comparisons of cohorts must utilize the same method of determining concordance. It is also apparent that the determination of concordance for an illness is a clinical judgment, with all of the problems and limitations of any clinical diagnosis in psychiatry.

The early twin studies demonstrated a significant difference in the concordance rate between monozygotes and dizygotes. These studies suffered from numerous methodological limitations, and it is therefore best to focus on more recent studies. Three twin studies were done in different Scandinavian countries by Tienari,[4] Kringlen,[5] and Fischer,[6] and two elsewhere in Europe by Gottesman and Shields[7] and Pollin et al.[8] While these studies differed in important ways and utilized different populations, they were consistent in their findings. There is an approximately threefold increase in the concordance rate of monozygotic twins over that of dizygotic twins. This is a highly significant difference.

The twin studies also found no difference in concordance rate as a function of sex and no difference in the concordance rate of dizygotic twins as a function of being of the same or different sexes. These are important negative findings, because they allow the extrapolation of studies restricted to males to the general population of twins and furthermore fail to support the hypothesis of the blurring of ego identity. The twin studies also revealed that twin pairs discordant for schizophrenia were no less likely to produce schizophrenic offspring than were twin pairs concordant for schizophrenia. Of even greater importance was the finding that the discordant twin was just as likely to produce schizophrenic children as was the schizophrenic twin. Finally, it has been found that identical twins reared separately have a concordance rate for schizophrenia that does not differ significantly from that found in monozygotic twins reared together.

There are limitations to the twin method that must be recognized. Monozygotic twins share not only their genome but also a unique psychological environment. Furthermore, individual differences in the evoking environments and the timing of genetic activations during the intrauterine and early postnatal periods have different effects on the genome.

There are other biological differences between fraternal and identical twins that make their direct comparison a problem. Monozygotes, when compared with dizygotes, tend to have more developmental problems, higher infant death rates, and increased perinatal morbidity. Monozygotes and dizygotes, therefore, do not represent a perfect natural experiment.

The adoptive method involves the comparison of the incidence of the disorder in the offspring of probands raised by the natural parents with that in the offspring of probands raised by adoptive parents. A further refinement of the adoptive method is to identify the index cases and then look for the incidence of the disorder in their biologic and adoptive relatives. Both of these techniques allow for an assessment of the different effects of genetic makeup on the occurrence of the illness.

The first published study by Heston[9] showed that the offspring of schizophrenic women who were adopted had approximately the same incidence of the disorder as they would have had if they had been reared by their natural mothers. A series of studies conducted in Denmark under the leadership of Kety[10] and Rosenthal[11] confirmed and extended this finding. The reported results consistently showed that what mattered with respect to the incidence of the disorder was who bore the child and not who reared it.

The adoptive studies are also not free of sources of error. The samples are small, and the question of reliability of diagnosis is always present. It is important to recognize that one cannot speak of proof in psychiatric research; one can speak only of evidence. The weight of the evidence from these three described lines of genetic research is consistent and compelling.

While much research through the years has gone into the search for morphologic and biochemical origins of the schizophrenias, this work has thus far proven disappointing. There are findings, but the consistency of these findings is not strong.[12]

Environmental Factors

The evidence for the role of personality factors as etiologic agents is not persuasive. No single personality type has been found in the premorbid histories of persons with schizophrenic illnesses. It is true that people who show autistic tendencies or a schizoid personality premorbidly have a poor prognosis, but many people who carry a poor prognosis do not show such tendencies. There is a broad range of premorbid personalities and adjustment patterns, none of which are inevitably associated with a schizophrenic illness.

A number of reports have correlated season of birth and schizophrenic psychosis. A disproportionate number of people in the northern hemisphere who develop a schizophrenic illness are born between January and April. Similarly, in the southern hemisphere there is a disproportionate number of schizophrenic births during their winter season. The meaning of this finding is not clear, but most likely lies in a yet undetermined relationship between intrauterine development and environmental demands.

The social-class studies in schizophrenia go back over 40 years. Initially, it was reported[13] that the inner or central city — in particular the transitional zones — had the highest rates for hospital admissions. The central city was populated primarily by those from the lower social classes. Clark[14] studied the rates of schizophrenia as a function of occupation. He reported that the highest rates of schizophrenia were to be found in the lower-status occupations. It has consistently been shown that there is an inverse and linear relationship between social class and prevalence of schizophrenia in large urban areas. This relationship holds for cities of over a million population. In cities of under 100,000 people, there is no relationship between social class and prevalence of schizophrenia. In cities between 100,000 and 500,000 in size, there is a concentration of cases in the lowest social class, but the relationship does not hold for the other social classes. These data can, of course, be interpreted in terms of downward social drift. In a competitively oriented society, people who drop out and do not compete tend to drift to the lower social classes. It is true that the relationship between social class and prevalence of schizophrenia weakens and even disappears when the class of origin is utilized rather than the social class of the patient.

There is a suggestive relationship between the stress of recent life events and the frequency of schizophrenia. A number of studies have reported that schizophrenics have had more stressful events in the year before their decompensation than have control groups. The life-event work may help to explain the social-class findings, because people from the lower social classes seem more likely to be exposed to many stressful life events. The group differences between schizophrenics and normals have been small, the number of persons studied has been modest, and the method has been retrospective. It is clear, therefore, that caution is necessary in interpreting these results.

The emotional climate in the home in which the patient lives would appear on the face of it to be important in mental decompensation. Brown et al.[15] reported that relapse rates in male schizophrenics living in the parental home were significantly related to three measures of expressed emotionality: critical comments, hostility, and emotional overinvolvement. Homes were rated as either high or low in expressed emotionality (EE), and the relapse rates of high- and low-EE homes were compared. It was found that the relapse rate was significantly higher in high-EE homes and that separation of the patients from the family members in such homes lowered the relapse rates. This initial work was replicated and extended by Vaughn and Leff.[16] The results of their study were consistent with those of the earlier studies. Again, caution must be utilized in interpreting these data because the patients were restricted to unmarried males living in the parental home. The generalizability of these results to other populations of schizophrenics remains to be determined.

Conclusions

The schizophrenic disorders are now recognized as a highly heterogeneous group that have certain clinical phenomena in common. It is not known whether the shared clinical phenomena are the important and unifying ones; they are merely the ones that are most visible and that have traditionally been used for diagnosis. Any diagnostic criterion utilized will be multidetermined as to its etiology and pathogenesis. An auditory hallucination will not necessarily have the same etiopathogenesis in different persons. The underlying mechanisms for symptom formation must ultimately be the unifying principle and not the final symptomatic end state. Symptoms do not constitute the basis of scientific classifications, although they may be useful for diagnostic groupings.

At least some of the disorders lumped under the rubric of schizophrenia are genetically loaded. This means that something is being transmitted that is essential in the etiopathogenesis of the illness. It is not the schizophrenic illness that is transmitted but, rather, a characteristic that is necessary but not sufficient for illness. Not everyone who has the capacity for a schizophrenic psychosis becomes ill. The identical-twin studies suggest that, at most, 50% of those who have the capacity for the illness manifest it; the figure is probably closer to 30%. It is in these genetically loaded individuals that the interaction of environmental and biologic factors can be understood most clearly.

Genes are encoded instructions that must be activated before they can have an effect. It is the environment that activates the gene. Many genes are never activated; therefore, in a very real sense, the accidents of development determine which of the many genetic potentials an individual has will actually be "turned on" and which will be allowed to remain dormant. The environment activates the gene by altering the biochemical "bath" in which the gene sits. It is that union of the gene and its immediate chemical environment that determines the characteristics of the individual. There is reason to believe that the genes that are activated in the preschizophrenic are not inherently pathologic but merely will contribute to the form that psychosis takes if that person decompensates. The relatives of schizophrenics are not at greater risk for mental illness. They are at greater risk for schizophrenia only if they become mentally ill. There is excellent evidence that they are at reduced risk for depressive and manic disorders. In other words, they are not more likely to become psychotic, but if they become psychotic they are almost certainly going to manifest it with symptoms that are categorized as schizophrenic.

It is essential to understand that the etiology of schizophrenic disorders that have a biologic component in fact reflects a combination of biologic and nonbiologic factors. The best evidence for the existence of environmental factors remains that genes require them in order to be activated. As with most battles of doctrine, the battle between the biologically oriented and environmentally oriented investigators is more reflective of their value system than of a true scientific conflict. It is perhaps ironically appropriate in the study of the schizophrenic psychoses that the investigators suffer from irrationality as well.

References

1. Rüdin E: *Zur Vererbung und Neuentstehung der Dementia Praecox*, Springer, Berlin, 1916.

2. Schultz B: Zur Erbpathologie der Schizophrenie. *Z. Gesamte Neurol. Psychiatr.* 143:175, 1932.

3. Kallmann FJ: *The Genetics of Schizophrenia*, Augustin, New York, 1938.

4. Tienari, P: Schizophrenia in monozygotic male twins. In Rosenthal D, Kety SS (Eds.): *The Transmission of Schizophrenia*, Pergamon Press, London, 1968, p. 27.

5. Kringlen E: *Heredity and Environment in the Functional Psychoses*, William Heinemann, London, 1967.

6. Fischer M: Genetic and environmental factors in schizophrenia. *Acta Psychiatr. Scand. (Suppl.)* 238:1, 1973.

7. Gottesman II, Shields J: Schizophrenia in twins: 16 years' consecutive admissions to a psychiatric clinic. *Br. J. Psychiatry* 112:809, 1966.

8. Pollin W, Allen MG, Hoffer A, Stabenau JR, Hrubec Z: Psychopathology in 15,909 pairs of veteran twins. *Am. J. Psychiatry* 126:597, 1969.

9. Heston LL: Psychiatric disorders in foster home reared children of schizophrenic mothers. *Br. J. Psychiatry* 112:819, 1966.

10. Kety SS, Rosenthal D, Wender PH, Schulsinger F, Jacobsen B: Mental illness in the biological and adoptive families of adopted individuals who have become schizophrenic: A preliminary report based on psychiatric interviews. In Fieve RR, Rosenthal D, Brill H (Eds.): *Genetic Research in Psychiatry*, Johns Hopkins University Press, Baltimore, 1975, p. 147.

11. Rosenthal D, Wender PH, Kety SS, Schulsinger F, Welner J, Østergård L: Schizophrenics' offspring reared in adoptive homes. In Rosenthal D, Kety SS (Eds.): *The Transmission of Schizophrenia*, Pergamon Press, Oxford, 1968, p. 377.

12. Wyatt R, Cutler N, DeLisi L, Jeste D, Kleinman J, Luchins D, Potkin S, Weinberger D: Biochemical and morphological factors in the etiology of the schizophrenic disorders. In Grinspoon L (Ed.): *Psychiatry 1982: The American Psychiatric Association Annual Review*, American Psychiatric Press, Washington, 1982, p. 112.

13. Faris REL, Dunham HW: *Mental Disorders in Urban Areas: An Ecological Study of Schizophrenia and Other Psychoses*, University of Chicago Press, Chicago, 1939.

14. Clark RE: The relationship of schizophrenia to occupational income and occupational prestige. *Am. Sociol. Rev.* 13:325, 1948.

15. Brown GW, Birley JLT, Wing JK: Influence of family life on the course of schizophrenic disorders: A replication. *Br. J. Psychiatry* 121:241, 1972.

16. Vaughn CE, Leff JP: The influence of family and social factors on the course of psychiatric illness: A comparison of schizophrenic and depressed neurotic patients. *Br. J. Psychiatry* 129:125, 1976.

4

The Subtyping of Schizophrenia

Nancy C. Andreasen

EDITOR'S NOTE

The real nature of schizophrenia continues to defy our understanding. Nonetheless, to study this condition and treat patients suffering with its manifestations, we must continue our efforts to clarify its diagnostic parameters. As the author points out, contemporary redefinition of this illness has begun to facilitate identification of neurological and neurophysiological factors that may be etiologically significant.

Kraepelin was perhaps the first to systematically evaluate forms of mental illness by means of a longitudinal approach, studying the course of the condition rather than the symptomatology exclusively. Bleuler then focused on dementia praecox, renaming it schizophrenia. Influenced by the interest in associative psychology prominent in his time, he concluded that the most important deficit in schizophrenia was a disruption of associative thought processes.

More recently, Schneider's work has begun to preempt that of Bleuler. He emphasizes first-rank symptoms — specific types of delusions and hallucinations — that tend to be tied together by the common thread that patients perceive themselves as losing the autonomy of their thoughts, feelings and even their bodies. His system seems to provide greater definition, a need that became quite apparent when studies of reliability in diagnosing schizophrenia revealed serious differences among psychiatrists in different countries.

The best approach to the definition of schizophrenia is polythetic rather than monothetic. It is viewed as a disorder with a wide range of symptoms, none specific to it alone, none diagnostic unto itself. *DSM-III-R* incorporates symptomatic, cross-sectional aspects as well as longitudinal ones. For example, to make a diagnosis, psychotic symptoms must have been present for at least one week, and continuous signs of disturbance for at least six months. Affective symptoms cannot dominate the picture, nor can symptoms be explained on an organic basis. On the whole, the concept of schizophrenia has indeed been narrowed.

Two subtypes of the disorder have also been proposed. The positive form is characterized by prominent symptoms, such as delusions, hallucinations, and a formal thought disorder; a more episodic course; a more acute onset; a better prognosis and responsiveness to major tranquillizer treatment. Negative schizophrenia is characterized by flattening of affect, poverty of speech or thought, and avolition, a more chronic course, and a poor response to treatment; moreover, such patients appear to reveal diffuse, irreversible structural brain abnormalities, such as ventricular enlargement and cortical atrophy, as measured by CT scan. The implications for research and patient management are discussed.

Historical Background

Our modern nosological system for classifying schizophrenia and affective disorders derives from Kraepelin. Most of his ideas are summarized in a set of textbooks on the major psychiatric illness that went through many editions between 1883 and 1926: *Dementia Praecox and Paraphrenia* and *Manic-Depressive Insanity and Paranoia*.[1,2] In these textbooks, Kraepelin synthesized much previous thinking concerning the classification of mental illness and developed the first really useful method of subdividing the major psychoses. Before Kraepelin, there was little agreement as to which psychoses had symptoms that "ran together" to form a syndrome. Kraepelin's approach emphasized longitudinal course rather than cross-sectional symptoms. Because the course was episodic and the outcome good, Kraepelin recognized that the two poles of what we now call bipolar disorder were essentially similar and considered manic-depressive insanity to be a single psychosis. Although this concept is now sometimes questioned, it has served a useful purpose for nearly 100 years.

In retrospect, it is sometimes difficult to recognize the creativity of Kraepelin's grouping. He was able to perceive that illness with great cross-sectional differences, such as mania and depression, in fact were related to one another because of their longitudinal similarity. Dementia praecox differed from manic-depressive insanity because its course was chronic rather than episodic and because its prognosis was poor. Kraepelin saw dementia praecox as an illness beginning early in life ("praecox"), having a relatively chronic rather than episodic course, and having a poor outcome ending in deterioration or dementia.

Kraepelin's texts contain probably the clearest, most complete, and most vividly portrayed description of the symptoms of manic-depressive illness and schizophrenia ever written. In both *Manic-Depressive Insanity and Paranoia* and *Dementia Praecox and Paraphrenia*, Kraepelin describes a wide variety of symptoms, many of which may occur in either disorder. He does not appear to consider any particular symptom or group of symptoms to be specific or pathognomonic.

The concept of specific or pathognomonic symptoms began with Bleuler, who focused on dementia praecox and renamed it "schizophrenia."[3] Unlike Kraepelin, who was interested primarily in describing underlying causes, Bleuler was preoccupied with understanding the basic mechanisms that caused schizophrenic symptoms. His search led him to what are now sometimes referred to as the "Bleulerian four A's": associative loosening, affective blunting, autism, and ambivalence. Bleuler worked in an era when "associative" psychology was preeminent. Psychological theorists were preoccupied with determining how thoughts were encoded or formulated in the mind. The prevailing theory was that the process of thinking and remembering was guided by associative links between ideas and concepts. Bleuler believed that the most important deficit in schizophrenia was a disruption of associative threads:

Certain symptoms of schizophrenia are present in every case and at every period of illness even though, as with every other disease symptom, they must have attained a certain degree of intensity before they can be recognized with any certainty. . . . For example, the peculiar association disturbance is always present, but not each and every aspect of it. . . . Besides these specific permanent or fundamental symptoms, we can find a host of other, more accessory manifestations such as delusions, hallucinations, or catatonic symptoms. . . . As far as we know, the fundamental symptoms are characteristic of schizophrenia, while the accessory symptoms may also appear in other types of illness.

Bleuler clearly believed that associative loosening was a specific or pathognomonic symptom. That is, it was present in every case, and if it was not present, the disorder could not be considered schizophrenia. Indeed, Bleuler's name for the disorder, "schizophrenia," means "split-mind," and Bleuler chose the name as the most apt term to refer to the disruptive associative thinking that characterizes the disorder.

Until quite recently, many of Bleuler's ideas prevailed over Kraepelin's. His new name for the disorder became standard, and for decades residents have been taught to recite the Bleulerian four A'S, to distinguish between fundamental symptoms (such as associative loosening) and accessory symptoms (such as delusions and hallucinations), to recognize that fundamental symptoms occur only in schizophrenia while accessory symptoms occur in other disorders, and to see thought disorder as the *sine qua non* of schizophrenia.

More recently, Bleulerian symptoms have diminished in popularity, and a third European psychiatrist has become influential: Kurt Schneider.[4,5] Like Bleuler, Schneider was interested in identifying pathognomonic symptoms. He developed a description of a set of "symptoms of the first rank," which were specific for schizophrenia and diagnostic of it. Schneiderian first-rank symptoms have been introduced to the English-speaking world primarily through the work of British psychiatrists, especially Frank Fish and John Wing.[6,7] They were incorporated in the Present State Examination, the interviewing instrument developed for the International Pilot Study of Schizophrenia, which remains perhaps the most widely used research instrument for documenting schizophrenic symptoms. Schneiderian first-rank symptoms are specific types of delusions and hallucinations, such as thought insertion, thought broadcasting, and delusions of control. They tend to be tied together by the common thread that the patient perceives himself as losing the autonomy of his thoughts, feelings, and body.

Schneiderian first-rank symptoms have enjoyed their recent popularity for several reasons. They can be defined very specifically. Unlike the Bleulerian four A's, which tend to be on a continuum with normality, delusions and hallucinations tend to be discrete phenomena that are clearly pathological. Therefore, many clinicians and investigators have believed that Schneiderian first-rank symptoms could be defined much more reliably than could the Bleulerian four A's. Thus, the emphasis on the use of Schneiderian first-rank symptoms to define schizophrenia was likely to lead to improved reliability. A concern with reliability became particularly important after the U.S/U.K. Study and the International Pilot Study of Schizophrenia revealed wide discrepancies in diagnostic practice around the world, and particularly that American psychiatrists tended to have a very broad and perhaps less precise view of schizophrenia.[8]

Finally, Schneiderian first-rank symptoms have been made an integral part of several standard structured interviews, such as the Present State Examination[9] and the Schedule for Affective Disorders and Schizophrenia.[10] They have also been introduced into widely used diagnostic criteria, such as the Research Diagnostic Criteria[11] or the *Third Diagnostic Manual* of the American Pyschiatric Association (DSM-III).[12] These interviews and criteria, although they make brief reference to more classic Bleulerian symptoms, depend very heavily on the recognition of delusions and hallucinations and particularly on Schneiderian first-rank symptoms.

In the past decade, however, a number of investigators have begun to reevaluate the descriptive psychopathology of affective disorders and schizophrenia. This reevaluation has shed considerable doubt on the specificity of both Bleulerian and Schneiderian symptoms. It has led to a more balanced view of descriptive psychopathology, one that gives more equal weight to the contributions of Kraepelin, Bleuler and Schneider. This work suggests that the best approach to the definition of schizophrenia is polythetic rather than monothetic; that is, schizophrenia is a disorder characterized by a wide range of symptoms, none of which is specific to it alone and many of which may also occur in the affective disorders. No single symptom is diagnostic. The clinical diagnosis of schizophrenia depends on a combination of longitudinal course and the patterning of symptoms rather than the presence of a single symptom. This point of view has been applied to the classification of schizophrenia as presented in *DSM-III*.

In addition, "neo-Kraepelinian" approaches to the classification of schizophrenia have been developed quite recently. These approaches have traditions that reach back into 19th and early 20th century neuropsychiatry, but most of the data supporting them are very recent and postdate the development of *DSM-III*. This new approach to subtyping schizophrenia incorporates the strengths of the Kraepelinian-Bleulerian-Schneiderian tradition by emphasizing careful descriptive phenomenology. However, this approach also attempts to relate subtypes of schizophrenia to important etiological constructs — specifically to neurochemical and structural brain abnormalities. This approach to subtyping schizophrenia divides it into two or three groups. The two extreme groups are variously called type I versus type II, positive versus negative, and florid versus deficit schizophrenia. Some investigators also add a third or "mixed" group.

DSM-III *Subtypes of Schizophrenia*

The criteria for schizophrenia in *DSM-III* combine longitudinal and cross-sectional features. The most important longitudinal criterion is the requirement that symptoms of schizophrenia be present for at least six months. The cross-sectional criteria enumerate characteristic symptoms of schizophrenia. These symptoms are primarily a mixture of Schneiderian first-rank symptoms (such as delusions of control or voices commenting) and other types of delusions and hallucinations. Bleulerian symptoms tend to be deemphasized, but do appear in the last of the symptomatic criteria, which refer to abnormalities of affect and thinking. Finally, in order to narrow the concept of schizophrenia by excluding patients with schizoaffective or affective disorder, there is a criterion stressing that affective symptoms cannot dominate the clinical picture. In addition, in order to rule out organic causes such as drug intoxication, an exclusion criterion requires that the symptoms cannot be explained on an organic basis.

DSM-III also employs both longitudinal and cross-sectional approaches to subtyping schizophrenia. Schizophrenia is to be classified longitudinally as subchronic, chronic, subchronic with acute exacerbation, chronic with acute exacerbation, or in remission. The patient with subchronic schizophrenia has been ill from six months to two years, while the chronic patient has been ill for more than two years. The qualifier "with acute exacerbation" refers to whether florid psychotic symptoms are currently prominent, as they might be in a patient early in the course of hospitalization.

The cross-sectional classification of schizophrenia subdivides the patients into four major symptomatic groups. Disorganized schizophrenia is characterized by prominent incoherence and affective disturbance, as well as an absence of systematized delusions. Catatonic schizophrenia is characterized by a variety of catatonic symptoms, such as stupor, negativism, abnormal movements, and excitement. Paranoid schizophrenia is characterized by prominent delusions, whether they be persecutory, grandiose, or jealous. Undifferentiated schizophrenia refers to patients who do not meet criteria for any of the other subtypes or who meet criteria for more than one subtype. As was the case with *DSM-III*, most schizophrenics seen in clinical practice are likely to be classified as undifferentiated.

The *DSM-III* classification is closely modeled after those of Kraepelin and Bleuler, who used essentially the same subtypes. The Bleulerian subtype, "simple schizophrenia," has not been included among the schizophrenias in *DSM-III*, but corresponds roughly to schizotypal personality disorder. Schizoaffective disorder, a subtype first described by Kasanin,[13] has also been moved outside the schizophrenias and reappears either as affective disorder with mood-incongruent psychotic features or as schizoaffective disorder under the heading "Psychoses Not Elsewhere Classified." These changes represent a narrowing of the concept of schizophrenia in *DSM-III*, as compared to *DSM-II*. In *DSM-III* the concept of schizophrenia is limited to patients who have been clearly psychotic at some time (thereby excluding simple schizophrenia) and who do not have prominent affective features (thereby excluding schizoaffective disorder).

Positive Versus Negative Schizophrenia

The *DSM-III* approach to classifying schizophrenia is purely descriptive. It attempts to define a group of patients who are likely to be homogeneous in terms of course and response to treatment; it has thus eliminated the older "acute schizophrenias," many of which are now reclassified (and usually treated clinically) as affective disorders.

Since the publication of *DSM-III*, a new approach to classifying schizophrenia has been developed. This approach, which draws on the distinction between positive and negative symptoms originally described by Hughlings-Jackson,[14] was first developed by Crow.[15] It is summarized in Table 1. This new, and perhaps more powerful, approach to the classification of schizophrenia is based on the assumption that the schizophrenic syndrome is composed of a set of heterogeneous but related disorders that have somewhat different characteristic symptoms, course, pathophysiology, and etiology. It is also based on the presumption that schizophrenic symptoms must ultimately be understood in terms of brain structure and function and that

TABLE 1
Type I vs. Type II Schizophrenia

	TYPE I	TYPE II
Characteristic symptoms	Positive (delusions, hallucinations, positive FTD)	Negative (flat affect, negative FTD, loss of drive)
Response to neuroleptics	Good	Poor
Outcome	Sometimes good	Usually poor (defect state)
Course	Sometimes acute	Usually chronic
Intellectual impairment	Absent	Sometimes present
Postulated pathological process	Increased dopamine receptors	Cell loss and structural changes in the brain

Adapted from Crow.[15]

the different and varied clinical pictures of schizophrenia are due to different types of brain abnormality. This approach to the classification of schizophrenia offers a fresh perspective that has considerable heuristic value, in that it leads to testable hypotheses concerning the nature of brain dysfunction in schizophrenia and concerning its causes, course, and outcome.

Briefly, this approach proposes that the schizophrenic syndrome can be initially divided into two broad subtypes. Positive or florid schizophrenia is characterized by prominent positive symptoms (e.g., delusions, hallucinations, bizarre behavior, and positive formal thought disorder), a more episodic course, a more acute onset, a better prognosis, and a greater sensitivity of its characteristic symptoms to treatment with neuroleptics. Positive schizophrenia is presumed to be caused by some type of focal brain abnormality that is probably neurochemical. Specifically, it may be due to an abnormality in dopaminergic transmission.

Negative or defect schizophrenia, on the other hand, is characterized by prominent negative symptoms (e.g., affective flattening, poverty of speech or thought, and avolition), a more chronic course, and poor response of its characteristic symptoms to treatment. It is presumed to be due to diffuse and irreversible structural brain abnormalities, such as ventricular enlargement and cortical atrophy, which can be measured by CT scan. Negative schizophrenia is very similar to Kraepelin's "dementia praecox," in that it is a "dementing" illness that begins early in life. It is also quite similar to Bleuler's concept of schizophrenia, since the characteristic negative symptoms are those that Bleuler stressed, such as disorganized thinking, affective flattening, and avolition.

Andreasen[16,17] has attempted to operationalize this approach to the classification of schizophrenia by providing standardized definitions of characteristic negative symptoms (affective flattening, alogia or poverty of speech, avolition-apathy, anhedonia-asociality, and attentional impairment), as well as developing diagnostic criteria for positive, negative and mixed schizophrenia. The criteria for these three subtypes are as follows:

POSITIVE SCHIZOPHRENIA

1. At least one of the following is a prominent part of the illness.
   a. Severe hallucinations that dominate the clinical picture (auditory, haptic, or olfactory). (The judgment of severity should be based on various factors, such as persistence, frequency, and effect on lifestyle.)
   b. Severe delusions (may be persecutory, jealous, somatic, religious, grandiose, or fantastic). (The judgment of frequency should be made as described for severity.)
   c. Marked formal thought disorder (manifested by marked incoherence, derailment, tangentiality, or illogicality).
   d. Repeated instances of bizarre or disorganized behavior.
2. None of the following is present to a marked degree.
   a. Alogia
   b. Affective flattening
   c. Avolition-apathy
   d. Anhedonia-asociality
   e. Attentional impairment

NEGATIVE SCHIZOPHRENIA

1. At least two of the following are present to a marked degree.
   a. Alogia (e.g., marked poverty of speech, poverty of content of speech)
   b. Affective flattening
   c. Anhedonia-asociality (e.g., inability to experience pleasure or to feel intimacy, few social contacts)
   d. Avolition-apathy (e.g., anergia, impersistence at work or school)
   e. Attentional impairment
2. None of the following dominates the clinical picture or is present to a marked degree
   a. Hallucinations
   b. Delusions
   c. Positive formal thought disorder
   d. Bizarre behavior

MIXED SCHIZOPHRENIA

This category includes patients that do not meet criteria for either positive or negative schizophrenia, or meet criteria for both.

In their early work demonstrating CT scan abnormalities in schizophrenia, Johnstone et al.[18] observed a relationship between negative symptoms and ventricular enlargement, as well as evidence of cognitive impairment among schizophrenics with ventricular enlargement. These findings have been extended by the work of other investigators. Weinberger et al.[19-21] have also identified a subgroup of schizophrenics with ventricular enlargement and noted that these patients tend to have poor premorbid adjustment and a poor response to treatment. Applying the above criteria to a group of 52 schizophrenics, Andreasen and Olsen[17] found the negative-symptom schizophrenics to have significantly more ventricular enlargement, poorer premorbid adjustment, poorer performance on standardized mental status testing, and more impairment both at admission and at discharge. Thus, a substantial amount of evidence has been amassed to suggest that this new approach to classifying schizophrenia may have greater predictive validity than the older, Kraepelinian approaches. Nevertheless, considerably more research is needed before this new method of subtyping the schizophrenic syndrome replaces the Kraepelinian-Bleulerian approach.

Conclusion

Most clinicians and investigators agree that the group of disorders called schizophrenia is heterogeneous. In *Dementia Praecox* and *Paraphrenia*, Kraepelin described various subtypes of this disorder and suggested that they might reflect different cerebral localizations in such areas as the frontal or temporal lobes. Bleuler emphasized the importance of subtypes by subtitling his book *The Group of Schizophrenias*.

American psychiatry has also emphasized the importance of subtyping, although there has been little consensus about the best system. As a consequence, the history of the nosology of schizophrenia is one of competing systems of classification, none of which has yet emerged as preeminent. Traditional Kraepelinian-Bleulerian subtypes — hebephrenic, catatonic, paranoid, and undifferentiated — still form the basis of *DSM-III*. Other subtypes have also been proposed, such as acute versus chronic, process versus reactive, or good versus poor prognosis. Yet none of these systems has well-documented predictive power for estimating outcome or facilitating the search for causes. Until recently, surprisingly few attempts had been made to relate classification to functional brain systems, such as language or visual or auditory perception, or to other possible etiological constructs.

The subdivision of schizophrenia into positive versus negative seems to suggest a way for solving some of these problems. This subdivision, which is reminiscent of Bleuler's distinction between fundamental and accessory symptoms, is one that clinicians who treat large numbers of schizophrenic patients have recognized for some time. Even among chronic schizophrenics, some are clearly floridly psychotic, while others appear to be "burned out." Although the florid or positive symptoms can be relieved with aggressive treatment, negative symptoms tend to be treatment-refractory and ultimately more crippling.

Recent research on this approach to subtyping suggests that this difference in symptoms and in treatment response may be due to underlying differences in brain function and structure. Patients with negative symptoms may suffer from some type of atrophic process that is reflected by ventricular enlargement on CT scanning, as well as poorer performance on tests of cognition. Since many of these patients have poor premorbid adjustment, this brain abnormality may be due to a pathological process beginning early in life; one explanation is some type of viral illness affecting the brain. Positive symptoms, which tend to be reversible through treatment with neuroleptics, tend to occur in patients with normal CT scans. The brain abnormality in these patients may be due to a neurochemical defect, presumably hyperdopaminergic, that responds well to blocking with neuroleptics.

While this approach to subtyping schizophrenia needs considerably more study and evaluation, it offers exciting opportunities to understand subtypes of schizophrenia in terms of underlying pathophysiology.

References

1. Kraepelin E: *Dementia Praecox and Paraphrenia*, Barkley RM (transl.), Robertson GM (ed.), E. & S. Livingstone, Edinburgh, 1919.

2. Kraepelin E: *Manic-Depressive Insanity and Paranoia*, Barkley RM (transl.), Robertson GM (ed.), E. & S. Livingston, Edinburgh, 1921.

3. Bleuler E: *Dementia Praecox or the Group of Schizophrenias*, Zinkin J (transl.), International Universities Press, New York, 1950.

4. Mellor CS: First-rank symptoms of schizophrenia. *Br. J. Psychiatry* 34:810–813, 1977.

5. Koehler A, Guth W, Grim G: First-rank symptoms of schizophrenia in Schneider-oriented German centers. *Arch. Gen. Psychiatry* 34:810–813, 1977.

6. Hamilton M (ed.): *Fish's Clinical Psychopathology: Signs and Symptoms in Psychiatry*, John Wright & Sons. Bristol, 1974.

7. Wing JK: A standard form of psychiatric Present State Examination (PSE) and a method for standardizing the classification of symptoms. In Hare EH, Wing JK (eds.): *Psychiatric Epidemiology*, Oxford University Press, London, 1970.

8. Kendell RE, Cooper JR, Gourlay, AJ, et al.: Diagnostic criteria of American and British psychiatrists. *Arch. Gen. Psychiatry* 25:123–130, 1971.

9. Wing JK, Cooper JE, Sartorius N: *Measurement and Classification of Psychiatric Symptoms*, Cambridge University Press, Cambridge, 1974.

10. Endicott J, Spitzer RL: A diagnostic interview: The Schedule for Affective Disorders and Schizophrenia (SADS). *Arch. Gen. Psychiatry* 35:837–844, 1978.

11. Spitzer RL, Endicott J, Robins E: Research diagnostic criteria: Rationale and reliability. *Arch. Gen. Psychiatry* 35:773–782, 1978.

12. American Psychiatric Association, Committee on Nomenclature and Statistics: *Diagnostic and Statistical Manual of Mental Disorders*, Third Edition, American Psychiatric Association, Washington, D.C., 1980.

13. Kasanin J: The acute schizoaffective psychoses. *Am. J. Psychiatry* 90:97–126, 1933.

14. Hughlings-Jackson J: *Selected Writings*, Taylor J (ed.), Hodder & Stoughton, London, 1931.

15. Crow TJ: Molecular pathology of schizophrenia: More than one disease process? *Br. Med. J.* 280:66–68, 1980.

16. Andreasen NC: Negative symptoms in schizophrenia: Definition and reliability. *Arch. Gen. Psychiatry* 39:784–788, 1982.

17. Andreasen NC, Olsen S.: Negative *v.* positive schizophrenia: Definition and validation. *Arch. Gen. Psychiatry* 39:789–794, 1982.

18. Johnstone EC, Crow TJ, Frith CD, et al.: Cerebral ventricular size and cognitive impairment in chronic schizophrenia. *Lancet* 2:924–926, 1976.

19. Weinberger DR, Torrey EF, Neophytides AN, et al.: Lateral cerebral ventricular enlargement in chronic schizophrenia. *Arch. Gen. Psychiatry* 34:735–739, 1979.

20. Weinberger DR, Bigelow LB, Kleinman JD, et al.: Cerebral ventricular enlargement in chronic schizophrenia: Its association with poor response to treatment. *Arch. Gen. Psychiatry* 37:11–18, 1980.

21. Weinberger DR, Cannon-Spoor E, Potkin SG, et al.: Poor premorbid adjustment and CT scan abnormalities in chronic schizophrenia. *Am. J. Psychiatry* 137:1410–1413, 1980.

5

Psychophysiological Nature of Schizophrenia:
I. Peripheral Nervous Systems Research

Terry Patterson and Herbert E. Spohn

EDITOR'S NOTE

Schizophrenia has long been considered a group of illnesses rather than a single diagnostic entity. The more we understand the psychophysiological parameters of the schizophrenia, the more we can deal with such patients and use available therapeutic techniques efficiently.

Learning more about the schizophrenias can be accomplished by integrating concepts and experiments from the field of cognitive psychology with those from the neurosciences. For example, cognitive science has slowly assembled a stage theory of information processing that describes the sequential steps of information transduction between stimulus input and response organization. A widely accepted hypothesis considers certain schizophrenics as suffering with information input dysfunction, a defect in the early stages of such processing.

Physiological research has been examined in relation to cognitive processes. Skin potential or conductance, for instance, involves surface recording from the hands to examine the activity of the sweat glands. Skin conductance response can be divided into latency, risetime, amplitude, and recovery time. Findings among schizophrenic patients include a large number of nonresponders who, in general, show a significant degree of withdrawal and thought disturbance and respond poorly to a variety of treatment measures.

Pupillometrics represents another psychophysiological method of study, one in which schizophrenics commonly fall outside the normal range on light/dark reflex parameters.

One important theory of cardiovascular responsiveness holds that cardiac deceleration — reduced heart rate — facilitates information intake from the environment; conversely, cardiac acceleration seems to facilitate closing out external perceptions in favor of increased attention to internal states or processes. Many schizophrenics display elevated resting heart rate levels, as if defending against environmental overload.

Finally, abnormal smooth pursuit eye movement has been observed among schizophrenics, reflecting a defect in involuntary attention processes. The observation that significant visual perceptual dysfunction can occur in schizophrenics and is amenable to diagnosis and correction bears important clinical significance.

"Mechanisms," "Subclassification," and the Level of Explanation

In the constellation of mental disorders known as the schizophrenias it is almost universally accepted that more than one illness is present. However, the subclassification of schizophrenia into diseases of different etiologies has not been possible because positive identification of causal mechanism(s) has not been achieved. If schizophrenics are subclassified into any assortment of groups, the basis of the subclassification could well be a statement about mechanism(s) underlying the condition. Similarly, if a statement about mechanism is made (at the biochemical, electrophysiological, or behavioral level), then it is imperative that the investigator ask, "To which schizophrenics is this mechanism applicable?" If the experience of the past half century can be relied upon, it will almost certainly not be applicable to all schizophrenics. It therefore follows that investigation into schizophrenia must carry these two arms of inquiry in parallel and that conceptualization in one area must be checked for applicability in the other. At present we cannot say how many subdivisions may be appropriate in schizophrenia, and for this reason we cannot say how many different mechanisms may ultimately be identified. By the same token, we are at risk for misidentifying the differential expression of a single mechanism as multiple mechanisms.

The strategy which has emerged in recent years is to find schizophrenics who are homogeneous with respect to either cognitive, electrophysiological, or neurochemical measures and to explore the possibility that these homogeneous subgroups will show systematic differences on other variables also. If this is successful then a "predictive subclassification" will have been achieved. For example, supposing schizophrenics were to be dichotomously subgrouped into those who show poor eye tracking when following a target and those who do not; these subgroups could be compared, for example, on simple reaction time and sustained attention ability. Suppose the poor eye trackers show significantly slower reaction time and inability to sustain attention over time, and the good eye trackers do not differ from the normal. In this case we would be able to state that (a) not all schizophrenics had slow reaction time and that some could sustain attention as well as normal subjects; both slow reaction time and difficulty in sustaining attention seem to be linked. Furthermore, we would be able to state that (b) at the electrophysiological (eye tracking) level we could "predict" these cognitive behaviors. We would then have a "predictive subclassification" from the psychophysiological level to the cognitive level.

Let us further suppose that neuro-opthalmologists could tell us that poor eye tracking is "caused" by a defect in cortically downward inhibitory control of certain brainstem structures that normally prevent saccades from intruding into eye tracking. In this instance we would be able to formulate a "mechanistic" understanding of a defect (applicable to some schizophrenics, but not all), in which the control of both attentional variables and certain motor functions (both eye tracking and reaction time) are seen in terms of defects in specific brain structures. The wider explanative framework might well be that all attentional control is achieved by a selective attenuation of incoming sensory "channels" by cortical inhibitory pathways that operate on brainstem reticular structures. In this example, the achievement of mechanistic understanding of schizophrenic deficit that isolates and describes the cognitive deficits in one specific subgroup of schizophrenics necessitates the involvement of cognitive science, psychophysiology, and neuroscience. Furthermore, it is evident that "subclassification" could originate from the neurological, the behavioral, or the psychophysiological level.

There is still considerable hope that an "explanation" of schizophrenia may be achieved at the neurochemical level. However, early enthusiasm has waned somewhat as the complexity of synaptic processes has unfolded.[1] For example, a catecholamine mechanism may be involved in some schizophrenias[2] but methods that would determine (in vivo) the involvement of release mechanisms (which are themselves profoundly complicated), as distinct from receptor abnormalities or "second messenger" anomalies, have not as yet been developed. In the recent decade a growing feeling has emerged that biochemistry cannot "go it alone" in explaining the roots of mental illness. There is nothing inherently wrong with biochemical explanation; rather, the subtle sophistication of biochemical tools must be directed to problems that are identified by behaviorally more sophisticated investigation in mental illness.

Cognitive Science and Neuroscience

Throughout the remainder of this chapter and the one that follows we will be describing psychophysiological investigation into schizophrenia. It is our contention that psychophysiology is placed in a highly integrative role between cognitive science and neuroscience and may thus bring the concepts of both disciplines to bear on both the mechanism(s) and subclassification of schizophrenia. In the investigative strategy outlined above, one "tactical" possibility is to begin subclassificatory procedures at the psychophysiological level. This can be diagrammatically represented as follows:

Neuroscience		Cognitive Science
Biochemical & Physiological Controlling Mechanisms	Psychophysiological Variables Brain & Periphery	Behavioral Subclassification in Schizophrenia

It must be emphasized that the explanation of schizophrenia in terms of the neurochemical control of behavior will come about secondarily to the understanding of how these processes work in normal individuals (perhaps of different species). Research in mental illness depends upon fundamental advances in both neuroscience and cognitive science.[3]

Within cognitive science[4] the development of information-processing theory has provided powerful concepts and methodologies for the analysis and description of cognition. Early investigation in schizophrenia yielded the tenable hypothesis that schizophrenic cognition could be described as subtle abnormalities in the control of attention.[5-9] This information rendered it possible to apply the powerful signal detection methodology to the schizophrenics' ability to sustain attention over time. The signal detection statistic of d' (sensitivity of the nervous system) can be separated from β (the subjectivity set criterion of signal present/absent) and both measures have yielded refined understanding of attention control in schizophrenia. These measures will be referred to below in conjunction with psychophysiological variables.[10]

Cognitive science has also laboriously assembled a "stage" theory of information processing[11-13] which describes, conceptually and temporally, the sequential steps of information transduction between stimulus input and response organization.[14-19] A gross oversimplification of this conceptualization calls for an early (sometimes called "iconic")[20] stage—of vast capacity but fast decay—that lasts no longer than a few hundred milliseconds. Extraction of information from this stage may lead to a short-term or working memory stage that is acted upon by central processing in conjunction with retrieval from existing hierarchically organized memory store. This is followed by organization of response.

A special attraction of this model is that it has time-dependent sequential aspects to its operation. One logical consequence is that defect at early stages may be the direct cause of later stage performance breakdown. It should be noted at this point that a widely accepted hypothesis of schizophrenic cognitive dysfunction is that there is "input dysfunction," i.e., defect in early stages of processing. From this it can be seen that information-processing methodology may have much to offer schizophrenia research at the behavioral level. Sophisticated electrophysiology in turn, when coupled with this methodology, may be capable of detailing the physiological/neurological events that coincide with specific information-processing stages.

Psychophysiological Studies

At this juncture we recommend to the interested reader the study of a general "psychophysiology in schizophrenia" review paper such as Spohn and Patterson.[21] Such a paper will give a more integrated comprehensive, and detailed review than is possible here. The remainder of this chapter will summarize research in electrodermal recording, pupillometry, cardiovascular measurement, and smooth pursuit eye movement.

A word of caution is appropriate at this point. Much early research in peripheral electrophysiology was conducted within the framework of concepts such as "arousal." Thankfully this trend has abated and psychophysiologists now appear more comfortable discussing their findings in terms of the actual variables recorded. Consequently, groups that display different levels of skin conductance or heart rate are referred to in terms of the parameters of such variables, and not as groups that display altered levels of "arousal."

The reader is urged to be especially vigilant when amorphous concepts such as "arousal" or "states of consciousness" are held to be derivable from peripheral psychophysiology and when discussion then takes place in terms of ill-defined concepts instead of the original data. It may be possible at some time in future to use psychophysiological variables to index some higher order concepts but only when much more is known about the biochemical and physiological controlling mechanisms of the variables.

Electrodermal Research: Methodological Issues

Surface recording from the hands examines the activity of the eccrine sweat glands, usually as skin potential or skin conductance. Because the response may be multiphasic, quantification problems attend comparison of skin potential records between subjects. Consequently, most electrodermal recording uses skin conductance (SC), and often, the orienting paradigm (skin conductance orienting response). A large amount of literature on the skin conductance orienting response (SCOR) in schizophrenia has recently been synthesized by Bernstein et al.[22] It should also be pointed out that methodological variability has rendered much of the early data in this area noncomparable between studies. However, methodological standardization has progressed following Venables and Christie's[23] and Lowry's[24] contributions, in addition to recommendations of the Society for Psychophysiological Research.[25]

The skin conductance response, in the orienting paradigm or any other experimental manipulation, can be divided into latency, risetime, amplitude, and recovery time. In practice the last of these measures is usually half-recovery time or the time taken to reduce from full amplitude of response to halfway back to prestimulus level. These separate measures are often referred to as "fractionated components." Further discussion is given by Spohn and Patterson.[21] This is a significant development in that findings of potential importance to schizophrenia have been due to careful and systematic examination of these components.

The orienting paradigm previously referred to is usually a series of innocuous tones of about 1000 Hz with a controlled rise and decay time, presented at pseudorandom intervals. Instructions to the subject are usually something to the effect of, "Relax, don't fall asleep; you may hear some tones; if so, you don't have to do anything, just sit and relax." This is usually what is termed a "non-signal significance" condition and the main variable that is measured is the number of responses (SCOR's) before the subject meets habituation criterion of two or three trials of nonresponse. The whole series is usually about 15 trials, and may be run to the same effect with visual as well as auditory stimuli. SC recording is often from the medial phalanges of both hands, and the responses subjected to fractionated component data reduction. Electrodermal measurement is best used in those experimental paradigms where a specific response (latency usually less than three seconds) is known to be driven by an experimenter-controlled, specific stimulus and where the onset of the stimulus can be precisely measured. Those paradigms which require sustained subject involvement without further stimulation, such as mental arithmetic for example, have not produced results of outstanding interest. Having said this, however, it would be perfectly appropriate to present orienting stimuli in the presence or absence of a parallel task such as mental arithmetic or auditory shadowing. Such an experiment would address concepts of parallel processing and channel attention in information-processing terms.

Conceptual Issues

The orienting response (OR) has received much attention from psychologists and electrophysiologists for very good reasons. The OR is considered by many to be a most fundamental aspect of organismic cognitive processing and attention, encompassing as it does the fundamental processes of stimulus registration, significance assessment and/or novelty factors, psychological and physiological response components, and habituation processes. All of these components are now known to be much more complex than initially supposed when the OR was first described in detail by Sokolov. Further discussion of this concept is given by Bernstein[26-28] and Barry.[29-30] In addition, a most interesting formulation of both psychological and neurological aspects of orienting is given by Pribram and McGuinness.[32] This latter paper discusses the OR in terms of the concepts of cognitive effort and proceeds to speculate on the critical role of the hippocampus as it is linked into an amygdala-to-forebrain circuit in a "gating-in and gating-out" manner. This Pribram and McGuinnes speculation follows in a long line of OR studies that derive from pioneering work by Bagshaw et al. (see Spohn and Patterson)[21] on limbic involvement in orienting.

Venables[33,34] has been a consistent and influential source of data and theory in electrodermal investigations in schizophrenia. His involvement with Mednick, Schulsinger and associates produced one of the most important early discoveries. These investigators examined a large population of "children at risk" for schizophrenia in Denmark, followed them longitudinally, and discovered that in many of the subjects who eventually became schizophrenic an abnormally fast SC recovery could be seen in their premorbid SCOR records. This finding led Venables[35] to formulate an "attentional gating" hypothesis wherein schizophrenics were seen to be exceptionally open to environmental stimulation, as distinct from other pathological populations such as psychopaths/sociopaths, who were hypothesized to show exceptional "closedness" to environmental stimulation and who displayed abnormally long SC recovery in the SCOR. The value of this formulation is that it is directly testable within the framework of information-processing and has led to stringent examination of "preattention" and "iconic" information-processing stages in schizophrenia.[36-41] As noted earlier, Venables has consistently advocated such an "input dysfunction"[42] in schizophrenia. Further reference will be made to this concept when cortical evoked potentials are discussed.

One of the most robust findings in the electrodermal study of schizophrenia has been the discovery of a large nonresponding subpopulation of schizophrenics. In the orienting paradigm only about 8% of normal subjects do not show a stimulus-driven skin conductance response. In the schizophrenic population, however, this figure may be as high as 50%. Is this, therefore, a possible basis for a predictive subclassification in schizophrenia? If so, two additional questions must be asked. First, what is known of the neurological controlling mechanisms of the SCOR, and secondly, do schizophrenic responders and nonresponders differ in other behaviors?

The earliest systematic exploration of nonresponding by Gruzelier and Venables[43,44] suggested a limbic explanation of the data in terms of lesion studies in monkeys by Bagshaw et al.[21] However, this position cannot be strongly upheld unless additional factors such as peripheral mechanisms can be ruled out as possible explanations. In short, with regard to neurological controlling mechanisms, simple peripheral cholinergic blockade will remove the response. Also, some subjects may have very low activity in the eccrine glands due to specific skin conditions. Until peripheral mechanisms are more fully understood, it is not possible to do other than speculate about neurological control of the SCOR.

Research examining linkages between SCOR responding/nonresponding and information-processing tasks have also been theoretically productive. Gruzelier and Venables[45-47] examined the two-flash-fusion threshold (2FFT) of responders and nonresponders and found some evidence for higher 2FFT values in nonresponders. This finding may be of considerable potential interest in that 2FFT is believed to index some aspect of steady-state central nervous system "activation" at the cortical level.[48,49] As such it may speak to aspects of inadequate brainstem "filter" or "attenuation" mechanisms. This possibility will be further discussed with reference to cortical evoked potentials.

Some suggestive clinical correlates of the responders/nonresponders dimension have also been identified. Differential therapeutic drug response has been found in responders and nonresponders as reported by Schneider[50] with neuroleptics and Gruzelier[51] and Yorkston[52,53] with adrenergic beta blockers.

Moreover, schizophrenic subjects who do not habituate the SCOR are reported by Frith et al.[54] to have a particularly poor prognosis. Straube et al.[55] have suggested nonresponders show greater withdrawal and thought disturbance than responders.

Patterson and Venables[10] investigated sustained attention ability in subgroups of schizophrenics, where the subgroups were defined by SCOR performance, and found that a "fast habituator" group, who showed only one or two responses in the SCOR, did not differ from normal subjects in signal detection d' (stimulus sensitivity) over a 30-minute vigilance task. This finding may be of some importance in that it is commonly believed that all schizophrenics have defective sustained vigilance. In this experiment nonresponder schizophrenics showed the worst vigilance performance and responder schizophrenics an intermediate level of performance. A relationship between SCOR and attention is further suggested by Schuri and Von Cramon[56] with neurological patients.

An especially provocative finding with nonschizophrenic subjects, by Nielsen and Petersen,[57] showed that those subjects who placed high on a "schizophrenism" questionnaire manifested a SCOR pattern similar to the schizophrenics premorbid pattern in longitudinal Danish studies. An attempt to directly manipulate fractionated components of the SCOR by Patterson and Venables[58] used centrally active drugs in normal subjects and showed that dopaminergic blockade in normals led to SCOR waveforms that resembled those of Nielson and Petersen's high "schizophrenism" subjects. Patterson and Venables also demonstrated that cholinergic blockade rendered all normal subjects, in their sample, SCOR nonresponders. This finding may suggest one of several different mechanisms whereby SCOR nonresponding is observed.

In conclusion, electrodermal study of schizophrenia has yielded sufficiently consistent data bearing on subclassification and sufficiently suggestive data in relation to mechanism(s) to further justify investigation. Fundamental neurobiological controlling mechanisms are still not fully understood and more work is required to ascertain additional ways in which schizophrenic subgroups (as determined by SCOR variables) may be different from each other and from normal controls. The current state of the art in this area is presented by Bernstein.[158]

Pupillometrics

Consideration of the pupil of the eye as a psychophysiological system can be dated back to pioneering work of Lowenstein and Loewenfeld in the early 1950s.[59-63] These investigators gave a fine account of how the sympathetic and parasympathetic nervous systems shaped the course of dilation and constriction reflexes in response to darkness and light. From a neuroscience research point of view a special attraction of the pupil is that it is a dually innervated organ where cholinergic parasympathetic pathways control constriction and adrenergically innervated sympathetic pathways control dilation. This is in contrast to speculation about control of the eccrine sweat glands where it is held that a single innervation of cholinergic pre- and post-ganglionic synapses controls these glands.

Methodological issues. Not as much work has been done with pupillo-metrics in schizophrenia as with other psychophysiological systems, in part because of the considerable difficulty of acquiring the data. Since, for certain purposes, pupillometric data must be recorded in darkness either as a dark reflex or during dark adaptation, infrared (IR) light and IR sensitive film must be used. This poses many technical problems, not the least of which is focusing a photographic system whose lenses are often distance-calibrated for visible light and not for IR. A further problem attends data reduction in studies where investigators have projected the film frames of the eye and measured the diameter of the pupil, thereby adding another data point to a time/size curve. Since the pupil is not completely circular in its dynamics of constriction/dilation, some investigators have used area analy-sis of the pupil with an image-analyzing computer.[64,65] The latter procedure also has inherent problems in that film negative emulsion may lack the contrast density for image contrast reversal in such a system, with the result that each frame must be hand printed at constant magnification. An alto-gether more modern approach is to use a raster scan device fed by an IR television camera and connected to a pixel-analyzing computer-based sys-tem. Such systems are described by Kollarits et al.[66] and Watanabe,[67] and some are commercially available. Their use is totally justified for psy-chophysiological investigation and their data are probably more accurate than photographic-based methodology, as well as being faster.

Parametric studies in schizophrenics and normal subjects. Many different parameters of pupil reflex can be measured. The light reflex examines the effects of light flashes on a dark-adapted pupil,[68,69] and the light/dark reflex plots the time/size curves of adaptation to darkness from the light-adapted state and its corresponding reconstriction to light again.[64-65] A long series of studies with schizophrenics was conducted by Rubin and associates in the 1960s.[70-75] This led to the somewhat spectacular conclusion that all schizo-phrenics fall outside the normal range on light/dark reflex parameters. Such findings were not totally confirmed by Stilson et al.,[76] but nonetheless rean-alysis of Rubin's[72] data by Sutton et al.[77] still indicates that many schizo-phrenics may possess light/dark reflex parameters more extreme than most of those in the normal range.

Pupil constriction parameters appear to be the most sensitive to differ-ences between schizophrenics and controls,[78,79] although schizophrenics do not differ from those in the normal range in consistent direction. Pupil constriction as a function of light intensity[80] illustrates that distinct subgroups of schizophrenics may be identified by means of this measure. Pupillometric measurement in conjunction with other physiological measures such as SCOR have yielded significant light/dark reflex differences between SC responders/nonresponders and schizophrenics, with slow and fast SC recovery in the orienting paradigm.[64,65] A second area of pupillometric investigation has used pupillary dilation and constriction as a dependent variable in information-processing tasks which have systematically varied the information-processing load upon the subject. This type of investigation has concentrated almost entirely upon normal subjects, with very consistent results.[81-83]

Thorough review of this area is given by Goldwater,[84] Tyron,[85] and, most recently, by Juris[86] and Beatty.[87] Credit for much of the early investigation in this area must go to Kahneman,[88-93] whose theoretical integration of information-processing concepts and the use of pupillometry to index both processing load and processing resources is refined and updated by Beatty.[87,94]

In conclusion, the area of pupillometrics has offered tantalizing prospects of elucidation of reflexive differences between schizophrenics and normal subjects and also the prospect of identification of functional subgroups within schizophrenia. Information-processing methodology, which has been developed to great effect within cognitive science, has also made use of the pupil as a dependent variable. In our view, it is unfortunate that so very few investigators have systematically explored reflexive pupillometric variables in psychosis and that almost none has applied the paradigms of Kahneman and Beatty to schizophrenia. Much of this neglect is undoubtedly due to technical difficulty; however, with the modern computer-aided pupillograph this should no longer be a problem. In addition, strong application of information-processing methodology to the understanding of schizophrenic cognition is really just beginning. It is greatly hoped that such psychophysiologically proven variables as pupillometry will find a place in this exploration in the near future.

Cardiovascular Research

A fairly comprehensive review of cardiac research in schizophrenia is given by Spohn and Patterson[21] and it would be redundant to duplicate this material here. The remainder of this section will deal with broader issues pertinent to cardiac controlling mechanisms and information-processing, some of which may not yet have been directly applied to schizophrenia research at this time.

Much credit for the adaptation of cardiac recording to a psychophysiolo-

gical system for elucidating the physiological aspects of information processing must be attributed to John and Beatrice Lacy.[95,96] A simplified ver-
sion of the Lacys' early theoretical framework sees cardiac deceleration (a
reduction in heart rate) as a facilitating mechanism to information intake
from the environment. Deceleration is also considered the cardiac component of the orienting response. Conversely, cardiac acceleration (increase in
heart rate) is thought to facilitate environmental "close-out" or rejection in
favor of increased attention to internal states or processes, such as mental
computation.[97] Much cardiac research in the past decade either has used this
conceptual framework as a dependent variable structure in cognitive manipulation or has sought to challenge or refine it.[98-100] The position of cardiac
decelerative activity as a component of a more generalized orienting response originally proposed by Graham & Clifton,[160] as well as cardiac accel-
erative activity as an index of defensive reflexes,[160] has come under strong
criticism by Barry & Maltzman.[161]

At this point it is worthwhile to be aware of the distinction between
steady-state or "tonic" heart rate and "phasic" or driven cardiac change as a
function of stimulation. Here the additional concept of "law of initial value"
must be considered. This law states that a negative correlation will exist
between tonic heart rate levels and the magnitude of stimulus-driven cardiac
change, and is predicated on the recognition that change in a physiological
system, functioning near its upper limits, is necessarily smaller than at lower
levels of functioning. This is especially important in schizophrenia, where
the general consensus of research is that many if not most schizophrenics
display elevated tonic heart rate levels, even after such confounding variables
as neuroleptic medication have been taken into account by research design.[21]
The finding of chronically elevated tonic heart rate fits very well into a
"Venables type" of "sensory flooding" theoretical framework (see section on
electrodermal activity), where the elevated heart rate may be considered to
be a defense against environmental overload, possibly caused by a defective
input "filtering" mechanism of putative brainstem or limbic origin. There is
also evidence from somatosensory cortical evoked potential studies in schizophrenia to support such a contention (this will be discussed in the following
chapter).

Studies of cardiac response to either "neutral" or "signal" stimulation in
schizophrenics have been aptly summarized by Spohn and Patterson.[21] It
may be mentioned here that many abnormalities in the heart rate response in
schizophrenics and normal subjects have been found.[101,102] Schizophrenics
who respond to neutral stimulation with heart rate acceleration are not
uncommon (normal subjects usually show transient bradycardia), and correspondingly, schizophrenics who show deceleration when stimulated by loud
tones (normal subjects would characteristically manifest a "defensive" accel-

eration) have also been found. Extension of the SCOR responder/nonresponder dichotomy is manifest in heart rate phasic change; responders show acceleration and nonresponders very brief deceleration to moderate intensity neutral tones.

Patterson[103] demonstrated that the speed of pupil constriction, from the dark-adapted state, could predict the intensity of cardiac orienting response seen in both normal subjects and schizophrenics. Those with fast pupil constriction showed the most rapid cardiac deceleration and those with the slowest constriction showed slower and less extensive deceleration. Subjects with "mid" pupil constriction speed showed an intermediate position. These findings may well suggest a cholinergic mediating mechanism, as pupil constriction is at least partly controlled by acetylcholine (ACH) pathways and cardiac decelerator pathways are also cholinergically coded. ACH is known to have strong effects on "attention" variables as directly manipulated by Warburton and associates.[104]

Cholinergic function is also implicated in a highly important technical paper by the Lacys.[95] These investigators have convincingly demonstrated that the type of cardiac phasic response is dependent upon the period within the cardiac cycle in which the stimulus onset occurs. This discovery renders it possible to reconcile conflicting findings from previous research, but by implication it also renders future cardiac research more difficult.[105] In order to present stimulation at an exactly prescribed cardiac period, the ongoing cardiac activity must be monitored by high speed automated processes. This will undoubtedly reduce the number of investigations in this area in the same way that technical difficulties have reduced pupillometric investigation. However, the obverse view is that those which are conducted will be all the more powerful. A related but novel form of psychophysiological measurement, the mean arterial pressure (MAP) has been used in an exploratory study by Hsiao et al[162] to show that many schizophrenics do not elevate their MAP when they speak, in comparison to psychiatric controls and normals. Such findings require replication and extension and may have added interest in light of current conceptualizations from Crosson & Hughes[163] concerning the subcortical control of speech mechanisms.

In conclusion, cardiac variables have an acknowledged place in information-processing research and have played a valuable part in permitting conceptualization of schizophrenic cognitive dysfunction in psychophysiological terms. This, in turn, demonstrates the psychophysiological-to-cognitive science link described in the introduction. Neuroscience research, which illuminates the neurological controlling mechanisms of cardiac control, has also taken place at a rapid rate.[106-116,159] There is, therefore, considerable reason for optimism concerning the explanatory power of cardiac research in more sophisticated information-processing application to schizophrenia in the future.

Smooth Pursuit Eye Movement

In less than a decade, smooth pursuit eye movement (SPEM) has become
one of the most interesting psychophysiological measurements in schizophrenia. Much of this work may be directly attributed to Holzman and
associates, who first focused attention on disturbed SPEM in schizophrenia
and suggested that it may represent a genetic marker.[117-123] Material available
in this field up to the late 1970s has been reviewed,[21,121] and the interested
reader is pointed in that direction for the early history and development of
this research. Spohn and Patterson[21] address five issues: the role of voluntary attention in eye tracking dysfunction (ETD); the genetic marker hypothesis; diagnostic specificity of ETD; the role of neuroleptic medication;
and methodological issues of recording and scoring. The remainder of this
section will build upon these previous articles and will detail mechanistic
and technical developments since then.[124]

The most usual paradigm for smooth pursuit eye movement recording
is that of the sinusoidally oscillating target. This target can be a simple
pendulum or a preprogrammed light spot on a cathode ray tube (CRT).
Normal subjects can track with smooth pursuit targets up to about 40 de-
grees/sec. without intrusion of saccadic "jumps" into the smooth pursuit
record. Studies with schizophrenics vs. normal subjects have characteristically used a target of about 30 degrees/sec. (well within normal smooth
pursuit capability) and discovered that many, but not all, schizophrenics
cannot do this task without saccadic intrusion. The ETD is not totally
limited to schizophrenics and can be seen in other diagnostic groups. It is
most surprisingly seen in up to 45% of the first-degree relatives of schizophrenics; hence, the preoccupation with ETD as a genetic marker for
schizophrenia.[125-129,164]

Some research has been conducted with psychotic patients and controls
in the past few years, using the optokinetic[130] and vestibular nystagmus,[131,132]
as well as smooth pursuit eye movements[133-136] and saccades.[137-140] Luckily,
the neurological controlling mechanisms of all of these eye movement factors have become partially elucidated[141-148] due to the interest of visual perception psychologists and engineers. A particularly readable review of the
most recent findings is given in *Schizophrenia Bulletin* (Vol 9, No. 1, 1983).
This publication provides multiple articles by most of the major contribu-
tors to this area and a summary of findings too extensive and detailed to be
summarized here. ETD directly addresses the concepts of voluntary/invol-
untary control of attention in schizophrenia, and the provision of mechanistic controlling concepts provides an excellent example of neuroscience (brain
mechanisms) being brought to bear on a cognitive science (control of attention) description of schizophrenia through the "interfacing" mechanism of

psychophysiology (SPEM), the idea with which this chapter was introduced.

The current consensus is that SPEM studies reflect defects in involuntary attention processes in schizophrenia and that these conclusions hold good even after contaminants of inattentiveness, distractibility, lack of motivation, or medication effects have all been allowed for by experimental design.[149,150] The way is therefore clear to apply further rigorous information-processing protocols to subgroups of schizophrenics defined by eye tracking and other ocular variables. Experiments derived from the concept of automatic vs. controlled processes[151] might be especially relevant here. It also further vindicates study of the "preattention" and initial stimulus registration stages of information processes in schizophrenia.[36-41]

The next decade of ETD investigation in psychosis will see even greater emphasis on neuro-opthamological data from which hypotheses will be derived for behavioral testing. It is currently the conclusion of the Holzman group that SPEM dysfunction is likely to be mediated by structures above the level of the brainstem and probably at the cortex.[124,152,165,166] The very exciting possibility exists, bolstered by increasing confidence in a strong genetic component in SPEM defects, that a neuro-opthalmological battery could be devised that would test the functioning of fairly specific neural controlling structures. For example, the oculocephalic reflex (tested by fixed target and rotating head) may examine a pathway from the vestibular nuclei and the medial longitudinal fasciculus to the oculomotor nuclei, via the cranial nerves to the extraocular muscles.[153] Similarly, tests of the optokinetic nystagmus may test (a) a subcortical component in which temporonasal direction of stimulation predominates in eliciting the nystagmus with different weights to the crossed and incrossed retinal fibers, and (b) a cortical component responsible for a symmetrical optomotor response involving the same retinal fibers.[154] It would appear that control of saccadic eye movement is not the same as those ocular phenomena mentioned above and that a brainstem generator that includes the substantia nigra (pars reticulata) superior colliculus and cerebellum is involved.[155,167]

In conclusion, large areas of cortex, thalamus, basal ganglia, and cerebellum are differentially involved in the control of the various ocular phenomena.[155] Exact exploration of these ocular movements to determine which are intact and which are dysfunctional[156] holds great promise for defining subgroups of schizophrenics,[157] which will then constitute independent variables in rigorous information-processing analysis to define the nature of their dysfunctional cognition. It cannot be emphasized too strongly that continued advance in this area depends fundamentally upon advances in neurosciences and cognitive science.

General Conclusion

There has been a veritable explosion of exciting research in the psychophysiology of schizophrenia over the past decade. What marks this research as worthy of optimism is the fact that much of it is theory-driven, a great advance over the atheoretical research of the previous decade. Cognitive scientists now find it possible to "neurologize" about mechanisms underlying their findings and neuroscientists have found the incorporation of behavioral data a necessary adjunct to their exploration.

References

1. Iversen LL: The chemistry of the brain. *Sci. Am.* 241:134–149, 1979.

2. Lechen F et al.: Positive symptoms of acute psychosis: Dopaminergic or noradrenergic overactivity? *Res. Commun. Psychol. Psychiatr. Behav.* 8:23–54, 1983.

3. Wasserman GS, Kong KL: Absolute timing of mental activities. *Behav. Brain Sci.* 2:243–304, 1979.

4. Estes WK et al.: The science of cognition. In: *The 5-Year Outlook on Science and Technology*, NSF US Gov. Printing Office, Washington, D.C., 1981, pp. 75–92.

5. Stuss DT et al.: Leucotomized and nonleucotomized schizophrenics: Comparison on tests of attention. *Biol. Psychiatry* 16:1084–1100, 1981.

6. Callaway E, Naghdi S: An information processing model for schizophrenia. *Arch. Gen. Psychiatry* 39:339–347, 1982.

7. Caudrey DJ et al.: Perceptual deficit in schizophrenia: A defect in redundancy utilization, filtering or scanning. *Br. J. Psychiatry* 137:352–360, 1980.

8. Asarnow RF, MacCrimmon DJ: Attention/information processing, neuropsychological functioning, and thought disorder during the acute and partial recovery phases of schizophrenia: A longitudinal study. *Psychiatr. Res.* 7:309–319, 1982.

9. Gjerde PF: Attentional capacity dysfunction and arousal in schizophrenia. *Psychol. Bull.* 93:57–72, 1983.

10. Patterson T, Venables PH: Auditory vigilance: Normals compared to chronic schizophrenic subgroups defined by skin conductance variables. *Psychiatr. Res.* 2:107–112, 1980.

11. McClelland JL: On the time relations of mental processes: An examination of systems of processes in cascade. *Psychol. Rev.* 86:287–330, 1979.

12. Simon HA: Information processing models of cognition. *Ann. Rev. Psychol.* 30:363–396, 1979.

13. Posner MI, McLeod P: Information processing models – in search of elementary operations. *Ann. Rev. Psychol.* 33:477–514, 1982.

14. Holtzman JD, Gazzaniga MS: Dual task interactions due exclusively to limits in processing resources. *Science* 218:1325–1327, 1982.

15. Hunt E: Intelligence as an information-processing concept. *Br. J. Psychol.* 71:449–474, 1980.

16. Anderson JR: Retrieval of information from long-term memory. *Science* 220:25–30, 1983.

17. Murdock BB Jr.: A theory for the storage and retrieval of item and associative information. *Psychol. Rev.* 89:609–626, 1982.

18. Pylshyn ZW: Computation and cognition: Issues in the foundations of cognitive science. *Behav. Brain Sci.* 5:111–169, 1982.

19. Anderson JR: Acquisition of cognitive skill. *Psychol. Rev.* 89:369–406, 1982.

20. Haber RN: The impending demise of the icon: A critique of the concept of iconic storage in visual information processing. *Behav. Brain Sci.* 6:1–54, 1983.

21. Spohn HE, Patterson T: Recent studies of psychophysiology in schizophrenia. *Schizophr. Bull.* 5:581–611, 1979.

22. Bernstein AS et al.: An analysis of the skin conductance orienting response in samples of American, British and German schizophrenics. *Biol. Psychiatry* 14:155–211, 1982.

23. Venables PH, Christie MJ: Mechanisms, instrumentation, recording techniques and quantification of responses. In Prokasy WF, Raskin DC (Eds.): *Electrodermal Activity in Psychological Research*, Academic Press, New York, 1984, pp. 1–124.

24. Lowry R: Active circuits for direct linear measurement of skin resistance and conductance. *Psychophysiology* 14:329–331, 1977.

25. Fowles DC et al.: Publication recommendations for electrodermal measurement. *Psychophysiology* 18:232–239, 1981.

26. Bernstein AS, Taylor KW: The interaction of stimulus information with potential stimulus significance in eliciting the skin conductance orienting response. N.A.T.O. Conference on Orienting, Amsterdam, Netherlands, 1978.

27. Bernstein AS: The orienting reflex as a research tool in the study of psychotic populations. In Ruttkay-Nedecky I et al. (Eds.): *Mechanisms of Orienting Reaction in Man*, Slovak Academy of Sciences, Bratislova, 1967, pp. 257–266.

28. Bernstein AS: To what does the orienting response respond? *Psychophysiology* 6:338–350, 1969.

29. Barry RJ: The effect of "significance" upon indices of Sokolov's orienting responses: A new conceptualization to replace the O.R. *Physiol. Psychol.* 5:209–214, 1977.

30. Barry RJ: Failure to find evidence of the unitary OR concept with indifferent low-intensity auditory stimuli. *Physiol. Psychol.* 5:89–96, 1977.

31. Barry RJ: Physiological changes in a reaction-time task: Further problems with Sokolov's dimension of stimulus "significance." *Physiol. Psychol.* 6:438–444, 1978.

32. Pribram KH, McGuinness D: Arousal, activation and effort in the control of attention. *Psychol. Rev.* 82:116–149, 1975.

33. Venables PH: The recovery limb of the skin conductance response in "high-risk" research. In Mednick SA et al. (Eds.): *Genetics, Environment and Psychopathology*, North-Holland/American Elsevier, Amsterdam, Netherlands, 1975, pp. 117–134.

34. Venables PH, Fletcher RP: The status of skin conductance recovery time: An examination of the Bundy effect. *Psychophysiology* 118:10–16, 1981.

35. Venables PH: The electrodermal psychophysiology of schizophrenics and children at risk for schizophrenia: Current controversies and developments. *Schizophr. Bull.* 3:28–48, 1977.

36. Braff DL, Callaway E, Naylor H: Very short-term memory dysfunction in schizophrenia. *Arch. Gen. Psychiatry* 34:25–30. 1977.

37. Braff DL, Saccuzzo DP: Information processing dysfunction in paranoid schizophrenia—a 2-factor deficit. *Am. J. Psychiatry* 138:1051–1056, 1981.

38. Braff DL, Saccuzzo DP: Effect of antipsychotic medication on speed of information processing in schizophrenic patients. *Am. J. Psychiatry* 139:1127–1130, 1982.

39. Saccuzzo DP, Schubert DL: Backward masking as a measure of slow processing in schizophrenia spectrum disorders. *J. Abnorm. Psychiatry* 90:305–312, 1981.

40. Saccuzzo DP, Braff DL: Early information processing deficit in schizophrenia. *Arch. Gen. Psychiatry* 38:175–179, 1981.

41. Long GM: Iconic memory: A review and critique of the study of short-term visual storage. *Psychol. Bull.* 88:785–820, 1980.

42. Venables PH: Input regulation in psychopathology. In Hammer M et al. (Eds.): *Psychopathology*, John Wiley & Sons, New York, 1973.

43. Gruzelier JH, Venables PH: Skin conductance orienting activity in a heterogenous sample of schizophrenics. *J. Nerv. Ment. Dis.* 155:277–287, 1972.

44. Gruzelier JH, Venables PH: Skin conductance responses to tones with and without attention significance in schizophrenic and nonschizophrenic psychiatric patients. *Neuropsychologia* 11:221–230, 1973.

45. Gruzelier JH, Venables PH: Relations between two-flash discrimination and electrodermal activity, re-examined in schizophrenics and normals. *J. Psychiatr. Res.* 12:77–85, 1975.

46. Gruzelier JH, Venables PH: Two-flash threshold, sensitivity and beta in normal subjects and schizophrenics. *Q. J. Exp. Psychol.* 26:594–604, 1974.

47. Gruzelier JH, Venables PH: Two-flash thresholds, heart rate, skin temperature and blood pressure in schizophrenics with and without skin conductance orienting responses. *Bull. Br. Psychol. Soc.* 25:48–49, 1972.

48. Robinson TN, Zahn TP: Covariation of two-flash threshold and autonomic arousal for high and low scores on a measure of psychoticism. *Br. J. Soc. Clin. Psychol.* 18:431–441, 1979.

49. Claridge G, Clark K: Covariation between two-flash threshold and skin conductance level in first-breakdown schizophrenics: Relationships in drug-free patients and effects of treatment. *Psychiatr. Res.* 6:371–380, 1982.

50. Schneider SJ: Electrodermal activity and therapeutic response to neuroleptic treatment in chronic schizophrenic inpatients. *Psychol. Med.* 12:607–613, 1982.

51. Gruzelier JH et al.: Influence of D-propranolol or DL-propranolol and chlorpromazine on habituation of phasic electrodermal responses in schizophrenia. *Acta Psychiatr. Scand.* 60:241–248, 1979.

52. Yorkston NJ et al.: Propranolol in the control of schizophrenic symptoms. *Br. Med. J.* 4:633–635, 1974.

53. Yorkston NJ et al.: DL-propranolol and chlorpromazine following admission

for schizophrenia—a controlled comparison. *Acta Psychiatr. Scand.* 63:13–27, 1981.

54. Frith CD et al.: Skin conductance responsivity during acute episodes of schizophrenia as a predictor of symptomatic improvement. *Psychol. Med.* 9:101–106, 1979.

55. Straube E, Heimann H: Untersuchungen zur Psychophysiologie der schizophrenie. *Drug Res.* 28:1485–1489, 1978.

56. Schuri U, Von Cramon D: Electrodermal response patterns in neurological patients with disturbed vigilance. *Behav. Brain Res.* 4:95–102, 1982.

57. Nielsen TC, Petersen NE: Electrodermal correlates of extraversion, trait anxiety, and schizophrenism. *Scand. J. Psychol.* 17:73–80, 1976.

58. Patterson T, Venables PH: Bilateral skin conductance and the pupillary light-dark reflex: Manipulation by chlorpromazine, haloperidol, scopolamine and placebo. *Psychopharmacology* 73:63–69, 1981.

59. Lowenstein O, Loewenfeld IE: Mutual role of sympathetic and parasympathetic in shaping of the pupillary reflex to light. *Arch Neurol. Psychiatry* 64:341–377, 1950.

60. Lowenstein O, Loewenfeld IE: Role of sympathetic and parasympathetic systems in the reflex dilation of pupil. *Arch. Neurol. Psychiatry* 64:313–340, 1950.

61. Lowenstein O, Loewenfeld IE: Types of central autonomic innervation and fatigue. *Arch. Neurol. Psychiatry* 66:580–599, 1951.

62. Lowenstein O, Loewenfeld IE: Disintegration of central autonomic regulation during fatigue and its reintegration by psychosensory controlling mechanisms. I: Disintegration. Pupillometric studies. *J. Nerv. Ment. Dis.* 115:1–21, 1952.

63. Lowenstein O, Loewenfeld IE: Disintegration of central autonomic regulation during fatigue and its reintegration by psychosensory controlling mechanisms. II: Reintegration. Pupillographic studies. *J. Nerv. Ment. Dis.* 115:121–145, 1952.

64. Patterson T: Skin conductance responding/nonresponding and pupillometrics in chronic schizophrenia: A confirmation of Gruzelier and Venables. *J. Nerv. Ment. Dis.* 163:200–209, 1976.

65. Patterson T: Skin conductance recovery and pupillometrics in chronic schizophrenia. *Psychophysiology* 13:189–195, 1976.

66. Kollarits CR et al.: The pupil dark response in normal volunteers. *Curr. Eye Res.* 2:255–259, 1982.

67. Watanabe T, Oono S: A solid-state television pupillometer. *Vision Res.* 22:499–505, 1982.

68. Lidsky A, Hakerem S, Sutton S: Pupillary reactions to single light pulses in psychiatric patients and normals. *J. Nerv. Ment. Dis.* 153:286–291, 1971.

69. Wyatt HJ, Musselman JF: Pupillary light reflex in humans: Evidence for an unbalanced pathway from nasal retina, and for signal cancellation in brainstem. *Vision Res.* 21:513–525, 1981.

70. Rubin LS: Pupillary reactivity as a measure of adrenergic-cholinergic mechanisms in the study of psychotic behavior. *J. Nerv. Ment. Dis.* 130:386, 1960.

71. Rubin LS: Patterns of pupillary dilation and constriction in psychotic adults and autistic children. *J. Nerv. Ment. Dis.* 133:130–142, 1961.

72. Rubin LS: Patterns of adrenergic-cholinergic imbalance in the functional psychoses. *Psychol. Rev.* 69:501–519, 1962.

73. Rubin LS: Autonomic dysfunction as a concomitant of neurotic behavior. *J. Nerv. Ment. Dis.* 138:558–574, 1964.

74. Rubin LS, Barry TJ: Dysautonomia in schizophrenia remission. *Psychosomatics* 11:506–512, 1970.

75. Rubin LS: Pupillary reflexes as objective indices of autonomic dysfunction in the differential diagnosis of schizophrenia and neurotic behavior. *J. Behav. Ther. Exp. Psychiatry* 1:185–194, 1970.

76. Stilson DW et al.: Pupillary response to light as an indicator of functional psychoses: A failure to replicate. *J. Nerv. Ment. Dis.* 143:438–442, 1966.

77. Sutton S: Personal communication.

78. Rubin LS, Barry TJ: Autonomic fatigue in psychoses. *J. Nerv. Ment. Dis.* 147:211, 1968.

79. Rubin LS, Barry TJ: The effects of conjunctival instillation of eserine and homatropine on pupillary reactivity in schizophrenics. *Biol. Psychiatry* 5:257–269, 1972.

80. Rubin LS, Barry TJ: Amplitude of pupillary contraction as a function of intensity of illumination in schizophrenia. *Biol. Psychiatry* 11:267–282, 1976.

81. Bradshaw JL: Pupil size and problem solving. *Q. J. Exp. Psychol.* 20:116–122, 1968.

82. Simpson HM, Hale SM: Pupillary changes during a decision-making task. *Percept. Mot. Skills* 29:495–498, 1969.

83. Stanners RF, Hedley DB: Pupil size and instructional set in recognition and recall. *Psychophysiology* 9:505–511, 1972.

84. Goldwater BC: Psychological significance of pupillary movements. *Psychol. Bull.* 77:340–355, 1972.

85. Tyron WW: Pupillometry: A survey of sources of variation. *Psychophysiology* 12:90–93, 1975.

86. Juris M, Velden M: Pupillary response to mental overload. *Physiol. Psychol.* 5:421–424, 1977.

87. Beatty J: Task-evoked pupillary responses, processing load, and the structure of processing sources. *Psychol. Bull.* 91:276–292, 1982.

88. Kahneman D et al.: Pupillary, heart rate and skin resistance changes during a mental task. *J. Exp. Psychol.* 79:164–167, 1969.

89. Kahneman D, Onuska D, Wolman RE: Effects of grouping on the pupillary response in a short-term memory task. *Q. J. Exp. Psychol.* 20:309–311, 1968.

90. Kahneman D, Peavler WS, Onuska L: Effects of visualization and incentive on the pupil response to mental activity. *Can. J. Psychol.* 22:186–196, 1968.

91. Kahneman D, Peavler WS: Incentive effects and pupillary changes in associative learning. *J. Exp. Psychol.* 79:312–318, 1969.

92. Kahneman D, Beatty J: Pupil diameter and load on memory. *Science* 154:1583–1585, 1966.

93. Kahneman D, Wright P: Changes of pupil size and rehearsal strategies in a short-term memory task. *Q. J. Exp. Psychol.* 23:187–196, 1971.

94. Beatty J, Wagoner BL: Pupillometric signs of brain activation vary with level of cognitive processing. *Science* 199:1216–1218, 1978.

95. Lacey BC, Lacey JI: Two-way communication between the heart and the brain: Significance of time within the cardiac cycle. *Am. Psychol.* 33:99–113, 1978.

96. Lacey BC, Lacey JI: Change in heart period: A function of sensorimotor event timing within the cardiac period. *Physiol. Psychol.* 5:383–393, 1977.

97. Friedman D, Tusky B, Erlenmeyer-Kimling L: Evoked cardiac waveform components during aversion and detection procedures. *Physiol. Psychol.* 8:497–502, 1980.

98. Daily W, Valtair J, Amsel A: Bidirectional heart-rate change to photic stimulation in infant rats: Implication for orienting/defensive reflex distinction. *Behav. Neur. Biol.* 35:96–103, 1982.

99. Fredrikson M, Ohman A: Heart-rate and electrodermal orienting responses to visual stimuli differing in complexity. *Scand. J. Psychol.* 20:37–41, 1979.

100. Coles MGH, Duncan-Johnson CC: Cardiac activity and information processing: The effect of stimulus significance and detection and response requirements. *J. Exp. Psychol.* 1:418–428, 1975.

101. Gruzelier JH, Venables PH: Evidence of high and low levels of physiological arousal in schizophrenia. *Psychophysiology* 12:66–73, 1975.

102. McCormick DJ, Broekema WJ: Size estimation, perceptual recognition and cardiac rate response in acute paranoid and nonparanoid schizophrenics. *J. Abnorm. Psychol.* 87:385–398, 1978.

103. Patterson T: The pupil as predictor of attentional control in normals and schizophrenics. Paper presented at the 10th Symposium on the Pupil, City University, New York, New York, 1977.

104. Warburton DM, Wesnes K: Cholinergic mechanisms and attentional dysfunction. In Perris C, Strune G, Jansson B (Eds.): *Biological Psychiatry*, Elsevier/North Holland, Amsterdam, Netherlands, 1981.

105. Turpin G, Sartory G: Effects of stimulus position in the respiratory cycle on the evoked cardiac response. *Physiol. Psychol.* 8:503–508, 1980.

106. Kalia M: Brainstem localization of vagal preganglionic neurons. *J. Autonom. Nerv. Sys.* 3:451–481, 1981.

107. Brooks CMcC: Introduction: Control of the autonomic nervous system and the multiple integrative roles it plays in regulating cardiovascular functions. *J. Autonom. Nerv. Sys.* 4:115–120, 1981.

108. Lokhandwala MF: Presynaptic receptor systems on cardiac sympathetic nerves. *Life Sci.* 24:1823–1832, 1979.

109. Gold MR, Cohen DH: Modification of the discharge of vagal cardiac neurons during learned heart rate change. *Science* 214:345–347, 1981.

110. Loewy AD: Descending pathways to sympathetic and parasympathetic preganglionic neurons. *J. Autonom. Nerv. Sys.* 3:265–275, 1981.

111. Akselrod S et al.: Power spectral analysis of heart rate fluctuation: A quantitative probe of beat to beat cardiovascular control. *Science* 213:220–222, 1981.

112. Kollai M, Koizumi K: Reciprocal and non-reciprocal action of the vagal and sympathetic nerves innervating the heart. *J. Autonom. Nerv. Sys.* 1:33–52, 1979.

113. Elliott JM: The central noradrenergic control of blood pressure and heart rate. *Clin. Exp. Pharmacol. Physiol.* 6:569–579, 1979.

114. Haroutunian V, Campbell BA: Neural control of the heart-rate-orienting response in preweanling rats. *Behav. Neur. Biol.* 36:24–39, 1982.

115. Brezenoff HE, Giuliano R: Cardiovascular control by cholinergic mechanisms in the central nervous system. *Ann. Rev. Pharmacol. Toxicol.* 22:341–381, 1982.

116. Richardson JS, Chiu EKY: The regulation of cardiovascular functions by monoamine neurotransmitters in the brain. *Int. J. Neurosci.* 20:103–148, 1983.

117. Holzman PS, Proctor LR, Hughes DW: Eye tracking patterns in schizophrenia. *Science* 181:179–181, 1973.

118. Holzman PS et al.: Eye tracking dysfunction in schizophrenic patients and their relatives. *Arch. Gen. Psychiatry* 31:143–151, 1974.

119. Holzman PS et al.: Smooth pursuit eye movements and diazopam, CPZ and secobarbital. *Psychopharmacologia* 44:111–115, 1975.

120. Holzman PS, Levy DL, Proctor LR: Smooth pursuit eye movements, attention and schizophrenia. *Arch. Gen. Psychiatry* 33:1415–1420, 1976.

121. Holzman PS, Levy DL: Smooth pursuit eye movements and functional psychoses: A review. *Schizophr. Bull.* 3:15–28, 1977.

122. Holzman PS et al.: Abnormal pursuit eye movements in schizophrenia. Evidence for a genetic indicator. *Arch. Gen. Psychiatry* 34:802–805, 1977.

123. Holzman PS et al.: Deviant eye tracking in twins discordant for psychosis — a replication. *Arch. Gen. Psychiatry* 37:627–631, 1980.

124. Lipton RB et al.: Eye movement dysfunction in psychiatric patients: A review. *Schizophr. Bull.* 9:13–72, 1983.

125. Holzman PS et al.: Deviant eye tracking in twins discordant for psychosis. *Arch. Gen. Psychiatry* 37:627–631, 1980.

126. Iacono WG, Lykken DT: Comments on "smooth-pursuit eye movement": A comparison of two measurement techniques by Linsey, Holzman, Haberman and Yasillo. *J. Abnorm. Psychol.* 88:678–680, 1979.

127. Iacono WG, Lykken DT: Electro-oculographic recording and scoring of smooth-pursuit and saccadic eye tracking: A parametric study using monozygotic twins. *Psychophysiology* 16:94–107, 1979.

128. Iacono WG, Lykken DT: Eye tracking and psychopathology. *Arch. Gen. Psychiatry* 36:1361–1369, 1979.

129. Iacono WG, Lykken DT: Eye tracking in normal twins. *Behav. Genet.* 12:517–526, 1982.

130. Latham C et al.: Optokinetic nystagmus and pursuit eye movements in schizophrenia. *Arch. Gen. Psychiatry* 38:997–1003, 1981.

131. Baloh RW, Yee RD, Honrubia V: Internuclear opthalmoplogia. II. Pursuit, optokinetic nystagmus and vestigulo-ocular reflex. *Arch. Neurol.* 35:490–493, 1978.

132. Buizza A, Schmid R: Visual-vestibular interaction in the control of eye movement: Mathematical modelling and computer stimulation. *Biol. Cybern.* 43:209–223, 1982.

133. Siever LJ et al.: Smooth pursuit eye tracking impairment — relation to other markers of schizophrenia and psychologic correlates. *Arch. Gen. Psychiatry* 39:1001–1005, 1982.

134. Cegalis JA, Sweeney JA: Eye movements in schizophrenia: A quantitative analysis. *Biol. Psychiatry* 14:13–26, 1979.

135. Schmid-Burgk W et al.: Disturbed smooth pursuit and saccadic eye movements in schizophrenia. *Arch. Psychiatr. Nervenkr.* 232:381–389, 1982.

136. Levin S et al.: Identification of abnormal patterns in eye movements of schizophrenic patients. *Arch. Gen. Psychiatry* 39:1125–1130, 1982.

137. Hershey LA et al.: Saccadic latency measurements in dementia. *Arch. Neurol.* 40:592–593, 1983.

138. Levin S et al.: Saccadic eye movements in psychotic patients. *Psychiatry Res.* 5:47–58, 1981.

139. Levin S et al.: Saccadic eye movements in schizophrenic patients measured by reflected light technique. *Biol. Psychiatry* 17:1277–1287, 1982.

140. Bahill AT, Stark L: The trajectories of saccadic eye movements. *Sci. Am.* 240:108–117, 1979.

141. Tedeschi G et al.: Effect of amphetamine on saccadic and smooth pursuit eye movements. *Psychopharmacology* 79:190–192, 1983.

142. Waespe W, Cohen B, Raphan T: Role of the flocculus and paraflocculus in optokinetic nystagmus and visual-vestibular interactions: Effects of lesions. *Exp. Brain Res.* 50:9–33, 1983.

143. Collewijn H: Sensory control of optokinetic nystagmus in the rabbit. *Trends Neurosci.* 3:277–280, 1980.

144. Godaux E, Laune JM: The saccadic system and the vestibulo-ocular reflex in the cat do not share the same integrator. *Neurosci. Let.* 38:263–268, 1983.

145. Harris LR, Cynader M: Modification of the balance and gain of the vestibulo-ocular reflex in the cat. *Exp. Brain Res.* 44:57–70, 1981.

146. Optican LM, Robinson DA: Cerebellar-dependent adaptive control of primate saccadic system. *J. Neurophysiol.* 44:1058–1076, 1980.

147. Kaneko CRS, Evinger C, Fuchs AF: Role of cat pontine burst neurons in generation of saccadic eye movements. *J. Neurophysiol.* 46:387–408, 1981.

148. Hikosaka O, Wurtz RH: Visual and oculomotor functions of monkey substantia nigra pars reticulata. *J. Neurophysiol.* 49:1230–1301, 1983.

149. Pivik RT: Smooth pursuit eye movements and attention in psychiatric patients. *Biol. Psychiatry* 14:859–879, 1979.

150. Cegalis JA, Sweeney JA: The effect of attention on smooth pursuit eye movements of schizophrenics. *J. Psychiatr. Res.* 16:145–161, 1981.

151. Schneider W, Shiffrin RM: Controlled and automatic human information processing: I. Detection, search and attention. *Psychol. Rev.* 84:1–66, 1977.

152. Jones AM, Pivik RT: Abnormal visual-vestibular interactions in psychosis. *Biol. Psychiatry* 18:45–61, 1983.

153. Lipton RB, Levin S, Holzman PS: Horizontal and vertical pursuit eye movements, the oculocephalic reflex, and the functional psychoses. *Psychiatr. Res.* 3:193–203, 1980.

154. Montarolo PG, Precht W, Strata P: Functional organization of the mechanisms subserving the optokinetic nystagmus in the cat. *Neuroscience* 6:231–246, 1981.

155. Fuchs AF, Kaneko CRS: A brain stem generator for saccadic eye movements. *Trends Neurosci.*, 1981.

156. Iacono WG, Tuason VB, Johnson RA: Dissociation of smooth-pursuit and saccadic eye tracking in remitted schizophrenics — an ocular reaction time task that schizophrenics perform well. *Arch. Gen. Psychiatry* 38:991–996, 1981.

157. Bartfai A, Levander SE, Sedvall G: Smooth pursuit eye movements, clinical symptoms, CSF metabolites, and skin conductance habituation in schizophrenic patients. *Biol. Psychiatry* 18:971–987, 1983.

158. Bernstein AS: Orienting response research in schizophrenia: Where we have come and where we might go. *Schizophr. Bull.* 13:623-641, 1987.

159. Morilak DA, Fornal C, Jacobs BL: Single unit activity of noradrenergic neurons in locus coeruleus and serotonergic neurons in the nucleus raphe dorsalis of freely moving cats in relation to the cardiac cycle. *Brain Res.* 399:262-270, 1986.

160. Graham FK, Clifton RK: Heart rate change as a component of the orienting response. *Psychol Bull.* 65:305-320, 1966.

161. Barry RJ, Maltzman I: Heart rate deceleration is not an orienting reflex — heart rate acceleration is not a defensive reflex. *The Pavlovian Journal of Biological Sciences* 20:15-28, 1985.

162. Hsiao JK, Lynch JJ, Foreman PJ, Gross HS: Cardiovascular response to speaking in schizophrenics. *Psychiatr. Res.* 22:69-79, 1987.

163. Crosson B, Hughes CW: Role of the thalamus in language: Is it related to schizophrenic thought disorder? *Schizophr. Bull.* 13:605-621, 1987.

164. Helmchen H, Henn FA: *Biological Perspectives of Schizophrenia*, John Wiley & Sons, Chichester, England, 1987.

165. Levin S: Frontal lobe dysfunctions in schizophrenia — I. Eye movement impairments. *J. Psychiatr. Res.* 18:27-55, 1984.

166. Levin S: Frontal lobe dysfunctions in schizophrenia — II. Impairments of psychological and brain functions. *J. Psychiatr. Res.* 18:57-72, 1984.

167. Sparks DL: Neural cartography: sensory and motor maps in the superior colliculus. *Brain Behav. Evolution.* 31:49-56, 1988.

6

Psychophysiological Nature of Schizophrenia:

II. Brain Electrical Activity

Terry Patterson and Herbert E. Spohn

EDITOR'S NOTE

The usual electroencephalographic study does not reveal much of value in deepening our understanding of the schizophrenias. However, the use of fast Fourier transform and various digital filtering algorithms have rendered it possible to quantify the EEG record into a mathematical statement of the power available; with such sophisticated methodology it has been possible to detect abnormalities among these patients. For example, they often show an increase in delta and theta activity, and a reduction in both the amplitude and frequency of peak alpha; this is characteristically seen in the presence of significantly reduced early beta activity and a significant increase in late beta activity.

A significantly higher proportion of schizophrenics with a family history of disorder (72%) showed severe thought disorder and a significantly lower proportion of EEG abnormalities than patients without family history of disease (43%). This may be an important clue, differentiating a kind of schizophrenia in which illness is learned as a result of skewed perceptions and communication in a family structure from a form of the illness which is primarily biological in origin.

EEG studies have been correlated with information-processing systems in normals and schizophrenic subjects. A variety of unusual findings suggest abnormalities in information-processing systems at various levels among the latter. For example, using evoked potential techniques, one observer noted alterations indicative of a marked reduction of normal inhibitory mechanisms in schizophrenics.

The mind-body relationship is the psychiatrist's unique terrain. Studies such as these will not only lead to new, exciting treatment approaches; they may also offer explanations about the efficacy of psychological treatment measures and new ways to sharpen psychotherapy's effectiveness.

Introduction

In the previous chapter, we reviewed peripheral nervous system psychophysiology in schizophrenia. In this one we will examine current conceptualizations of brain electrical activity in schizophrenia, with the same question in mind as previously, i.e., what can electrophysiological studies tell us about the subclassification and mechanism(s) underlying schizophrenia? Electrophysiological phenomena are particularly important for schizophrenia research in that they provide the neuroscientific "underpinnings" to psychophysiological measures. However, as we previously described, the combination of electrophysiology and an information-processing conceptualization derived from cognitive science provides a particularly excellent framework for theoretically driven research in schizophrenia. It will therefore be apparent that psychopathology research borrows heavily from cognitive science and neuroscience and that its productivity is vindicated by whatever light it can shed on the twin unknowns of schizophrenia: mechanism(s) and subclassification.

Surface-recorded in vivo brain electrical activity has undergone massive technical development in the past decade; there has also been increased clarification of the correlation of specific brain events with specific behaviors. It must be strongly stated at this point that the key word here is *correlated* and not *caused*. The correlation of brainwaves with behavior is simply one aspect of an effort at "functional specification" of the neurological/neurochemical control of behavior, including the aberrant behavior of schizophrenia. Its value may ultimately lie only in "targeting" more sophisticated neuroscience-developed techniques.

As conceptualization has rarefied, data have fractionated. This is nowhere more apparent than in research with cortical evoked potentials. At one time it may have been possible to talk about the evoked potential (EP) in schizophrenia; now one must specify which time period (or epoch) within the EP is under discussion. For this reason EP data will be discussed in three separate sections: (a) brainstem and early EP, (b) the "mild" components of the EP, and (c) the "late" EP components. Happily, we can report that this fractionation carries with it the exciting possibility of using the EP components to index the neurological events correlated with specific information-processing "stages," as far as these are currently known. Before evoked potentials are discussed we will briefly review research with the electroencephalogram (EEG), and after the discussion of EP we will present data from brain magnetic waves.

EEG Studies

The electroencephalogram has been in evolution for over half a century. Its use in the study of the psychoses has been reviewed elsewhere.[1-4] Consequently, here we will concentrate on significant developments since the late 1970s. First it should be mentioned that clinical EEG, which is usually a visually interpreted paper readout of up to 20 channels of polygraph recording, is not the same as in most modern research EEG studies, which make use of power spectral analysis.[1,5] The clinical EEG is most usually a search for lesion-related activity and involves the "impressions" of an experienced electroencephalographer. The most that this type of approach has been able to tell us is that in any given study of schizophrenics vs. normal subjects, a greater percentage of patients will show "nonspecific diffuse activity," "weak alpha," "general dysrhythmia," and possibly an increase in "spikes."[2,6] Lamentably, these "impressionistic" data have not been further refined in a clinical sense; this could be achieved by the investigation of subgroups of schizophrenics, defined by EEG variables, and subjected to cognitive processes analysis. Consequently, the significance of these findings cannot be ascertained, especially as the resting EEG dynamics of the "normal" population may be more variable than traditionally supposed.[7]

The use of fast Fourier transform and various digital filtering algorithms has rendered it possible to quantify the EEG record into a mathematical statement of the power available, usually in 1 Hz wide "steps," at any frequency in the range of approximately 0–40 Hz. This power spectral analysis has been widely used in schizophrenia research.[1,6] The general consensus is that many schizophrenics show an increase in delta activity (0–3.5 Hz) and theta activity (3.5–7.5 Hz), as well as a reduction in both the amplitude and frequency of peak alpha activity (8–13 Hz). This is characteristically seen in the presence of significantly reduced early beta activity (13.5–19 Hz) and a significant increase in late beta activity (19.5–40 Hz). Some authors take the view that the consistency with which increased power in high bands (19–40 Hz) has been found in schizophrenia may have diagnostic significance.[8] Indeed, such findings should, at the least, encourage the proponents of other forms of potentially predictive subclassification, from peripheral electrophysiology and cognitive processes, to systematically examine the power spectral EEG as part of the extension of subclassification.

A recent investigation has examined the EEG of schizophrenics with (familial) and without (sporadic) a family history of schizophrenia.[9] A significantly higher proportion of the familial schizophrenics showed severe thought disorder and a significantly lower proportion of EEG abnormalities (43%) than the sporadic group (72%). It would be especially interesting to see how these data would interact with the genetic implications arising from smooth pursuit eye movement dysfunction reviewed in Chapter 5.

It is of considerable interest to know what aspects of schizophrenic dysfunction represent steady-state or trait features and which aspects may be episodic or state features, correlated with psychotic episodes. This issue has been addressed by Stevens and Livermore, who used spectral analyzed EEG in free-moving patients.[10] In this study "ramp" spectra characterized by smooth decline from lowest to highest frequencies, previously found with subcortical spike activity in epilepsy but not in controls, appeared in the spectra of schizophrenics during hallucinatory periods, catatonic episodes, and certain visual tasks. The authors interpret their finding as indicating specific schizophrenic behaviors to be driven by, or interactive with, pathogenic brain processes. An alternative strategy has been used by Koukkou, who examined schizophrenics in a first acute episode and compared their EEG spectra to remitted patients and controls.[11,12] These studies are of particular interest in that EEG changes in reaction to stimulation were examined and showed that remitted schizophrenics and normal subjects responded in a similar manner but that the acute patients showed only a low frequency response. Interestingly, slowed reaction time and poor time estimation still differentiated the remitted patients from normal subjects. These data might be extremely useful when combined with subclassification based on other abnormal "orienting" behavior such as skin conductance. They also lend themselves to further investigation in more refined information-processing paradigms.

The fact that schizophrenics are not homogenous with respect to EEG spectra[13] is well-demonstrated by Etevenon et al.,[14] who cluster analyzed resting EEG spectra in subclassified schizophrenics. In this study "paranoid," "residual," and "other" schizophrenics could be differentiated, with the paranoid group showing greatest lowering of alpha power and frequency, and higher theta. This finding is reminiscent of early conflicting studies in skin conductance before the responder/nonresponder subclassification rendered the data more replicable between laboratories. There is a need for further investigation in this area, especially as the EEG spectra may index either enduring or episodic information-processing differences.[15,16]

In longitudinal studies in Denmark, a wide range of social and intellectual deviance was found in populations that also showed a high incidence of schizophrenia. Alcoholism was one such phenomena. This finding has led to EEG studies which directly compare alcoholics, drug abusers, and schizophrenics.[17-19] Much of this research is not directly comparable between studies due to large methodological differences, but there is a growing body of information that shows similarities of a nontrivial nature between alcoholics and schizophrenics. How far this may relate to trait variables in subjects who may be derived from a similar population will have to be defined by future studies. Current research on brain potentials and alcoholics has reached the exciting stage where perhaps a "genetic predisposition" to alcoholism, especially in males, may be "indexed" by alterations to both early and late components of the evoked potential.[80-92]

A study by Davis et al.[20] has directly utilized EEG occipital alpha blocking in a forced choice letter recognition study. This is a well-known information-processing paradigm and has showed the predicted slow reaction time and poor performance of schizophrenics vs. controls. However, the expected longer alpha blocking latency of schizophrenics did not materialize. The schizophrenics showed faster alpha blocking latencies than controls.

This finding is potentially of great importance in light of schizophrenics' well demonstrated slow reaction time. If information-processing is indeed a sequential process, then the results with occipital alpha blocking demonstrate that schizophrenics' information-processing may be intact up to that stage, and that the information-processing defect(s) that produce slow reaction time are to be found "downstream" of the alpha blocking stage. A similar and perhaps confirmational finding of this nature is that of the Holzman group (discussed in Chapter 5) with saccadic eye movements. The finding that the saccadic reaction time of a schizophrenic is not different from normal may demonstrate the same conclusion, i.e., that a schizophrenic's information-processing is not defective up to that stage and that deficit(s) occur "downstream." Thus, from two separate electrophysiological systems the hypothesis may be stated that stimulus "registration" and early processing stages may be intact, but that defects occur in later stimulus processing or perhaps the organization of response from competing alternative response strategies. Conversely, it is possible that the significantly faster alpha blocking latency may indicate some form of defect at an earlier information-processing stage. Davis et al. states:

To understand how excessive rapid blocking can be detrimental, the processes presumed to occur on a feature analysis task need to be examined. The stage of pre-attention (or feature extraction) is an active process that is guided by schemata, expectation and other active control processes. Efficient processing then requires rapid adjustment of the visual system (reflected in alpha blocking latency) along with a coordinated control system. Should these two operations become desynchronized, further processing would break down, or become fragmented.[21]

For the future, it is necessary to standardize methodology for recording "resting" EEG in schizophrenia and to relate such findings to potentially predictive subclassification derived from other areas. There is also a great need for further investigation similar to the Davis study where EEG is used as a dependent variable in tightly controlled information-processing tasks. This renders EEG spectra potentially capable of providing single trial data, which cannot be done with evoked potential measures which rely upon repeated trials and signal averaging. Sophisticated combination of EEG spectra and evoked potential methodology has already been fruitfully explored by Basar[22] and will hopefully be more widely and imaginatively applied to schizophrenia. In the past investigators have turned to the cortical evoked potential to access "time-dependent" brain response to stimulation. EEG epochs for spectral analysis typically cover periods of several seconds to several minutes and are therefore of limited usefulness in the investigation of information-processing stages (e.g., the "icon"), which may be over in a few hundred milliseconds. This criticism could also apply to regional cortical bloodflow (rCBF) studies, which also require several minutes over which to "integrate" data (or about 40 seconds in the case of O^{15} positron emission tomography). It would therefore appear that EP data may be complementary to EEG data, and that each is applicable to specific experimental paradigms depending upon the time-constant of the phenomenon under investigation. It is to studies of the evoked potential that we now turn.

Evoked Potential

If the stimulus (auditory, visual or somatosensory) is presented to a subject while an EEG is taken (usually less than 1 second), the EEG will show characteristic waveform changes beginning virtually at stimulus onset. This represents a single trial of cortical evoked potential. Usually the evoked waveform (signal) is very hard to see against the background EEG (noise) and so multiple trials are averaged together. As the background EEG is not in phase with the stimulation, it averages to zero and the signal waveform (which is in phase with the stimulation) steadily grows larger and therefore more visible. This represents the averaged evoked potential (AEP). Figure 1 gives an idealized waveform that represents most of the components of the AEP. A highly simplistic interpretation of these waveforms sees the brainstem EP (within the first 10 msecs) as the very earliest relay of information to the cortex. Each of the small waves in the brainstem corresponds to the function of known subcortical and brainstem structures[23] and is frequently used to detect possible brainstem lesion.

It was once thought that these early waves were not influenced by attentional factors,[24] but recent research casts doubt on this conclusion.[25] The

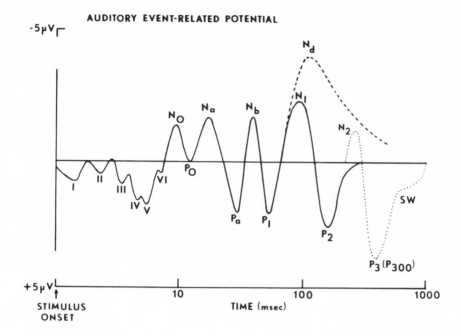

Figure 1: Highly idealized auditory EP waveform plotted on logarithmic time scale. Brainstem (waves I-VI) early and middle components (No, Po, Na, Pa, Nb, P1, N1, P2) some of which are task related, as are some of the later components (Nd, N2, P300, and slow wave).
(Adapted and redrawn from Hillyard, SA, Kutas, M: *Ann. Rev. Psychol.* 34:33-61, 1983.)

time epoch between the brainstem components and about 120 msecs is often referred to as "early" EP components, and simplistically, this region is thought to designate some aspects of stimulus "registration" at the cortex. The epoch from about 120 msecs to about 250 msecs is sometimes called the "mid" components of the EP, and these are the features that are most immediately recognized, more especially the N1 (or N100) to P2 (or P200) complex. These waveforms are thought to be sensitive to stimulus novelty and habituation factors and as such are said to be indicative of aspects of central processing. The region from about 300 msecs and later is called the "late" components and of these the P300 wave is perhaps the most exhaustively documented. Additional waves of note in this region include the "late positive complex" (or slow wave) around the 450 msec period, and later still the contingent negative variation. These late components are held to reflect decision processes, including response ambiguity and uncertainty. An over-simplified but perhaps useful distinction to bear in mind is that early components reflect more "hardwired" aspects of information handling and the later components come under progressively more "psychological" control. What we cannot say, with confidence, is how the "wraparound" may take place, by which processes indexed by the later components come to have an effect on earlier components. That this process does in fact take place we will shortly demonstrate. At this point it is well to bear in mind that investigators often specialize in just one of these time-dependent regions and consequently the experimental paradigms applicable to one are not necessarily relevant to the others, nor is the electronic equipment with which they are measured.

Within the past three years some especially exciting EP data have been acquired when EP measurement has taken place concurrent with information-processing tasks. In their review of these data, Hillyard and Kutas[26] state: " . . . EP's from the scalp make it possible to study cognitive and linguistic processes with greater precision than can be achieved with behavioral techniques alone. By providing a 'second window' into the information-processing activities of the human brain, EP data have proven helpful in tearing apart stimulus evaluation from response mobilization factors, in identifying hierarchical levels of stimulus selection, and in distinguishing serial from parallel stimulus analyses."[27] In the search for sophisticated elucidation of cognitive processing deficit in schizophrenia, it would be hard to overemphasize the potential importance of this development.

EP and Information-Processing

Renault et al.[28] report two types of N200 wave which are related in different ways to the same behavioral response: the duration of one increases with reaction time and the other remains constant. These waves peak at different times in different brain regions and seem to be related to the duration of perceptual processing. This processing negativity is more fully explored by Näätänen,[29] who provides integration with cognitive science concepts of selective attention and further suggests that these waveforms may represent separate pattern recognition and stimulus classification processes in the brain.[30] Principal components analysis of EP's in a letter/number information-processing task have identified a component at 250 msecs, which Chapman and associates term the "storage component."[31] This positive waveform is interpreted as being related to storage of information in short-term memory and may be similar to a P240 waveform reported to be sensitive to increased memory load when a second task was imposed upon a primary task of simple target detection.[32,33]

A recurrent finding with schizophrenic patients has been the tendency toward greater distractibility. A study of Wickens et al.[34] has shown that the EP may be an additional way to study this phenomenon. These authors used a primary and a secondary task; as the information-processing demands of the primary task increased, so did the amplitude of the EP components associated with it. Correspondingly, the EP components of the secondary task diminished in amplitude. This strongly indicates that there is reciprocity in the sharing of information-processing resources in the brain and that perhaps a defect in this capacity might characterize a subpopulation of schizophrenics. If this were found to be so, then it might well represent the neurological underpinnings of schizophrenic "distractibility."

The interaction between electrophysiology and information-processing cuts both ways. Recent EP evidence suggests that recognition memory may be a two-stage process.[35] Conversely, subtle manipulation of information-processing demands has indicated that the late positive component (sometimes called the slow wave) may in fact be composed of at least two different waves, which may interact with the P300 component.[33,36] EP data have been used to indicate the information-processing stage at which stroop interference effects occur. In this "stroop type" task the response time varies with congruence between the stimulus word and its color but the P300 latency remains constant, indicating that "response competition" is the primary source of interference.[37]

Throughout this chapter we have suggested that information-processing is conceptualized as a serial, stage-by-stage process. While this may largely be true, it has been suggested that the transfer between these stages happens continuously and that these processes are in "cascade."[38] (Imagine a fountain of many levels with the water continuously pouring from one to the other.) In this way it is possible to conceptualize a serial process which has many of the aspects of parallel processing. An implication of such a conceptualization is that the final stages should in turn be capable of influencing the primary stages. Recent EP data lend credence to this "wraparound" effect. For example, with stimulus repetition, changes in late negative waves seem to contribute to changes in amplitude of the earlier P270 waves.[39] In lexical decision tasks a P637 component covaries with reaction time, suggesting a parallel response preparation and stimulus evaluation process that influences an earlier N100-P187 component.[40] A particularly elegant study by Donald and Young[41] concludes that, with regard to successful selective attention (an area thought to be disrupted in many schizophrenics), neural selectivity proceeds in a "top-down manner," with the longer latency P300 showing a selective response sooner than the earlier N100. They also show evidence that the selectivity of N100 "tuning" increases over time with the continued focusing of attention.

EP research within an information-processing framework has been relatively recently applied to schizophrenia. However, two results of outstanding interest and profound implication are worth discussing at length. Adler et al.[42] presented acute, unmedicated schizophrenics and normal subjects with paired click stimuli that were separated by 0.5, 1.0, and 2.0 seconds and measured an early 50 msec positive component of the EP. When the stimuli were separated by 0.5 sec., the normal subjects showed a 90% decrement of response to the second stimulus, but the schizophrenics showed only a 15% decrement. When the stimuli were separated by 2.0 secs. the normal subjects showed a second response decrement of 30–50%, but the schizophrenics actually showed an increased response to the second stimulus.

These data are powerful evidence that normally present inhibitory mechanisms are markedly reduced in schizophrenics and that failure of these inhibitory mechanisms may be responsible for defects in sensory gating. This work directly supports the theories described above that suggest "input dysfunction" in schizophrenia. If these data are related to the "wraparound" concepts described in the previous paragraph, then it may be possible to see such an "input dysfunction" in terms of failures to selectively inhibit input channels, which are in turn a function of defective cortically downward mediation upon brainstem structures.

This concept is directly addressed by Baribeau-Braun et al.[43] These authors used a dichotic listening task (well-known in information-processing experiments) for both schizophrenics and normal subjects and measured both early and later EP components. Despite slow and inaccurate detections, the schizophrenic subjects were able to focus selectively to different ears but only at fast stimulation rates. The authors accept this as evidence for an intact early selective stage of information processing. However, the schizophrenics showed an abnormal late information-processing stage, which indicates inefficiency in processing information from a previously detected target.

Marked deficits in schizophrenics at slow stimulation rates and during divided attention suggests that the schizophrenic attention disorder is one of control or maintenance of a selective processing strategy, rather than one of general slowness or absence of selectivity. It is readily conceivable that the control or maintenance of attention has its neurological controlling mechanism in the activity of cortically downward pathways that selectively influence subcortical gating structures (e.g., the hippocampus, amygdala, thalamus, and aspects of the cerebellum). If this should prove to be the case, then a theoretical synthesis is possible between theories of schizophrenia that advocate "input dysfunction" and those which advocate intactness of early processing stages (and their neurological controlling structures) and opt for a hypothesis of later stage information-processing dysfunction, or "thinking defects" at the cortical level.

At this point a cautionary note is appropriate. Throughout this chapter we have implicitly assumed that the late EP components are dependent for their occurrence upon early brainstem EPs. However, this view may undergo radical change following demonstration that two major EP components from the temporal scalp (and underlying auditory cortex) are clearly visible in subjects with absent or markedly abnormal brainstem EPs.[44] Clearly we have much to learn about the neurological underpinnings to surface (scalp) recorded electrical activity. Data from evoked magnetic fields in the brain may be of some help here and are detailed below. We would also like to point out that conflicting reports between laboratories can often be attributed to differences in recording sites and that some of the more interesting findings outlined above show waves that peak at different times in different regions of the brain. For these reasons new techniques have been developed which allow visualization of "whole-scalp" electrical activity using computerized techniques and color graphic topography representation. Such a system is that of Duffy and associates, referred to as brain electrical activity mapping (BEAM).[45-47] This is an immensely important technical development and the equipment is currently commercially available.

EP and Schizophrenia

Research of EP in schizophrenia, as far as the late 1970s, has been reviewed by the present authors[2] and also, with respect to "early" evoked potentials, by Shagass,[48] "middle" EP components, by Buchsbaum,[49] and "late" EP waveforms, by Roth.[50] The remainder of this section will outline developments since then.

The brainstem evoked potential has fairly well-developed maturational indices[51] and has been used to show[52] that children at risk for central nervous system (CNS) disease depart from normal waveforms in a variety of ways. The implications of these findings for schizophrenia lie in the belief that childhood autism may be etiologically similar to schizophrenia but with a particularly early onset. Recent research with the brainstem EP indicates longer response latency in the auditory nerve and increased brainstem transmission time in autistic children.[53] Confirmation of these findings[54] leads to the tentative hypothesis that abnormal information input at a very early age may cause maldevelopment of brain systems subserving language and cognition. Although the brainstem EP has been shown to be sensitive to operant control,[25] acute ethanol administration,[55] history of alcoholism,[56] and Alzheimer's disease,[57] very little work has been done with brainstem EP in schizophrenia. A consensus of the available data suggests no differences between schizophrenics and normal subjects and no differences between schizophrenics and depressives.[59] For the moment it may be tentatively concluded that the brainstem EP does not provide much information about the sources of abnormal information-processing in schizophrenia, although it should continue to be researched as an extension of subclassification as abnormalities may be applicable to a specific subgroup. The main problem with work in this area is that published data is from a very small number of schizophrenics. For example, the report of Brecher and Begleiter[93] is based on only nine patients, although it concludes that brainstem EPs are within normal limits in schizophrenia. The report by Lindstrom et al.[94] is based on more than twice that number and concludes that a specific subgroup (those with active auditory hallucinations) have clear brainstem EP abnormalities.

More research using early EP's (after 10 msec but not shorter than 120 msecs) has been conducted with schizophrenics and is reviewed by Shagass.[60] Shagass and associates produced the particularly interesting finding (subsequently confirmed) that early components of the somatosensory EP showed an increase in amplitude in schizophrenia and that the latter components were attentuated. This finding fits very well with "input dysfunction" hypotheses (see Chapter 5) and suggests that selective attenuation (stimulus gating) by subcortical structures is inadequate in many schizophrenics and that information may reach the cortex of these patients with too much force, resulting, perhaps, in sensory flooding. This in turn requires active inhibitory processes at the cortical level, as indexed by the smaller "mid" and "late" EP components. However, as these later components also index the "processing" of the stimulus, it may be concluded that schizophrenics' active inhibitory processes, to reduce the effect of abnormal cortical bombardment, are "bought" at the cost of defective central processing. This hypothesis has many attractions in light of the ideas presented in the information-processing section, but it also has its limitations, in that increased somatosensory EP early components are not paralleled by similar findings with visual or auditory stimulation.[60] Further research is required to assess the significance of these findings, but at present perhaps the increased early somatosensory EP components might speak most directly to concepts of distorted body image in schizophrenia.

Findings of reduced "mid" EP components are fairly common in schizophrenia[60,49] and their precise significance is currently not known. However, interesting data have been reported when stimulus intensity has been manipulated and schizophrenics have been shown to produce either no increase or a paradoxical decrease in amplitude (as compared to normal subjects) with increasing intensity of stimulation.[61] The application of variable demand information-processing paradigms with concurrent EP measurement may well lead to sophisticated theorizing in this area, as shown by Parasuraman.[62] This study demonstrated convincingly that "mid" components (N100) are strongly interactive with slow negative shifts and that the relationship between these different components is the principal factor responsible for variations in the effects of attention on the EP with changes in information-processing demands. Perhaps more information will be obtained on abnormal "mid" EP components in schizophrenia by studying the later EP components and the interaction of both.

An exciting review of the complexity of the component structure underlying the N100 wave is given by Näätänen and Picton.[95] Added interest for schizophrenia research is given by the report of Patterson et al.[96] in which a negative going component, 70–105 msecs following stimulation (possibly the N100 wave) is markedly and specifically absent from schizophrenic brains during a backward masking task. As these brain events occurred before the onset of the masking stimulus in this experiment, then the strong implication is that schizophrenics' well-known deficit in this task[97] may be due to subcortical failures in early information "assembly" rather than to "gating" failures which allow the backward masking stimulus to degrade ongoing processing of a target. (See *Schizophrenia Bulletin*, 1987, Vol. 13, No. 4, for a more detailed presentation of these arguments.)

Late components of the EP have been widely used in experiments with controls and schizophrenics. In the space available we can only refer to a few of the recent developments.[36,63-65] In general, when methodological issues of controlling for latency or amplitude variability have been taken into account, the consensus, across studies, is that schizophrenics show significantly reduced P300 components under almost all conditions that are appropriate to elicit the P300 waveform.[66] In many studies of late EP components, the contingent negative variation (CNV) is also often recorded. This cortical negativity is best seen in experiments where a stimulus (S1) is given as a warning, or preparatory interval, or to signify some other aspects of a second stimulus (S2) to which some psychological response (e.g., simple reaction time) must be made. The separate information-processing-related waveforms seen in the late components is well demonstrated by Ruchkin et al.,[36] where principal components analysis of late EP data in a signal detection paradigm shows energy accountability of CNV, 30%, P300, 21%, and slow wave, 40%. These authors also demonstrated that P300 (varimax rotated) weighting coefficients increased monotonically with increased detection accuracy whereas slow wave weighting coefficients decreased monotonically with increased acccuracy. CNV, however, did not show this accuracy related variability. This type of experiment might be very illuminating if conducted with schizophrenics. CNV research with schizophrenics suggests a complex picture of abnormalities related to brain region and timing onset of the CNV. Significant interactions with severity of pathology may be seen.[67] The time epoch of CNV following response to the second (S2) stimulus is referred to as postimperative negative variation (PINV) and this waveform has also been shown to be significantly different from normal in 94% of acute and 43% of remitted schizophrenics.[68]

The correlation of late EP and CNV waveforms with specific stages in information-processing is proceeding rapidly.[69-72] Information already exists to further suggest P300 deficits in schizophrenics irrespective of motivational factors[73] and CNV abnormalities independent from treatment methods.[74] Clearly, exciting results are imminent in this area.

Brain Magnetic Waves

To our knowledge, there have been no magnetic evoked potential (MEP) studies conducted with schizophrenics, but we feel compelled to make the reader aware of their existence on the basis of their promise for the future. Many of the components of the surface recorded EP are known to have cortical and subcortical "dipole" generators,[75] and it is certainly conceivable that abnormalities of surface recorded EP waves could be attributed to alterations in the orientation of these dipoles.[76] Magnetic fields which are not subject to volume conduction distortion through brain tissue have been found to be effective in isolating epileptiform activity[77] and mapping the activity of the auditory cortex.[78]

Perhaps more importantly, the MEP allows brain electrical activity to be directly traced to subcortical structures without the tenuous and inferential steps involved with surface recorded activity.[98] Thus Okada et al.,[79] using MEP, have located the source of the N200-P300 complex seen in surface recorded EP within the hippocampal formation in the limbic brain. We remind the reader that limbic involvement with many aspects of schizophrenic abnormality has been hypothesized in the material which we have reviewed. The possibility of directly examining subcortical structures, in vivo during the performance of information-processing tasks, must be regarded as not only a possibility, but a very exciting current development.

General Conclusion

In recent years new noninvasive technologies have generated excitement at the possibility of examining heretofore inaccessible brain structures and processes. While new developments of nuclear magnetic resonance, position emission tomography, and regional cerebral blood flow have greatly enhanced the ability to see inside the living, functioning brain, these developments have not led to startling discoveries in schizophrenia, perhaps because the slow integrative nature of their data acquisition lends itself more to examination of anatomy than to examination of functioning. Schizophrenia research owes a great debt to cognitive-science information-processing theory, and within this theoretical structure the time-dependent nature of its "stages" requires examination of brain functioning with shorter time constants than the new technologies can provide. It is for these reasons that EEG and EP recording, with their inexpensive and noninvasive techniques and well-developed database, may provide a much needed "second window" into cognitive functioning in schizophrenia.

References

1. Itil T: Qualitative and quantitative EEG findings in schizophrenia. *Schizophr. Bull.* 3:61–79, 1977.

2. Spohn HE, Patterson T: Recent studies of psychophysiology in schizophrenia. *Schizophr. Bull.* 5:581–611, 1979.

3. Fink M: The electroencephalogram in clinical psychiatry. In Mendels J (Ed.): *Biological Psychiatry*, John Wiley & Sons, New York, 1973, pp. 331–344.

4. Haider M: Neuropsychology of attention, expectation and vigilance. In Mostofsky DI (Ed.): *Attention: Contemporary Theory and Analysis*, Century Psychology Series, A.C.C., New York, 1970, pp. 419–432.

5. Duffy FH, Burchfiel JL, Lombroso CT: Brain electrical activity mapping (BEAM): A method for extending the clinical utility of EEG and evoked potential data. *Ann. Neurol.* 5:309–321, 1979.

6. Itil TM, Saletu B, Davis S: EEG findings in chronic schizophrenics based on digital computer period analysis and analog power spectra. *Biol. Psychiatry* 5:1–13, 1972.

7. Goldstein L: Is a man, a man, a man? (or: Is an EEG, an EEG, an EEG?). Some remarks on the homogeneity of "normal subjects." *Pharmako-psychiatrie* 12:74–78, 1979.

8. Giannitrapani D, Kayton L: Schizophrenia and EEG spectral analysis. *EEG Clin. Neurophysiol.* 36:377–386, 1974.

9. Kendler KS, Hays P: Familial and sporadic schizophrenia—a symptomatic, prognostic and EEG comparison. *Am. J. Psychiatry* 139:1557–1562, 1982.

10. Stevens JR, Livermore A: Telemetered EEG in schizophrenia—spectral analysis during abnormal behavior episodes. *J. Neurol. Neurosurg. Psychiatry* 45:385–395, 1982.

11. Koukkou M: EEG and behavioral differences between first acute schizophrenic episode and remission. *Adv. Biol. Psychiatry* 6:35–40, 1981.

12. Koukkou M: EEG states of the brain, information processing, and schizophrenic primary symptoms. *Psychiatr. Res.* 6:235–244, 1982.

13. Tarrier N, Cooke EC, Lader MH: The EEG's of chronic schizophrenic pa-

tients in hospital and in the community. *EEG Clin. Neurophysiol.* 44:669–673, 1978.

14. Etevenon P et al.: Schizophrenia assessed by computerized EEG. *Adv. Biol. Psychiatry* 6:29–34, 1981.

15. Kemali et al.: Computerized EEG in schizophrenics. *Neuropsychobiology* 6:260–267, 1980.

16. Whitton JL, Moldofsky H, Lue F: EEG frequency patterns associated with hallucinations in schizophrenia and "creativity" in normals. *Biol. Psychiatry* 13:123–133, 1978.

17. Coger RW, Dymond AM, Serafetinides EA: Electroencephalographic similarities between chronic alcoholics and chronic nonparanoid schizophrenics. *Arch. Gen. Psychiatry* 36:91–94, 1979.

18. Dymond AM, Coger RW, Serafetinides EA: EEG banding and asymmetry in schizophrenics, alcoholics and controls: An objective comparison. *Res. Commun. Psychol. Psychiatr. Behav.* 5:113–122, 1980.

19. Kemali D et al: CEEG findings in schizophrenics, depressives, obsessives, heroin addicts and normals. *Adv. Biol. Psychiatry* 6:17–28, 1980.

20. Davis JR, Glaros AG, Davidson GS: Visual information processing and alpha blocking in schizophrenics and normals. *J. Psychiatr. Res.* 16:95–102, 1981.

21. Ibid., p. 100.

22. Basar E: *EEG-Brain Dynamics: Relation Between EEG and Brain Evoked Potentials*, Elsevier/North Holland, Amsterdam, Netherlands, 1980.

23. Cracco RQ, Cracco JB: Visual evoked potentials in man: Early oscillatory potentials. *EEG Clin. Neurophysiol.* 45:731–739, 1978.

24. Picton TW, Hillyard SA: Human auditory evoked potentials. II. Effects of attention. *EEG Clin. Neurophysiol.* 36:191–200, 1974.

25. Finley WW, Johnson G: Operant control of auditory brainstem potentials in man. *Int. J. Neurosci.* 21:161–170, 1983.

26. Hillyard SA, Kutas M: Electrophysiology of cognitive processing. *Ann. Rev. Psychol.* 34:33–61, 1983.

27. Ibid., p. 55.

28. Renault B et al.: Onset and offset of brain events as indices of mental chronometry. *Science* 215:1413–1415, 1982.

29. Näätänen R: Processing negativity: An evoked-potential reflection of selective attention. *Psychol. Bull.* 92:605–640, 1982.

30. Ritter W et al.: Manipulations of event-related potential manifestations of information processing stages. *Science* 218:909–911, 1982.

31. Chapman RM, McCrary, JW, Chapman JA: Memory processes and evoked potentials. *Can. J. Psychol.* 35:201–212, 1981.

32. Friedman D, Vaughan HG, Erlenmeyer-Kimling L: Event related potential investigations in children at risk for schizophrenia. In Lehmann D, Callaway E (Eds.): *Human Evoked Potentials: Applications and Problems*, Plenum Press, New York, 1979, pp. 105–120.

33. Friedman D, Vaughan HG, Erelenmeyer-Kimling L: Cognitive brain potentials in children at risk for schizophrenia: Preliminary findings. *Schizophr. Bull.* 8:514–531, 1982.

34. Wickens C et al.: Performance of concurrent tasks: A psychophysiological analysis of the reciprocity of information-processing resources. *Science* 221:1080–1082, 1983.

35. Warren LR, Wideman SS: Event-related potentials to match and mismatch letters in an immediate item recognition task. *Int. J. Neurosci.* 18:191–198, 1983.

36. Ruchkin DS et al.: Slow wave and P300 in signal detection. *EEG Clin. Neurophysiol.* 50:35–47, 1980.

37. Duncan-Johnson CC, Kopell BS: The stroop effect: Brain potentials localize the source of interference. *Science* 214:938–940, 1981.

38. McClelland JL: On the time relations of mental processes: An examination of systems of processes in cascade. *Psychol. Rev.* 86:287–330, 1979.

39. Kitajima S, Murohashi H, Kanoh M: Stimulus repetition and an amplitude increase of the occipital late positive component in the human visual evoked potential. *EEG Clin. Neurophysiol.* 55:567–574, 1983.

40. Rugg MD: Further study of the electrophysiological correlates of lexical decision. *Brain Lang.* 19:142–152, 1983.

41. Donald MW, Young MJ: A time-course analysis of attentional tuning of the auditory evoked response. *Exp. Brain Res.* 36:357–367, 1982.

42. Adler LE et al.: Neurophysiological evidence for a defect in neuronal mechanisms involved in sensory gating in schizophrenia. *Biol. Psychiatry* 17:639–654, 1982.

43. Baribeau-Braun J, Picton TW, Gosselin J-Y: Schizophrenia: A neurophysiological examination of abnormal information processing. *Science* 219:874–876, 1983.

44. Satya-Murti S et al.: Late auditory evoked potentials can occur without brain stem potentials. *EEG Clin. Neurophysiol.* 56:P304–308, 1983.

45. Duffy FH: Brain electrical activity mapping (BEAM) — computerized access to complex brain function. *Int. J. Neurosci.* 13:55–65, 1981.

46. Duffy FH, Bartels, PH, Burchfield JL: Significance probability mapping: An acid in the topographic analysis of brain electrical activity. *EEG Clin. Neurophysiol.* 51:455–462, 1981.

47. Morstyn R, Duffy FH, McCarley RW: Alterned P300 topography in schizophrenia. *Arch. Gen. Psychiatry* 40:729–734, 1983.

48. Shagass C: Early evoked potentials. *Schizophr. Bull.* 3:80–92, 1977.

49. Buchsbaum MS: The middle evoked response components and schizophrenia. *Schizophr. Bull.* 3:93–104, 1977.

50. Roth WT: Late event-related potentials and psychopathology. *Schizophr. Bull.* 3:105–120, 1977.

51. Mochizuki Y et al.: Developmental changes of brainstem auditory evoked potentials (BAEPs) in normal human subjects from infants to young adults. *Brain Dev.* 4:127–136, 1982.

52. Salamy A et al.: Contrasts in brainstem function between normal and high risk infants in early postnatal life. *Early Human Dev.* 4:179–185, 1980.

53. Student M, Sohmer H: Evidence from auditory nerve and brainstem evoked responses for an organic brain lesion in children with autistic traits. *J. Autism Childhood Schizophr.* 8:13–20, 1978.

54. Tanguay PE et al.: Auditory brainstem evoked responses in autistic children. *Arch. Gen. Psychiatry* 39:174–180, 1982.

55. Church MW, Williams HL: Dose- and time-dependent effects of ethanol on

brainstem auditory evoked responses in young adult males. *EEG Clin. Neurophysiol.* 54:161–174. 1982.

56. Chu N-S, Squires KC, Starr A: Auditory brain stem responses in chronic alcoholic patients. *EEG Clin. Neurophysiol.* 54:418–425, 1982.

57. Harkins SW: Effects of presenile dementia of the Alzheimers type on brainstem transmission time. *Int. J. Neurosci.* 15:165–170, 1981.

58. Pfefferbaum A et al.: Auditory brainstem and cortical evoked potentials in schizophrenia. *Biol. Psychiatry* 15:209–223, 1980.

59. Bolz J, Giedke H: Brainstem auditory evoked responses in psychiatric patients and healthy controls. *J. Neural Transm.* 54:285–291, 1982.

60. Shagass C et al.: Temporal variability of somatosensory, visual, and auditory evoked potentials in schizophrenia. *Arch. Gen. Psychiatry* 36:1341–1351, 1979.

61. Landau SG et al.: Schizophrenia and stimulus intensity control. *Arch. Gen. Psychiatry* 32:1239–1245, 1975.

62. Parasuraman R: Effects of information processing demands on slow negative shift latencies and N100 amplitude in selective and divided attention. *Biol. Psychiatry* 11:217–233, 1980.

63. Rockstroh B et al: *Slow Brain Potentials and Behavior*, Urban and Schwarzenberg, Baltimore, 1982.

64. Pritchard WS: Psychophysiology of P300. *Psychol. Bull.* 89:506–540, 1981.

65. Sanquist TF, Beatty JT, Lindsley DB: Slow potential shifts of human brain during forewarned reaction. *EEG Clin. Neurophysiol.* 51:639–649, 1981.

66. Roth WT et al.: P3 reduction in auditory evoked potentials of schizophrenics. *EEG Clin. Neurophysiol.* 49:497–505, 1980.

67. Van den Bosch RJ: Contingent negative variation and psychopathology: Frontal-central distribution and association with performance measures. *Biol. Psychiatry* 18:615–634, 1983.

68. Chouinard G et al.: Postimperative negative variation (PINV) in ambulatory schizophrenic patients. *Compr. Psychiatry* 16:457–460, 1975.

69. Begleiter H et al.: P3 and stimulus incentive value. *Psychophysiology* 20:95–101, 1983.

70. Tecce JJ et al.: CNV rebound and aging. *EEG Clin. Neurophysiol.* 54:175–186, 1982.

71. Stuss DT et al.: Event-related potentials during naming and mental rotation. *EEG Clin. Neurophysiol.* 56:133–146, 1983.

72. Fitzgerald PG, Picton T: Temporal and sequential probability in evoked potential studies. *Can. J. Psychol.* 35:188–200, 1981.

73. Brecher M, Begleiter H: Event related brain potentials to high-incentive stimuli in unmedicated schizophrenic patients. *Biol. Psychiatry* 18:661–674, 1983.

74. Rizzo PA et al.: Brain slow potentials (CNV), prolactin, and schizophrenia. *Biol. Psychiatry* 18:175–183, 1983.

75. Cohen D, Cuffin BN: Demonstration of useful differences between magnetic-encephalogram and electroencephalogram. *EEG Clin. Neurophysiol.* 56:38–51, 1983.

76. Kaufman L et al.: On the relation between somatic evoked potentials and fields. *Int. J. Neurosci.* 15:223–239, 1981.

77. Barth DS et al.: Neuromagnetic localization of epileptiform spike activity in the human brain. *Science* 218:891-894, 1982.

78. Romani GL, Williamson SJ, Kaufman L: Tonotopic organization of the human auditory cortex. *Science* 216:1339-1340, 1982.

79. Okada YC, Kaufman L, Williamson SJ: The hippocampal formation as a source of the slow endogenous potentials. *EEG Clin. Neurophysiol.* 417-426, 1983.

80. Chu N-S, Yang S-S: Somatosensory and brainstem auditory evoked potentials in alcoholic liver disease with and without encephalopathy. *Alcohol* 4:225-230, 1987.

81. Chu N-S: Computed tomographic correlates of auditory brainstem responses in alcoholics. *J. Neurol. Neurosurg. Psychiatry* 48:348-353, 1985.

82. Chu N-S, Squires KC: Auditory brainstem response study of alcoholic patients. *Pharmacol. Biochem. Behavior* 13:241-244, 1980.

83. Diamond I: Studies of acute and chronic effects of ethanol on early evoked potentials *Alcohol* 4:255-256, 1987.

84. Emmerson RY, Dustman RE, Shearer DE, Chamberlin HM: EEG, visually evoked and event related potentials in young abstinent alcoholics. *Alcohol* 4:241-248, 1987.

85. Freedman R, Waldo M, Waldo CI, Wilson JR: Genetic influences on the effects of alcohol on auditory evoked potentials. *Alcohol* 4:249-253, 1987.

86. Merikangas KR, Lechman JF, Prusoff BA, Pauls DL, Weissman MH: Familial transmission of depression and alcoholism. *Arch. Gen. Psychiatry* 42:367-372, 1985.

87. Oscar-Berman M: Alcohol-related ERP changes in cognition. *Alcohol* 4:289-292, 1987.

88. O'Connor S, Hesselbrock V, Tasman A, DePalma N: P3 amplitudes in two distinct tasks are decreased in young men with a history of paternal alcoholism. *Alcohol* 4:323-330, 1987.

89. Porjesz B, Begleiter H, Bihari B, Kissin B: The N_2 component of the event-related brain potential in abstinent alcoholics. *EEG Clin. Neurophysiol.* 66:121-131, 1987.

90. Porjesz B: Begleiter H, Bihari B, Kissin B: Event-related brain potentials to high incentive stimuli in abstinent alcoholics. *Alcohol* 4:283-287, 1987.

91. Porjesz B, Begleiter H: Human brian electrophysiology and alcoholism. In Tarter RE, Thiel DH (Eds.): *Alcohol and the Brain*, Plenum Press, New York, 1985, pp. 139-182.

92. Steinhauer SR, Hill SY, Zubin J: Event-related potentials in alcoholics and their first-degree relatives. *Alcohol* 4:307-314, 1987.

93. Brecher M, Begleiter H: Brain stem auditory evoked potentials in unmedicated schizophrenic patients. *Biological Psychiatry* 20:199-202, 1985.

94. Lindstrom L, Klockhoff I, Svedberg, A, Bergstrom K: Abnormal auditory brain-stem responses in hallucinating schizophrenic patients. *Br. J. Psychiatry* 151:9-14, 1987.

95. Näätänen R, Picton T: The N1 wave of the human electric and magnetic response to sound: A review and an analysis of the component structure. *Psychophysiology* 24:375-425, 1987.

96. Patterson T, Spohn HE, Hayes K: Topographic evoked potentials during backward masking in schizophrenics, patient controls and normal controls. *Prog. Neuropsychopharm. Biol. Psychiatry* 11:709–728, 1987.

97. Braff DL, Saccuzzo DP: The time course of information-processing deficits in schizophrenia. *Am. J. Psychiatry* 142:170–174, 1985.

98. Weinbert H, Brickett P, Robertson A, Harrop R, Cheyne, DO, Crispo D, Baff M, Dykstra C: The magnetoencephalographic localization of source-systems in the brain: Early and late components of event related potentials. *Alcohol* 4:339–345, 1987.

7

Individual Psychotherapy for Schizophrenia

Louis Linn

EDITOR'S NOTE

The basic approach to individual psychotherapy in schizophrenic patients is shaped by special intrapsychic and interpersonal dynamics commonly encountered among such patients. The author uses a rough, but relevant, sociobiological analogy to emphasize the importance of what Carl Jung called introversion in the personality makeup of the schizophrenic. Jung, of course, was describing a perceptual style, the introvert deriving much of his stimulation and succor from within himself rather than from others. The introversion of the schizophrenic seems to be a reflection of the extreme pain that can be activated by intimate human contact. At the same time, the patient experiences a need and longing for such contact. The net result is fear, loneliness, and ambivalence. Isolation and social withdrawal reflect this dilemma; so, too, may the creation of delusions or hallucinations as an alternative to an unbearable reality.

Outlining principles of psychotherapy, the author reminds us that no schizophrenic is ever totally out of touch with his environment. The skilled therapist can work his way into the patient's system of thought and feeling, always carefully balancing the therapeutic relationship between too much and too little closeness. Whether the patient uses mannerisms of speech, bizarre language, or eccentricities of dress and personal appearance to distance himself, the therapist can help him recognize the purpose of these devices and encourage him to adopt new and better ways of relating.

Many schizophrenic patients solve the loneliness problem by clinging to a single friend or by staying within the familiar framework of their original families. Attempts to forcibly evict them from family structure are rarely successful. If positive in nature, the family support system should be valued; if negative and disruptive to the patient's well-being and progress, gradual separation should be encouraged.

One of the greatest dangers in psychotherapy with schizophrenics is therapeutic overambitiousness. Setting too high a goal for a patient can lead to repeated episodes of defeat; on the other hand, a certain number of patients may surprise therapists by reaching substantial levels of accomplishment, particularly in careers that make few demands on social relationships and skills.

Countertransference issues are prominent. Certain features of the patient's personality and illness may be threatening to some therapists. Patience is indeed a virtue, since therapy may often be drawn out, with improvement occurring slowly and almost imperceptively, and the eventual outcome often being relatively modest in degree.

In Search of a Theoretical Basis for Therapy

There is an adage which says that a physician who practices medicine without a theory is like a sailor who goes to sea without a map or compass. Although commonly attributed to Osler, this saying really goes back to the 15th century and the writings of Leonardo da Vinci.[1] In any case, this injunction applies with particular force to the 20th century physician who undertakes to treat schizophrenia, that complex entity which remains enigmatic to this day.

Let us start with the fact that human existence in health and disease is biopsychosocial. That is, every moment of life is the outcome of a threefold force which is at once biological, psychological, and social. For the purposes of this discussion, I will allude only briefly to the biological component. There is surely a neurophysiological and a biochemical substrate to the schizophrenic disorder, the nature of which we are just starting to comprehend. For example, there is now convincing evidence that a hereditary component is involved, which surely operates through enzymes and other chemical systems.[2] In addition, potent medications can alter certain aspects of the disease. Finally, there is some biological evidence from an evolutionary point of view.

In the evolution of hunting techniques in the predatory mammalian world, two contrasting patterns have emerged — the solitary hunter, perhaps best exemplified by the tiger or the leopard, and the social hunter, best exemplified by the wild dogs of Africa. In general, it may be said that the solitary hunting mode seems best adapted to a jungle environment in which visibility is limited and large prey relatively scarce. Under these conditions, stealth, privacy, and the capacity to cope with isolation are particularly valuable adaptational qualities. On the other hand, when it comes to hunting in the open plains where the wildebeest and the antelope roam, group hunting strategies work best, and animals that are more sociable in their relationships are more successful here. Thus, the solitary hunter strives for privacy and accepts social contact only transiently for purposes of mating and caring for cubs. The social hunter, on the other hand, strives constantly for contact with his group.

Of some relevance here is the behavior of the domestic cat and the domestic dog, two species that have lived with man for over 10,000 years. Despite this commonly shared environment, each has preserved a distinctive pattern of socializing. The cat chooses limited social interactions involving largely one or more members of a single family. The dog, on the other hand, characteristically has a more generalized eagerness for social contact. It is my thesis that these divergent socializing patterns have hereditary roots in the hunting patterns of their ancestors and that human beings, too, carry hereditary traits for the same qualities, and for the same reasons. Although commonly present as a mixture in a given individual, they also occur in relatively pure forms as solitary types (i.e., "cat people") and social types (i.e., "dog people"). This fact has long been known. It was described in most detail by Carl Jung. He characterized these divergent patterns of adaptations as introversion and extroversion.[3]

These different behavior patterns, indiscriminate sociability versus highly selective sociability, are unquestionably associated with fundamental neurophysiological differences. Interestingly, there are differences in the way dogs and cats respond to psychoactive drugs. To cite a single familiar example, there is the action of morphine, which is sedative in the dog and excitatory in the cat.

It cannot be emphasized too strongly that these two patterns, introversion and extroversion, both occur well within the limits of normal human behavior and that each, in its own distinctive way, represents an adaptationally useful system for mankind. For example, it seems that creativity—the ability to break old modes and to strike out in new directions of thought or action—occurs more frequently in solitary types, whereas the qualities associated with the maintenance aspects of civilization are more likely to occur among the social types. It is my hypothesis that, when the extroverted type becomes psychotic, he is more likely to manifest the symptoms of the affective disorders, and that when the introverted type becomes psychotic, he usually manifests the symptoms of schizophrenia.[4-6] Thus, while the patient with an affective disorder yearns with pathological intensity for social contact, the patient with a schizophrenic disorder yearns with equal intensity to be left alone.

Even though Freud himself did not make use of Jung's terminology, he did regard schizophrenia as the outgrowth of an inability to tolerate intimate human contact.[7] Contacts that would ordinarily elicit pleasure or contentment elicit fear and dread in the schizophrenic patient. In an attempt to relieve this dysphoric state, the schizophrenic patient breaks off contact with people. In effect, he disconnects from the real world. This was what Freud called the process of decathecting reality.

While this disconnecting process may be accompanied by some transient sense of relief, disconnection is soon followed by feelings of intolerable loneliness. When the pain of loneliness becomes severe enough, the schizophrenic patient reaches out again to the real world — only to experience again his former state of terror, and so he retreats again. This, then, constitutes the schizophrenic patient's dilemma — to oscillate constantly between the intolerable pain of human contact and the equally intolerable pain of utter loneliness. This has been called "the schizophrenic's need-fear dilemma,"[8] and is the basis for the severe ambivalence that characterizes the schizophrenic condition.

During this period of oscillation, the schizophrenic patient may bewilder others with his display of contrasting thoughts and actions. This may appear as loosening of associations and periods of thought deprivation — that is, in the typical thought disorder of schizophrenia.

To resolve this dilemma, the schizophrenic may lapse into a state of total apathy — that is, into a state of flattened affect during which he seems to be totally unconcerned about others. This basic unconcern for human contact expresses itself in a pattern of social withdrawal that has been referred to as autism.

Our theoretical model has thus far made it possible to deduce, or to explain, a specific set of schizophrenic symptoms — namely, ambivalence, thought disorder, flattening of affect, and social withdrawal. These symptoms, sometimes called the "negative symptoms" of schizophrenia, constituted for Bleuler the core manifestations of the disorder. These are the symptoms that are always present in schizophrenia.

There is another way out of the schizophrenic dilemma. Since reality is unbearable and unacceptable, the patient may create a "new reality." Delusions, hallucinations, and ideas of reference emerge. These are elaborately rationalized and systematized until the patient finds himself living in a psychotic world. However complex or uncomfortable it may be, it is for the schizophrenic patient still more comfortable than the real world with which he has broken contact. Because of the primary state of disconnection from the real world, these patients are essentially inaccessible to psychotherapeutic intervention. The symptoms upon which the psychotic world are based were called by Bleuler the "secondary symptoms of schizophrenia."[9]

Just because the psychotic world is not as terrifying as the real world, these secondary symptoms play a problem-solving role, and for this reason Freud called them the "restitutive symptoms."[10] Bleuler cautioned that these secondary symptoms may occur in many psychotic states, and therefore they are not all pathognomic of schizophrenia. For example, they can occur in major affective disorders with psychotic features, in delirium, in schizophreniform psychotic reactions, or in borderline states. Ironically, although Bleuler coined the term "schizophrenia," his own criteria for defining the condition are currently downgraded. I refer to the prevailing emphasis on the "Schneiderian first-rank symptoms"[11] and to the *DSM-III* criteria for the diagnosis of schizophrenia.[12]

My proposed model has helped bring some order into our understanding of schizophrenic phenomenology. It remains to be seen if it is equally helpful as a guide to treatment.

The Role of Medications in Psychotherapy for Schizophrenia

Since medications have assumed a central role in the treatment of schizophrenia,[13] it is reasonable to start with that topic. Years of experience have confirmed the invaluable role of medications in the control of the secondary symptoms of schizophrenia. Leaving aside for the moment the theoretical question "How do these medications work?" we know that the so-called major tranquilizers do indeed reduce and even eliminate delusions, hallucinations, and paranoid trends in many cases. This is a matter of major significance. The psychotic point of view that is represented in the secondary symptom–complex has many socially unacceptable consequences. Many patients in the grip of secondary symptoms become frightening and even dangerous; as a result, they may require inpatient care. Furthermore, because he has abandoned the real world and is totally committed to his imagined world, the patient is unable to interact with the psychiatrist in a psychotherapeutically meaningful way. This was why Freud believed that these patients are not analyzable.

In any event, medications cannot be prescribed in a mechanical cookbook fashion. The patient must be carefully monitored. In settings of increased environmental stress, it is necessary to increase the dose; conversely, in settings of reduced stress, it may be possible to put the patient on a drug holiday.[14] Emerging signs of depression may signal the need to reduce the dose of a major tranquilizer. On the other hand, signs of increasing psychotic excitement may call for increased medication.[15] This is not the occasion to discuss the details of clinical psychopharmacology but, rather, to make the point that one cannot properly draw a sharp line between pharmacotherapy and psychotherapy. A truly professional approach calls for a sensitive integration of both modalities.

There is compelling evidence that medications that are invaluable for controlling acute psychotic flareups do not alter the long-term outpatient course of the disease as measured by improved social functioning.[16] This is not said to minimize the revolutionary significance of these medications. At the very least, they make outpatient management possible for many patients who would otherwise have to be forcibly confined to a hospital. In addition, medications make possible a more intensive psychotherapeutic approach.

The Elements of
a Psychotherapeutic Approach

No schizophrenic patient is ever totally out of touch with reality. I compare the floridly psychotic patient to a person in the grip of a nightmare. The latter tells himself, "This is only a dream and I can wake myself at any time." In this analogy, the sleeper wants to wake up. The schizophrenic patient, on the other hand, usually fears the real world more than he fears his waking dream world.

A skilled psychotherapist can work his way into the patient's psychotic system. First he must establish a relationship of trust. To accomplish this, a sophisticated psychodynamic approach is called for. Simple intuition is not enough. The psychotherapist must understand the nature of the patient's need-fear dilemma, and he must carefully walk a tightrope, approaching the patient by allaying his psychotic fears but not approaching him too closely lest his psychotic fears be intensified — a difficult but not impossible balancing act.

In general, I explain to the patient that our contact will be purely verbal. All we will do is talk. Therefore, no one can get hurt. "I can't hurt you and you can't hurt me. Under these guaranteed safe circumstances, we can trust each other and talk to each other." If this message can be convincingly communicated, one may be rewarded within a single session with the thrilling phenomenon of a transient psychotic remission, occurring right before one's eyes. Psychotic manifestations may recede, and a rational conversation may ensue. The contact so established may be brief and tenuous, but the therapist can build on it in successive sessions.

A minimal goal may be the use of this fragile relationship to persuade the patient to accept hospitalization. If there is a suggestion of actual danger to himself or to others, hospitalization is required. Hospitalization may be called for because the caretakers at home have experienced "burnout" in relation to the patient, or the home environment may be so clearly antitherapeutic or even actually schizophrenogenic that continued treatment in a setting of physical disconnection from the family or the community is imperative.

Over many years, I have had to hospitalize many patients. Not once have

I ever had to use formal commitment proceedings or even a show of force. Sufficient awareness of the need for help seems always present in the patient, and most patients can be persuaded to accept hospitalization on an informal basis. Formal commitment may be necessary, subsequently, to keep the patient in a therapeutic inpatient setting.

Regulating the Interpersonal Distance

In the grip of his need-fear dilemma, the patient's whole life is preoccupied with what I call the interpersonal distance-regulating mechanisms, which can be almost limitlessly varied. For example, there may be mannerisms of speech (too soft or too loud), unusual word choices, or bizarre language usage (loosening of association and neologisms).[17] There may be eccentricities of dress and personal appearances. The patient may not bathe and may deliberately cultivate a repulsive façade, which I call the "skunk maneuver." In the latter instance, I explain to the patient that the skunk has no intention of harming anyone. It uses its stench only to keep people at a safe distance. I may describe to the patient the porcupine and its quills in similar terms. Whenever any of these distance-regulating phenomena are recognized, they should be identified (interpreted) and the protective functions of these devices explained to the patient. He should be reassured that these defensive maneuvers are certainly not necessary during the therapy session.

Despite these explanations, the patient may choose to retain them, in which case one tries to accept them and to work along with them, if possible, or to indicate that they are not acceptable and that treatment cannot continue unless these specific objectionable defensive maneuvers are controlled. A certain number of patients will try to break off treatment at this point. Many, however, will exert the necessary self-control in order to stay in treatment with a therapist on whom they have now become dependent.

In any event, making a direct attack on a specific behavior pattern without first explaining to the patient its defensive function and the fact that this defense is now not necessary will almost always drive the patient away. Some eccentricities will, in time, have acquired the force of habit, and the patient will require a behavior modification approach to master it. For example, if the patient refuses to shave in the morning or to properly attire himself, he may respond to suitable rewards or good-humored cajolery. The advice of a skilled behavior modification therapist may be helpful here.

To overcome loneliness in the outside world, the patient may depend on a single friend, who may be a fellow psychotic or a phobic patient or someone who exploits the patient for financial or sexual gain. Most often the patient solves the loneliness problem by tenaciously clinging to the parental home, disrupting family life, and effectively keeping the parents prisoners in their own home. I try to explain to parents that they should take vacations and live as full a private life as they can despite the patient's presence. I assure them that the patient will manage perfectly well in their absence as long as he has enough food and money. On the other hand, efforts to evict the patient forcefully from the parental home (except for hospitalization) are rarely successful, as was tragically shown in the Hinckley case. A skilled psychiatrist may sometimes succeed in meeting the patient's delicately balanced needs and fears and help him, in a purely supportive way, to control the otherwise unbearable loneliness in settings away from home. In these instances, actual therapeutic sessions may be relatively infrequent, brief, and even confined to the telephone.

In response to a schizophrenic patient, family life may be twisted out of shape, or skewed, in order to accommodate the patient's eccentricities. This is one reason why the patient should be encouraged to take up separate residence. On occasion, the patient may himself create a schism by choosing to move to a distant city, where he lives alone, with or without a job. In such instances, I encourage the family to maintain contact by mail and occasionally by phone if the patient can tolerate it. I discourage actual visits unless the parents are invited by the patient. The patient should be assured of continued financial support even if he earns money on his own. The continued availability of family finances may be necessary to stabilize the fragile need-fear balance. Despite great yearning by parents to see their offspring, I try to inculcate respect for the patient's need for privacy.

The sex drive represents a special complication and source of danger to the schizophrenic patient. The psychosis commonly manifests itself at puberty, when the patient's fear of intimacy collides with the biologically urgent drive to establish physical contact. Because the outer world fills him with dread, he has to cope with his sexual dilemma within the home. As a result, incest fantasies may erupt and may acquire psychotic expressions with terrible feelings of guilt, fear of punishment, self-inflicted mutilation, tantrums, panic, attacks of rage, and assaultiveness against family members. It is important to inform families that these aggressive manifestations are generated not so much by hatred as by fear, and that the fear erupts whenever personal interaction has become too close for the patient's comfort. Thus, what looks like rage is really an interpersonal distance-regulating mechanism. Indeed, when a schizophrenic patient appears to be on the brink of an assault, the most effective calming device is to reassure him that he is not in physical danger and that no one will get close to him if he doesn't want that.

In these instances, psychotherapy should aim at increasing the interpersonal distance by encouraging the patient to accept separate living quarters, a day hospital, or a program like that of Fountain House in New York City, which seeks to engage the patient in activities and relationships away from home at interpersonal distances that the patient can tolerate.

The family itself is encouraged to reduce the emotional intensity of its interactions with the patient. Studies of schizophrenic patients at home have led to the division of families into two broad categories, those that are "emotionally expressive" (EE) and those that are "not emotionally expressive" (non-EE).[18] Families that can reduce their expectations concerning the schizophrenic member and can achieve an attitude of bland acceptance of the patient, with his eccentricities, are called non-EE. Subjects fare better in such family settings. A significant psychotherapeutic goal is to generate within the family a non-EE pattern of behavior, as far as is possible.

Until recently, the families of schizophrenic patients were regarded, in effect, as "poisonous" to the patient. The literature was full of allusions to "schizophrenogenic" mothers and familial "double binds." While these are realistic issues from time to time, the family's love and loyalty to the patient more often prevail despite the great suffering they may entail. The family of a schizophrenic is often a positive resource to be used by the psychiatrist in his treatment plan.

The Sick Role

One of the most difficult problems in treating schizophrenics is that many of them refuse to accept the fact that they are sick.[19] To accept "the sick role" is to agree voluntarily to intimate interactions with a network of helpers — precisely the kind of closeness with which these patients cannot cope. This attitude of rejecting the sick role applies not only to the psychiatrist as a physician but to all physicians. Many schizophrenic patients go to incredible lengths of personal neglect — involving mutilating malignancies, fractures, burns, myocardial infarctions, etc. — in order to avoid closeness with others. For some patients this is an impenetrable barrier, and treatment of any kind that calls for the voluntary cooperation of the patient becomes impossible.

When Freud said that these patients were not voluntarily treatable, he failed to appreciate that the schizophrenic disorder is really a spectrum of disorders and that tolerable interpersonal distances vary from case to case. For example, there are some schizophrenic patients who actually seem to improve or even to go into remission when they become physically ill because they find within the simplifications of the doctor-patient interaction an interpersonal distance they can tolerate. Thus, while there are hard-core cases that are probably not treatable except involuntarily, there are many patients with whom a workable distance can be achieved.

How to achieve a working interpersonal distance with a schizophrenic patient is a puzzle that always taxes the ingenuity of the therapist. For example, Schulman[20] found that mute schizophrenic patients would talk to him if they faced each other (patient and doctor) not directly but by looking at each other in a mirror. Under these circumstances, mute patients would often verbalize delusional material not previously communicated. Mute schizophrenic children will sometimes enter into conversations with a therapist if permitted to sit inside a large cardboard carton or to hide behind the door of a closet. Noncommunicating schizophrenic patients will occasionally speak up in the context of a foreign-language class although mute in their native tongue. Some schizophrenic patients relate more comfortably when talking to a tape recorder than when speaking directly to the psychiatrist.

Long ago, it was known that a mute catatonic will go briefly into remission and will eat and speak freely in response to intravenous amobarbital. Major tranquilizers produce longer-lasting periods of nonpsychotic responsiveness. These substances probably act as sensory filters or barriers against stimuli that reduce the intensity of the emotional effects of a human encounter and constitute, in effect, chemical interpersonal distance-regulating mechanisms.

What all these data emphasize is that schizophrenia is not a disease that dwells steadily inside the patient like a tumor, for example, but is a state that manifests itself transiently and variably, depending on the stress with which the patient has to cope. This principle is true not only for schizophrenia but also for many diseases, such as coronary heart disease, diabetes, hypertension, etc. Clinical manifestations vary as the environmental stresses vary. Thus, a major task for the psychotherapist is to identify the schizophrenic environmental stresses and to reduce their effect when he can.

Further Psychotherapeutic Goals

In psychotherapy for schizophrenia, the greatest danger is therapeutic overambitiousness — that is, setting long-term goals that are too high. The intelligence level in a population of schizophrenics is probably the same as that in the general population. That is, many schizophrenics are very intelligent, some are brilliant, and some may even have qualities of genius; yet the schizophrenic illness makes underachievement an almost unavoidable outcome. Brilliant high-school youngsters become schizophrenic as graduation approaches and the uncertainties of college life away from home loom ahead. College students may become schizophrenic as the end of their sheltered school years approaches and problems of occupational and marital choice loom ahead.

Family pressures on gifted young patients are often irresistible, and the result may be disastrous. The psychotherapist must support the patient in the choice of modest vocational goals, at least for a few years of treatment and time for further maturation. Later on, many patients may achieve great vocational success scientifically or artistically, particularly if the vocational endeavor requires solitude and no great dependency on tact or social grace. The patient may achieve great professional success, amass great wealth, and yet lack any of the qualities that are essential for marriage or parenthood. Thus, the therapist may have to steer the fragile patient away from an ill-advised marriage, and the patient may collapse if he is not properly protected.

However, one should not foreclose the possibility of marriage for the schizophrenic patient. There is a tendency for like to seek out like. An eccentric may be more tolerant of eccentricity in a partner, and a socially avoidant personality may be more tolerant of a spouse's yearning for privacy. A schizophrenic may find stability in such a marriage and may learn to grow emotionally and even to weather the stress of parenthood with a properly supportive mate. Thus, schizophrenic men who have the good fortune to mate with a "well" wife have more periods of remission and less tendency to chronicity.[21] Very often, however, it does not work out that way, and the psychiatrist may have to help the partners go their separate ways, often to their mutual benefit.

Countertransference Issues

Everyone who works with schizophrenia has to expect unusual countertransference experiences, because of the patient's need to preserve his privacy and to push the psychiatrist away. Schizophrenics are sometimes touted for their frankness and their merciless honesty. Some therapists are even inclined to idealize this quality, saying that schizophrenics are the only truly honest people in this corrupt world. Unfortunately, this romantic view does not hold up. The schizophrenic often zeros in on some personal vanity or weakness of his therapist and attacks it derisively, not really as a matter of principle but simply as a device to maintain distance.

At times the patient may be verbally abusive or even physically threatening, and it takes a certain amount of courage as well as clinical skill to reassure the patient that these hostile displays are unnecessary because he is in no danger during the psychotherapeutic session. At times heroic degrees of patience and compassion are called for when the schizophrenic goes out of his way to act repulsively, again in the service of his fear of intimacy. These difficult maneuvers demand expenditures of great emotional energy and self-control.

The therapist of the schizophrenic patient, like the patient's parents, must accept with humility his inability to completely cure the patient. He must provide the patient with substitute supports when he is not personally available. Some patients ask for a written receipt of payment, for example, not so much to keep their accounts straight as because the paper on which it is written serves as a transitional object that plays a reassuring role in the therapist's absence. Similarly, the voice of the therapist on the telephone answering machine or on a tape the patient takes home with him may play a stabilizing role.

It may be difficult to sustain the high level of therapeutic commitment required in the service of humble goals — for example, in the direction of simplifying the schizophrenic patient's environment in the knowledge that, as the environmental expectations recede, so will the florid psychotic manifestations. The therapist may have to be content with a simple role, relieving the patient's loneliness and helping his family deal with him more effectively.

References

1. da Vinci L: "Those who are enamored of practice without science are like a pilot who goes into a ship without rudder or compass and never has any certainty where he is going." From *Manuscript G*, Library of the Institut de France (translated by Edward MacCurdy in *The Notebooks of Leonardo da Vinci*, Vol. II, ch. XXIX). In *Strauss' Familiar Medical Quotations*, Little, Brown and Company, Boston, 1968. With thanks to William B. Ober, M.D., who found this for me.

2. Kety SS: What is schizophrenia? *Schizophren. Bull.* 8:597, 1982.

3. Jung CG: Introversion-extroversion. In *Collected Works*, Vol. 6, Second Ed., Princeton University Press, Princeton, N. J., 1971, pp. 330–337.

4. Kendler KS, Gruenberg AM, Strauss JS: An independent analysis of the Copenhagen sample of the Danish adoption study of schizophrenia. IV. The relationship between major depressive disorder and schizophrenia. *Arch. Gen. Psychiatry* 39:639–642, 1982.

5. Kety SS, Rosenthal O, Wender PH: The biologic and adoptive families of adopted individuals who became schizophrenic: Prevalence of mental illness and other characteristics. In Wynne L (Ed.): *The Nature of Schizophrenia*, John Wiley & Sons, New York, 1978, pp. 25–37.

6. Baron M, Gruen R, Asni L, Kane J: Familial relatedness of schizophrenia and schizotypal states. *Am. J. Psychiatry* 140:1437–1442, 1983.

7. Freud S: Psychoanalytic notes on an autobiographical account of a case of

paranoia. In *The Standard Edition of the Complete Psychological Worlds of S. Freud*, Vol. XII (1913), Norton, New York, 1961.

8. Burnham DL, Gladstone SI, Gibson RW: *Schizophrenia and the Need-Fear Dilemma*, International Universities Press, New York, 1969.

9. Bleuler E: *Dementia Praecox or the Group of Schizophrenics*, International Universities Press, New York, 1950.

10. Freud S: Neurosis and psychosis (pp. 149–153); the loss of reality in neurosis and psychosis (pp. 183–187). In *The Standard Edition of the Complete Psychological Works of S. Freud*, Vol. XIX (1923–25), Norton, New York, 1961.

11. Schneider K: *Klinische Psychopathologie*, Ninth Ed., Thieme, Stuttgart, 1971.

12. American Psychiatric Association: *Diagnostic and Statistical Manual of Mental Disorders*, 3rd Ed. Revised (DSM-III-R), American Psychiatric Association, Washington, D.C., 1980.

13. May PRA: Schizophrenia: Evaluation of treatment methods. In Freedman AM, Kaplan HI, Sadock BJ (Eds.): *Comprehensive Textbook of Psychiatry/II*, Vol. 1, 2nd Ed., Williams & Wilkins, Baltimore, 1975, pp. 923–938.

14. Wing JK: The social context of schizophrenia. *Am. J. Psychiatry* 135:1333–1339, 1978.

15. Ostow M: The psychodynamic approach to drug therapy. *Mental Health Materials Center*, the Psychoanalytic Research and Development Fund, New York, 1979.

16. Baldessarini RJ: *Chemotherapy in Psychiatry*, Harvard University Press, Cambridge, Mass., 1977.

17. Forest DV: Nonsense and sense in schizophrenic language. *Schizophren. Bull.* 2:286–301, 1976.

18. Leff JP: Developments in family treatment of schizophrenia. *Psychiatr. Q.* 51:216–232, 1979.

19. Talbott, JA, Linn L: Reactions of schizophrenics to life threatening disease. *Psychiatr. Q.* 50:218–227, 1978.

20. Schulman D: The use of the mirror as a diagnostic and therapeutic instrument in child psychiatry. (Unpublished manuscript)

21. Merikangas KR: Assortative mating for psychiatric disorders and psychological traits. *Arch. Gen. Psychiatry*, 39:1173–1180, 1982.

8

In-Hospital Family Treatment in Psychiatric Disturbances

John G. Howells

EDITOR'S NOTE

Family treatment has become a routine and useful adjunct in the management of in-patients. Additionally in hospital care programs, the family can often help by providing intimate knowledge of the patient as well as facilitating the patient's compliance to treatment measures.

In reviewing some of the more notable experiments in family care, the author begins with the early work that focused primarily on the mother-patient relationship, and then goes on to discuss some programs which have experimented with the unusual procedure of having key family members actually stay in or near the hospital during a patient's therapy; such involvement of the family in treatment programs may help reduce the likelihood of relapse after discharge. In Norway, the following criteria were established to indicate the desirability of in-hospital family care: mothers with post-partum illness; depression in a patient whose partner has contributed to the illness but has previously refused individual therapy; adolescents in conflict with parents; alcoholic index patients who have not responded to other therapies; and neurotically affected marriages. Other Norwegian studies add the following: an index psychotic patient in need of family support; geriatric patients; family problems centering around a child.

Although extensive involvement of families during the inpatient care of psychiatrically ill patients is often not feasible, one can extrapolate from these studies certain principles that can be employed to a lesser degree in other settings. Whether or not family interactions produce illness may be a subject for debate, but the fact that the interpersonal interactions within a family can significantly affect the patient's ability to recover and maintain his or her recovery has been clearly established, making family treatment a necessary part of planned care in many diagnostic situations.

Family Involvement During In-Hospital Care

In many societies families are closely involved with a psychiatric hospital in the care of a family member admitted to a hospital as a patient. In two-thirds of the world's countries relatives actually accompany patients on a full-time basis during hospitalization.[1] In 1963, the National Institute of Mental Health began an international study into the most important aspects of family-hospital relations. After an extensive review of the literature, the study progressed to investigate facilities involving families in 27 countries of Africa, the Middle East, and Asia.

Many benefits of family participation were revealed by Bell's study. The family members' opportunity to observe and monitor the patient, coupled with their intimate knowledge of his or her behavior, provided a valuable baseline of information for the staff. The handling of the patients became a two-way concern, with the staff and family learning from each other. The family and the patient worked together to understand the illness and its consequences. The informal communication between the relatives of one patient with relatives of others resulted in speedy adjustment to hospital rules and regulations, expectations, taboos, etc. The family brought community standards into the hospital, which they used to control the behavior of the patient. Families helped each other in caring for the patients, exchanged information, reduced isolation, and brought reassurance and opportunity for socializing. Staff-family communication facilitated treatment objectives and promoted the education of the family.

Communication between the patient and those members of the family left at home was also found to be an important link, as was the link between the family in the hospital and their home community. Social and psychological support was brought to the patient by the family—not as a separate action, but as an indirect consequence of family participation in the care of the patient during hospitalization.

The requirements for family participation, listed in Bell's study, were: the provision of space, ease of contact with patient, continuity of customary home functions, easy equipment to manipulate, open communication between families, sanitation and safety, ease of entry into hospital, special facilities for chronically ill patients (space for personal possessions, socialization, privacy, etc.), nonregimentation of colors and furnishings, areas for privacy, flow of communication with the community outside, flexibility of space, exposure of patients to "normal" people, and easy transportation between home and hospital.

There are advantages and disadvantages in family participation. On the positive side, both family and staff have exclusive contributions to make, as well as contributions that overlap. Among the advantages listed by Bell were a reduction of hospital costs, a greater responsiveness of the staff when the family was present, and a lessening of impersonal handling and callousness in working with the patient. In addition, there was an improved psychological condition of the patient resulting from a lessening of stress-producing changes in the environment and a reduction of anxiety among relatives. The patient was less passive and less confused after operative procedures such as an ECT. On the negative side, the indiscriminate interference of the family in treatment, diet, and assumption of staff tasks could be harmful.

In all 27 countries covered in the study, the individual patient alone receives treatment. In the last 30 years, however, there have been experiments in which the family itself receives treatment.

Treatment of the Family by Psychiatric Units

The key concept of family psychiatry[2] is that, in clinical practice, the family is the patient; it is as true of inpatient psychiatric practice as it is of outpatient practice.

There are, however, four gradations of hospital family treatment. The least structured entails attendance by the whole family at a day hospital or outpatient department for milieu therapy and/or family group therapy. The most highly confining requires the whole family — father, mother, children, and other family members — to be admitted to a ward or to a modified ward setting in a hospital or an ancillary building. This last gradation is explored in the following account.

Experiments have been conducted in at least three countries. Each has arisen spontaneously, the result of some local need or inspiration, and each is distinct.

The United States Experience

Washington, D.C. Bowen pioneered the admission of families into hospital care in the U.S. Then the chief of the family study section at NIMH, he conducted a project that lasted from 1954 to 1958, and in 1959 he surveyed the work.[3] The inspiration for the procedure came from the demands of research of adult schizophrenic offspring and their families, and was based on Bowen's earlier experiment at the Menninger Clinic. During the first year, the project was concerned with the mother-patient relationship. Three mothers lived on the ward with their offspring, and both the patients and the mothers had individual psychotherapy. By the end of the first year, however, the hypothesis for study changed, and the schizophrenic was seen as part of a total family problem. This led to the admission of whole families.

If the three original mother-patient dyads are included, 18 families participated in the research project, either in residence or as outpatients. At the core of the project were seven families who lived together in the ward as a group (father, mother, patient, and normal siblings). The longest stay was 33 months; the average stay was a few days under 12 months. Eight other families were seen on an outpatient basis. In addition, of course, there were the original three mother-patient families, two of whom had long periods in residence (25 and 35 months).

The ward accommodated two or three families at a time. As the ward could accommodate a greater number of small families, selection favored the small family. The family members were encouraged to live together as a unit. Parents cared for their schizophrenic family member, although the staff could give assistance. One parent could work during the day as long as the other cared for the patient and both attended the daily psychotherapy sessions for one hour. The nursing staff could "patient sit," so that the parents could have outings together. The patient was free to go with them, as long as the parents could provide adequate care.

The situation gave a unique and unequaled opportunity for family observation. The core of the treatment was the one-hour daily family psychotherapy session, supplemented, if required, by individual interviews with the family "leader." Family group therapy, which was highly nondirective, was supplemented by milieu therapy. Ward activities were geared to families rather than individuals. Important postulates regarding the family and schizophrenia arising from the research project were reported by Bowen[3,4] and have recently been reviewed.[5]

Galveston, Texas. Since the University of Texas Medical Branch Hospitals at Galveston lie on the edge of their catchment area, patients and their families must travel long distances; therefore, regular attendance is difficult. The Youth Development Project circumvented this situation with multiple impact psychotherapy, a new procedure that involved a family's moving into residential care and receiving the entire time and facilities of a team for up to two and one-half days. Twelve families were received from 1957 to 1958. From 1958 to 1962, 55 families with problem adolescents were seen. Reports appeared by team members,[6-9] and research findings were discussed by Serrano, McDonald, et al.[10] Indications for multiple impact therapy included difficulty in enlisting family cooperation in the treatment of the adolescents, especially from the father, the imminent breakdown of the family, and the exclusion of the adolescent from the community.

Both the referring agency and the family were oriented about the nature of the project before the treatment began, with emphasis placed on the need to exploit this opportunity fully. The family group included parents, the adolescent problem member, selected relevant siblings, a community representative, and occasionally, a relative who had become involved with the problem.

Individual interviews were held with parents while the adolescent underwent psychometric procedures. Multiple therapists were sometimes employed with an individual or with part of the family. The day's therapy ended with the team-family conference, after which the family spent the rest of the day together. The second day continued as the first.

In intransigent cases, the above procedure continued for another half day. With one-fourth of the cases, a further day's treatment was repeated in two months' time. In every case, there was a follow-up visit to the home in six months. Results were judged as being as good as with established methods.

During the multiple impact therapy, the family need not have stayed in a hospital but could have chosen to stay in a hotel or other nearby establishment. Residence in a hospital did, however, allow longer and more skilled observation.

Madison, Wisconsin. The program initiated in Madison concerned short-term multiple impact therapy with family groups in a hospital setting.[11] From March 1968 to July 1969, the inpatient psychiatric service at the University of Wisconsin Hospitals admitted additional family members to the hospital in the course of treating 100 patients. (This followed earlier work on admitting mothers, who were suffering from postpartum reactions, and their babies.) In 15% of the 100 families in treatment, both parents were admitted with the index patient. In 4% the family group involved the index child patient, parents, and one or more siblings. Another 3% of the family groups included the index adult patient, a spouse, and one or more children. In 7% of the cases one or more children of the patient, who was always the mother, were admitted. In 45% the husband, as the index patient, was admitted alone, while 26% involved wives alone.

The ages of the 100 index patients ranged from 17 to 64. The diagnostic pattern was similar to the usual run of patients in this inpatient unit: 32 schizophrenic disorders, 24 affective psychoses, 23 personality disorders, 16 neuroses, and 5 miscellaneous disorders. The average length of stay was 20 days.

The ages of additional family members who were admitted ranged from 2 months to 68 years. It is noteworthy that 70% of these additional family members manifested psychopathology. Usually the additional family members stayed for only a week, but frequently they needed to stay some days longer.

In many cases, the additional family members were admitted after a stalemate in the progress of the index patient — one of the main indications for this approach. This procedure allowed the family to receive as much attention as the index patient. In some cases, the index patients were so sick that outpatient care was ineffective and the family had to move into the hospital to use a family approach.

Following admission, several therapists worked collaboratively with each family. In addition to milieu therapy, with its scaffolding of ward meetings, sensitivity exercises, encounter groups, and group therapy meetings, there were available psychoactive drugs, behavior modification techniques, psychodrama, videotape playbacks, programmed learning, social engineering, and individual and group psychotherapy. Each family member was encouraged to recognize that he or she had contributed to the family's problem, needed to work on this contribution, and had the status of a patient.

Elaborate statistical evaluations were not available at the time the workers presented their report, but their "impression" suggests that the results were at least as good as with traditional procedures.

Los Angeles, California. Portner[12] described an intensive treatment program in which members of a family were hospitalized with their sick family member. The work was inspired by the Madison experiment. It was argued that when patients deteriorate after discharge, it indicates a family involvement in the illness that can only be handled by the admission of the family itself. The project was a research effort to establish whether patients treated in a hospital with their families remain out of the hospital longer than if treated by other methods, and whether patients resistant to traditional methods improve with this procedure.

It was also hoped that the study would identify the characteristics of patients who would respond to this procedure. Thus, the index patients had been hospitalized on at least one occasion or had been resistant to the traditional treatment.

The project took place in a 17-bed psychiatric unit of a general hospital between January 1 and December 1, 1975. All patients had voluntary status. Eleven families were included, six whole families and five families in which only one additional family member was admitted. Spouses shared the same room, and their children had the adjoining room. Infants always shared the same room as the same-sexed parent or had an adjoining room if they were not of the same sex. The cost of hospital care came from each family's insurance supplemented, if required, by the government's Hill-Burton program.

Treatment concepts were based on general systems theory and socialization theory. In practice, treatment was operated as task centered casework by teams consisting of a primary therapist (psychiatrist or social worker), two nurses, an occupational therapist, and a ward clerk. Only one family could be on the unit at any one time, as room had to be found for patients undergoing orthodox treatment.

Admissions took place on Monday mornings and started with the signing of consent forms before moving to the taking of a family history, which assisted with the planning of therapy. Two nurses undertook the continuous observation of family interactions. The family then attended a patient group meeting at which regular ward patients fixed their targets for the week. This prepared the family for its own target setting in a family group session that afternoon. There the family members set their goals for the entire period of hospital care and were given a target to be accomplished by the next day, often a nonthreatening occupational therapy project. Family sessions were scheduled once or twice a day, and task setting often concerned the areas which the family regarded as needing change.

The length of treatment ranged from three days to three weeks, with a median of seven days. The ages of the index patient ranged from 13 to 59 years. Of the eight male and three female patients, most suffered from nonpsychotic disorders. The size of family in the project ranged from two to six members. In terms of the relationship to the index patient, four mothers, three wives, two husbands, one father, one sister, and one daughter were hospitalized with the index patient. At least one member of each family worked, but all took time off work to participate in the treatment program.

In order to evaluate the results of the procedure, an assessment of each index patient's two major symptoms was made on admission and on discharge. It was assumed that an improvement in these was indicative both of changes in the family system and of changes in his or her personality. A follow-up was undertaken three months after the end of the project to determine if any index patients had been rehospitalized within that period. The results were encouraging, if we consider the dimensions selected for study:

1. The relapse rate was significantly improved. Six of eight patients who had previously relapsed within three months had not returned to the hospital within three months.
2. Two patients who had not shown improvement with conventional treatment improved and remained out of the hospital for three months.
3. Those who did best were hospitalized with their whole family rather than with part of it.
4. Those who stayed longest did best.

A picture emerged of those who might benefit from this procedure: a family prepared to cooperate and convinced that traditional methods had failed to work with their index family member. The author suggests that further work might show this procedure to be the treatment of choice for most patients.

The United Kingdom Experience

London, England. The Cassel Hospital was founded in 1920. Growing out of a World War I interest in functional nervous disorders, its aim was to explore the psychotherapy of the neuroses. The Cassel is unique in the U.K. — a hospital staffed entirely by psychoanalytically trained physicians whose work is based on the concept of the psychotherapeutic community. It has three interdependent units: one for children and adolescents, one for adults, and one for families. The family unit owes its existence to two factors: the concept of the psychotherapeutic community which emerged during the World War II and, in 1946, the leadership of Dr. T. F. Main.

As Main recalls, work was at first centered on individuals.[13] In 1948, when a woman patient asked to be allowed to bring her child to the hospital with her, permission was granted. The practice has since expanded, allowing mother and baby to be admitted together in instances of postpartum breakdown.

In 1955, the 100-bed hospital was divided into four therapeutic communities of 25 beds, each in the charge of a consultant psychiatrist and a senior nurse. Liberally supplied with small rooms, it could admit a mother and child among the other patients of each section and provide a room for each mother-child dyad with a child's cot and toys. Occasionally, a mother might be accompanied by more than one child. In common with the other patients, each mother was expected to participate fully in the life of the section, including the domestic work. The mother cared for the child with the assistance of staff and other patients. There were extra facilities for children, such as a playroom, playground, and special mealtimes. The average length of stay for a dyad was a little over six months. The mother and her family were prepared for the admission by a visit at home from a senior nursing officer.

Treatment consisted of milieu therapy and individual psychotherapy for the mother. Main was impressed by the changes in the mother and the improvement in her capacity to mother her children. He stressed this project as a unique opportunity to study the mother-child relationship.

Main reveals the beginning of an important development, which still persists: "Rarely, where the father too has been psychologically ill, we have admitted whole families." This procedure soon gathered momentum and led to the planned admission to the hospital of whole families.

Another shift in conceptualization occurred, from treating the mother-child dyad, accompanied by the husband, to treating the triad itself. Wilson takes up the account of this shift.[14] By 1980, the families have their own unit to accommodate 30 people. The psychoanalytic flavor continues, as does treatment through the psychotherapeutic community. The family has a "home," the parents' room, and the children sleep nearby. A two-to-three-week period of comprehensive assessment, including physical examinations, is emphasized. In addition to milieu therapy, there is individual therapy for adults (two hours a week) and for children, as well as supplementary therapies and procedures. The central aim is not research oriented, but clinical.

Oxford, England. The Park Hospital for Children, in Oxford, was founded in 1958 to deal with children's psychiatric and neurological problems. From its inception, it has included evaluation and therapy of family problems associated with children's disorders. In 1964, a bungalow was built on the hospital grounds to serve as a family unit for the psychotherapy of parents and siblings of irreversibly handicapped children. The increase in referral of child abuse cases in the late 1960s and early 1970s necessitated that the unit be employed to a great extent for the admission of families involved in child abuse. Teachers are provided in the hospital's own school. The emphasis is on informality and family-like atmosphere. Therapy varies according to each family's need.

Cupar, Scotland. Just north of Edinburgh lies Cupar, with its mental hospital, Stratheden. Here, during the postwar period, there developed a comprehensive psychiatric service for children and adolescents, from which emerged a service for the admission of whole families and by 1975, facilities for admitting three to four families at a time, with one to two families in the children's unit and two in houses built for this purpose.

The department of child and family psychiatry was founded in 1960 under the leadership of Dr. Douglas Haldane.[15] In 1975, it was possible to include, in the new inpatient unit for children, a family suite capable of taking one large or two small families. During the first year, five families were admitted. These families had some of the characteristics of multi-problem and one-parent families. Treatment was comprehensive and eclectic, family psychotherapy being given prominence.

Since August 1975, 35 families have used the facilities.[16] Before admission, families visit and view the family unit, and the unit staff may visit the home. Admission is not arranged unless inpatient care promises to improve upon the outpatient care of the family. There is careful assessment of the family prior to admission by the hospital and community staff.

Families eat in the children's inpatient-unit dining room, but as discharge nears the family can arrange to collect a meal from the hospital kitchen and serve the meal in their "home." The family participates in the therapeutic and domestic arrangements of the unit, with the children fully involved in the therapeutic, school, and play facilities. The main thrust of therapy is milieu therapy reinforced by individual psychotherapy, counseling, formal family psychotherapy in an interview setting, or spontaneous family psycho-therapy in the family "homes." Fathers may go to work from the unit or from their home, in which case they join the family for the weekend at the hospital. Families may have weekend breaks in their own homes. Duration of stay ranges from one week to nine months.

The Norwegian Experience

Vikersund. The Modum Bads Nervesanatorium, a private mental hospital, was founded in 1957 at what was previously a spa. Over the last 15 years it has been the scene of perhaps the largest experiment in family care in the world. Its progress up to 1967 was reviewed by its founder, Gordon John-sen.[17] His account began with the important statement that, "ideally, family treatment should take place in the home." He observed, however, that when there is a great distance between the home and the hospital — and this would apply to his hospital — there is a case for the inpatient care of the whole family, thus permitting the intensification of treatment and continuous observation.

Specific indications for admission given by Johnsen were:

1. Index patients who are mothers with postpartum disorder.
2. An index patient who is depressed and whose condition is caused by a partner who refuses treatment; a family admission brings the real index patient into treatment.
3. Adolescents in conflict with their parents.
4. Alcoholic index patients who have not responded to treatment.
5. Known deviant sexual propensities in an index family member.
6. Neurotic marriages.

From 1964 to 1967, Johnsen began admitting families for the summer months only. All the families contained patients previously known to the hospital. When the index patients were mothers, they were put in a separate house with their children. The husbands joined them for weekends or stayed in the house and worked from there. Treatment included individual psycho-therapy, family group therapy, and traditional group therapy, which under-scored the value of the arrangement for research in family dynamics. The admission period of a number of weeks was financed by national health service insurance. At the time of his report, there were five homes for families on the grounds of his hospital. Since 1968, further reports have been published by Holm and Rynning,[18] Eli Norbye,[19] and Ravnsborg.[20]

By 1967, eight homes were available for families throughout the year. It is now possible to admit five families, each in a home of its own, plus six married couples with two couples sharing a house. Meals are cooked in the hospital kitchen and served in the houses. A period of observation and investigation culminates in a staff evaluation conference that allows a plan of treatment to be worked out. A staff-family meeting follows. Milieu thera-py is supported by a comprehensive program of psychoanalytically based individual, dyadic, and family group therapy, as well as pastoral guidance, occupational therapy, educational facilities for children, and recreation. Family group therapeutic time amounts to three or four hours a week. The duration of stay is from three to seven weeks for married couples and from five to twelve weeks for families, followed by aftercare.

Oslo. Albretsen, who has in the past discussed the general need for family management for a number of groups of patients,[21-24] offers six indications for inpatient family treatment:

1. Postpartum disorders in the mother (sometimes admission before child-birth).
2. Family problems centering around the child.
3. An index psychotic patient needing the support of a relative.
4. Neurotic problems in an index patient, significantly affecting or affected by intrafamilial relationships.
5. Support for geriatric patients.
6. Death of a significant family member.

At the State Center for Child and Adolescent Psychiatry in Norway a further experiment has developed—admission of families with disturbed adolescents. Selnes and his group emphasize the necessity of making the family aware of the adolescent's problems if the adolescent is to be reintegra-ted into the family.[25] The center collaborates with referring agencies on admission and discharge. Families participate fully in the life of the unit. Milieu therapy is supplemented by cotherapy with individuals, parents, or whole families. The length of stay is about three weeks, and readmission is possible.

Analysis of Programs and Conclusions

Historically, it is of special interest that at least three experiments in admitting families to hospitals started over 20 years ago in the late 1950s and early 1960s—in Washington, London, and Galveston. One of these, in London, continues today. From available evidence it seems that in recent times, it was Bowen at NIMH, in 1955, who was the first to admit families to the hospital.

Indications for admission in the studies reviewed included geographical, research, and clinical considerations. The unusual location of the hospitals in Vikersund and Galveston made a family admission more desirable there, as outpatient management was difficult. This indication alone would not apply in urban areas and applies increasingly less as transportation and communication systems improve. Research was a paramount reason for the projects in Washington and in Los Angeles.

Clinical indications were both general and specific. General indications were: the belief that the family, rather than the index patient, was the real patient; no progress had been made with the index patient by any other procedure; outpatient treatment had failed either for the index patient or the family; the index patient could not be treated on a family basis as an outpatient due to the severe state of his or her illness; a patient had deteriorated on return to his or her own family.

Ironically, although theoretical concepts linking family dynamics with schizophrenia have received much attention, most units cited above concluded that inpatient family treatment was a procedure more suitable for neuroses than psychoses; nonprocess schizophrenia might also be an indication (nonprocess schizophrenia implies here schizophrenic-like states that appear at first glance to have affinity with true-process schizophrenia, but which on closer observation seem to be cases of a severe neurosis). Process schizophrenics are not likely to respond.

Particular clinical categories recommended for admission were: postpartum disorder in the mother, child abuse, adolescent disorder in the index patient, alcoholism in the index patient, deviant sexual propensities in the index patient, neurotic marriages, neurosis in a child index patient, neurosis in an adult index patient, death of a family member, and support for the index psychotic or geriatric patient. It is most likely that these indications were given because these categories were target categories of the particular hospitals involved at the time, or were of special interest to the workers. The whole range of psychiatric disorders may well be suitable targets in particular circumstances.

The number of families admitted at any one time varied from one family to as many as ten families (30 people). The constitution of the family admitted varied greatly, often depending on the age of the index patient. At

Galveston, other relatives were sometimes involved in addition to the nuclear family. Sometimes some, or all, of the children in the family were included; at other times, only a father, a mother, or frequently both parents were in the family group.

A number of the projects stressed the importance of observation and diagnosis. Occasionally, most of the attention went to the index patient, thus negating the concept of family psychiatry, in which the family should always be the patient in both treatment and diagnosis.

Treatment was almost always based on milieu therapy, supplemented by various forms of psychotherapy (sometimes only individual psychotherapy), and supported by various extra procedures. Rarely was an effort made to define the rationale of milieu therapy. The psychotherapies were sometimes used intensively; sometimes the duration of psychotherapy was so brief that its effectiveness seems unlikely.

There appeared to be agreement on some points of organization. The longest experiments emphasized the importance of preadmission preparation of the family and aftercare following treatment, with flexibility about the parents continuing to work. There was little agreement about desirable length of stay, which varied from two to two-and-one-half days at Galveston, to six to nine months in the United Kingdom. The Los Angeles experiment impressionistically suggests that the best results came from longer stay.

Most units had to make do with single rooms in existing wards of hospitals. Cupar had purpose-built accommodations and Vikersund had adapted very suitable accommodations. There may be some advantages in mixing families in ward populations and other advantages in segregation.

Results were generally a matter of impression. In Los Angeles a laudable attempt at systematic evaluation was made, but the patients in the study were very few. A mood of enthusiasm is very evident in the papers. At worst, results were as good as with other measures; in the small Los Angeles experiment, they seemed somewhat better for the chosen group. Results seemed best the longer the duration of admission and the more complete the family in the hospital.

Spontaneously in three separate countries, experiments with in-hospital family therapy have been undertaken. The work reviewed here supports only cautious optimism as to results. The overwhelming reaction must be that research is required to establish the value of such a procedure for clinical purposes. What are the advantages over the dramatically cheaper (and less stigmatized) outpatient care for the same group of families? What are indications for the admission of which group of index patients and families in what circumstances? What are the optimum requirements of accommodation? What are the desirable diagnostic and therapeutic facilities and procedures of preparation and aftercare? Inpatient care has advantages for family diagnosis and remains largely unexploited for this purpose. Investigation is clearly required to define more precisely the nature and effectiveness of milieu therapy and psychotherapy. Future research must be well planned with clear identification and control of variables, clear definition of categories, sufficient material for statistical purposes, and appropriate control groups.

No more experiments have been instituted since those described. This may have more to do with the difficulties of adapting living accommodations and the high cost of the procedure than the value of the procedure itself or unfamiliarity with family psychiatry. It may well be that all psychiatric facilities will someday provide accommodations for the admission of families, and that there should be a flexible arrangement whereby some families can be treated on an outpatient basis, some in a day hospital, some attending the outpatient department for family group therapy with the index patient, some attending the ward setting for family group therapy with the ward index patient, and some needing admission as a partial or whole family. The past 30 years of innovation are certainly only the end of the beginning of the approach to understand the role of family in psychiatric illness and the evolution of strategies to deal effectively with the whole family unit in treatment.

References

1. Bell JE: The family in the hospital: Experiences in other countries. In Harbin HT (Ed.): *The Psychiatric Hospital and the Family*, MTP Press, Lancaster, Eng., Spectrum Publications, Jamaica, N.Y., 1982.

2. Howells JG: *Family Psychiatry*, Oliver & Boyd, Edinburgh, 1963.

3. Bowen M: The family as the unit of study and treatment: Workshop 1959 — family psychotherapy. *Am. J. Orthopsychiatry* 31:40-60, 1961.

4. Bowen M: A Family Concept of Schizophrenia. In: D. Jackson (Ed.): *The Etiology of Schizophrenia*, Basic Books, New York, 1960.

5. Howells JG, Guirguis W: *The Family and Schizophrenia*, International Univ. Press, New York, 1985.

6. Schuster FP: Summary description of multiple impact psychotherapy. *Tex. Rep. Biol. Med.* 17:426-430, 1959.

7. Ritchie A: Multiple impact therapy: An experiment. *Soc. Wk.* 5:16-22, 1960.

8. Goolishian HA: A brief psychotherapy program for disturbed adolescents. *Am. J. Orthopsychiatry* 32:142, 1962.

9. MacGregor R: Multiple impact psychotherapy with families. In Howells JG (Ed.): *Theory and Practice of Family Psychiatry*, Oliver & Boyd, Edinburgh, 1968.

10. Serrano AC et al.: Adolescent maladjustment and family dynamics. In Howells JG (Ed.): *Theory and Practice of Family Psychiatry*, Oliver & Boyd, Edinburgh, 1968.

11. Abroms GM, Fellner CH, Whitaker CA: The family enters the hospital. *Amer. J. Psychiatry* 127:1364–1369, 1971.

12. Portner DL: Hospitalization of the family in the treatment of mental patients. *Health and Social Work* 2:111–122, 1977.

13. Main TF: Mothers with children in a psychiatric hospital. In Howells JG (Ed.): *Theory and Practice of Family Psychiatry*, Oliver & Boyd, Edinburgh, 1968.

14. Wilson AR: An outline of work with families at the Cassel Hospital. *Int. J. Fam. Psychiatry* 1:339–355, 1980.

15. Haldane D, McCluskey U, Peacey M: Development of a residential facility for families in Scotland: Prospect and retrospect. *Int. J. Fam. Psychiatry* 1:357–371, 1980.

16. Lindsay SF, Sethi PC: Personal communication, 1980.

17. Johnsen G: Family treatment in psychiatric hospitals (Proc. 7th Int. Congr. of Psychotherapy, Wiesbaden, 1967, Part IV: Family investigation). *Psychother. Psychosom.* 16:333–338, 1968.

18. Holm HJ, Rynning S: Experiences with a two weeks' stay of observation. *J. Norweg. Med. Assn.* 91:2495–2497, 1971.

19. Norbye E: Treatment of families: Village in Modum Bads Nervesanatorium. *Acta Psychiatr. Scand.* 265:34, 1976.

20. Ravnsborg IS: The inpatient care of families at Vikersund. *Int. J. Fam. Psychiatry* 1:373–392, 1980.

21. Albretsen CS: Hospitalization of postpartum psychotic patients, together with babies and husbands. *Acta Psychiatr. Scand.* (Suppl.) 203:179–182, 1968.

22. Albretsen CS: A closed multifamily group. *J. Oslo City Hosp.* 21:56–60, 1971.

23. Albretsen CS: Hospital admission of families. *Int. J. Fam. Psychiatry* 1:393–399, 1980.

24. Albretsen CS, Vaglum P: The alcoholic's wife and her conflicting roles: A cause for hospitalization. *Acta Socio-Medica Scand.* 1:41–50, 1971.

25. Selnes B, Undersrud G, Kolnes B: Brief residential treatment of families with adolescents. *J. Fam. Ther.* 4:23–24, 1976.

9

Expressed Emotion in Families

Julian Leff

EDITOR'S NOTE

The research that has been carried out during the past few years to identify the role that family attitudes play in determining the strength and duration of recovery among formerly hospitalized schizophrenic patients has proved to be groundbreaking; it possesses eminently practical implications too.

In essence, the more hostility the family feels and shows toward the patient in various critical ways, the more likely are relapses; overinvolvement with the patient seems to produce a similar effect. Emotional warmth, on the other hand, facilitates sustained improvement.

Using the Camberwell Family Interview system, it is possible to estimate the level of expressed emotion in the home; the higher the EE level, the higher the relapse rate. Only the continued use of prophylactic antipsychotic medication or a daily routine in which the patient spent much of his or her time out of contact with the family members served as some protection against the detrimental influences of a high level of critical hostility.

These findings do not appear to be unique for schizophrenic patients. Patients with neurotic depression and obesity have also been shown to do poorly in families with high levels of EE.

Experiments at intervention suggest that a combination of education, group sessions for relatives, and family therapy can reduce the EE level and increase the patient's chances of remaining stabilized and functioning reasonably well.

Introduction

The policy of custodial care for the mentally ill began to change in the late 1940s, and in some pioneering hospitals the number of occupied beds started to fall at that time. The trickle of discharges soon swelled to a tide, and in a relatively short period of time large numbers of psychiatric patients, many suffering from schizophrenia, were living outside of a hospital. A high readmission rate was noted and prompted a study of factors that might be associated with a return to the hospital. Brown and his colleagues[1] conducted a follow-up of 150 schizophrenic men discharged from psychiatric hospitals. They found that a key determinant of readmission was the type of living group to which the patients returned. Those who were discharged to relatives were more likely to be readmitted than those who lived alone or with a landlord. Brown considered it possible that the emotional relationship between relative and patient could influence the likelihood of the patient's relapsing. Consequently, in conjunction with Rutter,[2] he set about developing a technique for measuring emotional attitudes of relatives and patients.

The Camberwell Family Interview

After undergoing some modification,[3] the measure developed by Brown and Rutter is now the standard instrument for assessing a subject's level of expressed emotion (EE). It is named the Camberwell Family Interview (CFI) and consists of a semistructured questionnaire that covers the preceding three months. It has been administered most commonly at the time of a patient's admission to the hospital, but it can be given at any point in the patient's life. The same interview has been used for patients with psychiatric conditions other than schizophrenia, and the schedule has been adapted for use with patients suffering from nonpsychiatric illnesses such as diabetes and hemophilia.

The CFI consists of questions about the patient's symptoms and behavior. The interview has usually been conducted in the relatives' own home to put them more at ease, but it can be administered in an office. The interview is audio recorded, and the ratings are made later while listening to the recording.

There are five principal scales:

1. *Critical comments.* These are negative remarks made about the patient's behavior that are rendered critical by content or tone.
2. *Hostility.* This is rated as present either if there is a string of criticisms about unrelated areas of the patient's life or if negative remarks are made about the patient as a person.
3. *Emotional overinvolvement.* This complex scale is rated from 0 to 5, and consists of various components. They include excessive emotionality displayed during the interview, overprotective behavior reported by the relative,

unnecessary self-sacrifice, and an inability of the relative to lead a life independent of the patient.

4. *Warmth*. This is also rated on a scale from 0 to 5, and refers to warmth expressed about the patient. It is judged mainly by the respondent's tone of voice.

5. *Positive remarks*. These are statements expressing praise, approval, or appreciation of the behavior or personality of the patient. The number of positive remarks made during the interview is counted.

The interview takes about an hour to complete, and the ratings occupy about another hour and a half. Training is necessary in order to master the interviewing and rating techniques. Trainees are expected to exceed an interrater reliability of 0.8 on all scales, and this is commonly achieved by the end of a two-week training course.

The Expressed Emotion Index

In the first study to use the five scales, patients were followed up for nine months after discharge from the hospital, and any relapses were noted.[4] Relapses were not equated with readmission, but were defined as either Type I, a reappearance of schizophrenic symptoms in patients previously free of them, or Type II, a marked exacerbation of psychotic symptoms that persisted at discharge. The average length of stay of schizophrenic patients in hospitals in the U.K. exceeds two months, and the majority are free of psychotic symptoms by discharge. Consequently, most relapses observed in the British studies have been Type I in nature. The diagnosis of schizophrenia has been established using the Present State Examination (PSE) and the associated computer program, Catego.[5]

Brown and his colleagues[4] found that relapse was more likely if the patient returned to live with a relative who was excessively critical, or showed any hostility, or was highly overinvolved. In fact, hostility is almost invariably linked with a high degree of criticism, so for prediction of relapse it is redundant. Consequently, relatives are now categorized as high on an index of expressed emotion (EE) if they make six or more critical comments or are rated 3 or above on the overinvolvement scale. On the other hand, if relatives are rated as high on warmth in the absence of the negative expressed emotions, the patients are less likely to relapse. Thus, it appears that relatives may be able to influence the course of schizophrenia beneficially as well as adversely. This aspect of the work has tended to be ignored in the focus on the negative side of expressed emotion.

In most instances, the relatives interviewed were either parents or a spouse, though occasionally siblings were seen. It has been the convention to categorize a household as high EE even when only one member meets the necessary criteria.

Expressed Emotion and Relapse of Schizophrenia

When Brown and his colleagues assigned relatives to high or low EE categories, they found that patients in the two groups had significantly different relapse rates over the nine-month follow-up: 58% in high EE homes, 16% in low EE homes ($p < 0.001$). These findings have now been replicated in a number of centers in widely differing cultures, as shown in Table 1.

The difference in relapse rates between high and low EE homes is significant in every case, and the rates are remarkably similar across centers, with the exception of Chandigarh. The patients in the Indian sample were all making their first contact with the psychiatric services, whereas the other centers included readmissions as well as first admissions.

Although the relapse rates within high and low EE groups were almost uniform, the proportion of high EE relatives shows extreme variation across cultures, as can be seen from Table 2.

There appears to be a gradient from West to East, the highest proportion of high EE relatives being found among Californian Anglo-Americans, and a negligible number being identified among the peasant farmers of Chandigarh.[10] We can only speculate about the causes of these marked differences in the degree of tolerance of relatives for the problems presented by a schizophrenic patient in the household. Warner[11] has argued that market forces are a major influence on societal attitudes towards individuals disabled by schizophrenia. However, it seems likely that popular concepts of the origin of

TABLE 1
Relapse Rates of Schizophrenia over 9 Months in Various Studies

City	London		Los Angeles		Chandigarh
Ethnic group	British		Anglo-Americans	Mexican-Americans	Indians
Study	Brown et al.[4]	Vaughn & Leff[6]	Vaughn et al.[7]	Jenkins et al.[8]	Leff et al.[9]
High EE	58%	50%	56%	58%	31%
Low EE	16%	12%	17%	26%	9%

TABLE 2
Proportion of High EE Relatives in Different Cultural Groups

City	Los Angeles	London	Aarhus	Los Angeles	Chandigarh	
Ethnic group	Anglo-Americans	British	Danish	Mexican-Americans	Indians urban	rural
	67%	52%	54%	41%	30%	8%

mental illness also play a part. In many traditional cultures, mental illnesses are ascribed to outside influences — angered ancestral spirits or spells cast by enemies — and hence the patient is not held responsible for his disability. Although the determinants of relatives' EE remain to be identified, the consequences are of considerable importance for schizophrenia, since the greater acceptance of patients by their relatives provides an explanation for the markedly better outcome in developing countries.[12]

EE and Measures of Direct Interaction

Most of the studies of EE have employed a nine-month follow-up period, but this is a relatively brief interval in the life of a schizophrenic patient. Leff and Vaughn[13] extended their follow-up to two years and found that the relationship between relatives' EE and outcome remained significant. The relapse rates in high and low EE homes were 62% and 20%, respectively.

It will be appreciated that the ratings of EE are made from an interview with the relative alone. In relating these to the outcome of schizophrenia, we are making two assumptions: that the attitudes expressed to the interviewer closely reflect the actual behavior of the relative towards the patient, and also that they are representative of enduring relationships over time. The second assumption is supported by the findings of the nine-month and two-year follow-ups. The first assumption remained untested until recently.

Doane[14] has developed a method of coding direct interactions between patients and their relatives. Her coding categories include Benign Criticism, Harsh Criticism, Guilt Inducement, and Critical Intrusive Comments, all of which appear to be aspects of the EE ratings of critical comments and hostility. Another category, Neutral Intrusive Statements, overlaps somewhat with the symbiotic component of overinvolvement. Miklowitz and his colleagues[15] used Doane's Affective Style technique in parallel with EE ratings to study the families of 42 schizophrenic patients. They found that there was a close correspondence between the number of critical statements made in the interactional situation and EE ratings of high criticism. Furthermore, parents who were rated as high on overinvolvement made significantly more

Neutral Intrusive Statements than low EE parents and parents rated high on criticism.

Further evidence germane to this issue is provided by a study of the relatives of patients with anorexia nervosa.[16] In this trial of family therapy for anorexia nervosa, the EE levels of relatives were measured routinely. In addition, a family lunch in which a therapist joined the whole family for a meal was organized and the occasion was videotaped. Advantage was taken of these recordings to make EE ratings from the direct interactions between family members. High correlations were found between critical comments rated from the EE interview and those made during the family meal, though this relationship was stronger for mothers than fathers. However, there were low correlations between overinvolvement scores in the two settings.

Thus, the experimental data indicate a close correspondence between criticism expressed to the interviewer administering the CFI and criticism directed at the patient in interactional situations. The evidence concerning overinvolvement is more equivocal, possibly because the CFI elicits accounts of overinvolved behavior that occur outside of the interview and may not be observed in a relatively brief interactional situation.

The Nonspecific Nature of EE

In the preceding section we have referred to a study of EE in anorexia nervosa. Relatives' EE has now been measured in a variety of psychiatric and nonpsychiatric conditions, including depressive neurosis,[6,17] anorexia nervosa,[16] obesity,[18] mental subnormality, epilepsy in children, and diabetes. In each of these conditions, some relatives have been rated as high on critical comments, overinvolvement, or both. In the study of Vaughn and Leff,[6] relatives of depressed neurotic patients were rated as high on criticism as the relatives of patients with schizophrenia. When the threshold of six critical comments was applied, no difference was found between the relapse rates of depressed patients in high EE and low EE homes. However, when the threshold was lowered to two critical comments, a significant difference emerged between the relapse rates of the two groups of patients. This finding was treated cautiously until recently replicated by Hooley et al.[17] The results from the two studies are compared in Table 3. This table also includes the findings of a study of obese women conducted in California by Havstad.[18] She found that if the husband was at all critical of his wife, she was not likely to maintain the weight loss initially achieved by dieting.

We conclude from these results that it is not only schizophrenic patients whose condition is responsive to the emotional attitudes of relatives. In-

TABLE 3
**Relapse Rates of Patients with Depressive Neurosis and Women with Obesity
in Low and High Criticism Homes**

Condition	Depressive neurosis		Obesity
Study	Vaughn and Leff 1976	Hooley et al. 1986	Havstad 1979
High criticism (2+)	67%	59%	68%
Low criticism (0–1)	22%	0%	11%

deed, it appears that patients with depressive neurosis are even more sensitive to critical attitudes than patients with schizophrenia. The same would seem to apply to obese women. Follow-ups have still to be completed in the studies of the other conditions listed, but enough evidence already exists to indicate that high EE attitudes are by no means confined to the relatives of schizophrenic patients. Furthermore, they are associated with a poor outcome in conditions as different as schizophrenia, depressive neurosis, and obesity. It seems likely that high EE attitudes may develop in respect to any illness, whether psychiatric or not, that runs a chronic or relapsing course. If this proves to be the case for a number of nonpsychiatric conditions, then it opens up a new area of research into illnesses traditionally considered to be psychosomatic.

Protective Factors in High EE Homes

Returning to schizophrenia, one can see from Table 1 that, with the exception of the Indian center, about half the patients living in high EE homes remained well over a nine-month period. Two protective factors have been identified and appear to account for the well-being of these patients. One is regular maintenance with neuroleptic medication. Patients in high EE homes who remained on prophylactic drugs had a significantly lower relapse rate than those who took drugs irregularly or not at all. A protective effect of drugs was not apparent in low EE homes at the nine-month follow-up but emerged by the end of two years.[13]

The other protective factor concerns the amount of time patients spend in the company of high EE relatives. This was measured by constructing a time budget of a typical week and calculating how much time the patient and the relative spent in the same room together. This is termed face-to-face contact, and it is assumed to reflect the amount of social interaction between them. An arbitrary cutoff point of 35 hours of face-to-face contact per week was applied. Patients in high EE homes with an amount of contact greater than this did significantly worse than those with a lesser amount of contact. The degree of contact for those living with low EE relatives had no effect on the relapse rate.

Combining the data from the two British studies resulted in a large enough group of patients, totalling 128, to allow the relapse rates in subgroups to be studied. The relevant analysis is shown in Table 4, and indicates that there may be an additive effect between the two protective factors.

Either regular neuroleptic medication or low face-to-face contact appears to reduce the relapse rate of high EE patients from nearly 100% to about half, whereas if both protective factors are present, the relapse rate is as low as 15%. In the California study conducted by Vaughn and her colleagues,[7] prophylactic drugs and low contact provided no protection on their own but only in combination; that is, they exerted an interactive effect. The data from these studies suggest that patients in high EE homes can completely protect themselves against the dangers inherent in their environment by combining low social contact with regular maintenance drugs.

However, there are problems with this interpretation, since the data are derived from naturalistic studies in which the direction of cause and effect cannot be determined with any certainty. For instance, it is just as plausible to suggest that patients with a good premorbid personality have a large social network, which they can utilize to maintain low face-to-face contact with a high EE relative. In this interpretation, the benefit for the patients would derive from their personality assets and not from low contact with the relative. A powerful way to resolve the issue of cause and effect is to conduct an experiment. In this case, the aim would be to attempt to alter the family environment in a direction that theoretically should be beneficial and to look for an effect on the course of the patient's illness. This reasoning led to a study of intervention in the families of schizophrenic patients.

TABLE 4
Nine-month Relapse Rates of Schizophrenic Patients from Two British Studies[4,6]

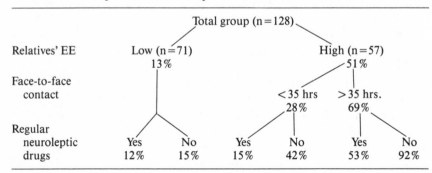

Before considering the intervention studies, it is necessary to point out that the factors usually identified as indicative of a good prognosis in schizophrenia also emerged as such in the EE studies. Thus, female sex, married status, and an acute onset of illness were each associated with a better outcome, regardless of the EE level of the home. However, when these were taken into account statistically, the association between EE and outcome remained significant.

Studies of Intervention in Families of Schizophrenic Patients

The first trial of social intervention to be based on the EE work involved the evaluation of a package of treatments for the families. It was considered unethical to withhold maintenance neuroleptics from patients, so that it was necessary to select a high-risk group who would be likely to have a high relapse rate even on regular medication. Thus, patients were deemed suitable for the trial if they were in high contact with high EE relatives. Such patients would be expected to show a 50% relapse rate over nine months while on medication (see Table 4). Of the 24 patients who entered the trial, 21 were maintained on depot neuroleptics. Once suitability for the trial had been determined, patients were randomly assigned to an experimental or control group. The control patients were given routine outpatient care, but their relatives were not offered any help by the research therapists. Of course, it was possible for them to have been given some form of assistance by the clinical team responsible for the patients, but only one relative received care comparable in amount to that offered to the experimental relatives.

The experimental intervention comprised three main components: an education program, a relatives' group, and family therapy. The education program consisted of two formal lectures given to the relatives in their home, which provided information on the etiology, symptoms, course, and management of schizophrenia. Education continued in an informal manner throughout the intervention. A Knowledge Interview was used to assess the effect of the education program on the relatives. It revealed that the program resulted in more of them knowing the diagnosis and in an increase in optimism.[19] The relatives' group included both high EE and low EE relatives, and was held every fortnight for an hour and a half. It was run by two therapists, their main aims being to determine from low EE members what effective coping strategies they had evolved and to attempt to persuade high EE members to adopt them. Other functions of the group included the relief of guilt and isolation, the expansion of relatives' social networks, and the serving as a safety valve to allow the expression of anger and anxiety in a supportive environment.[20]

The Schizophrenias

Patients were excluded from the relatives' group, but took part in family sessions, which were held in the home at first fortnightly and later monthly. They lasted an hour and were conducted by two cotherapists, almost always a male and a female. The family therapy complemented the relatives' group, but in addition enabled the therapists to tackle behavior and relationships in a more direct way than was possible in the group.

At the nine-month assessment it was found that there had been a significant reduction in critical comments made by experimental relatives, whereas the control relatives showed hardly any change. There was also some reduction in overinvolvement, but this did not reach significance, so it was concluded that the intervention made a much greater impact on criticism than on overinvolvement. In all, 6 of the 12 experimental families changed from high EE to low EE. Five altered from high to low face-to-face contact. However, there was some overlap between the two alterations, with the consequence that 9 of the 12 families became low EE and/or low contact by the nine-month follow-up.[21] All experimental patients continued taking their maintenance drugs, whereas 10 of the 12 control patients did so. Nevertheless, five (50%) of the control patients relapsed, as was anticipated from the figures in Table 4. Only a single experimental patient relapsed, a significant difference (exact $p=0.032$), which indicates that the therapeutic package conferred a substantial advantage on the experimental patients.

The primary aim of the study was to investigate the hypothesis that family attitudes exert a causal influence on relapse. The data germane to this purpose derive from those families in which EE and/or contact became low. In these nine families, no patient relapsed, an even more significant difference from the control group (exact $p=0.017$).

A later follow-up was conducted at two years and throws light on the sustained effect of the social intervention.[22] Between the two follow-ups, three more patients discontinued their regular neuroleptic medication, leaving 10 in the experimental group and nine in the control group. Seven of the nine (78%) control patients relapsed, compared with two of the ten (20%) experimental patients (exact $p=0.017$). However, the relapse rates underestimate the psychiatric morbidity of the experimental patients, two of whom committed suicide. If these are included as failures of treatment, the difference between experimental and control groups is no longer significant. Thus, there is some doubt about the effectiveness of the intervention over a two-year period.

Our subsequent experience has induced us to keep contact with the families, however tenuous, over much longer periods of time than we had at first planned. In relation to testing the causal hypothesis, both suicides occurred in families in which we did not achieve the aims of our intervention. Experimental patients on medication who lived in families in which one or both of the aims of therapy were attained did very well. Only one out of seven (14%)

relapsed in two years. This is significantly different (exact $p=0.20$) from the relapse rate in the control group, and provides evidence for the view that the deleterious effect of high EE attitudes on schizophrenia extends over at least two years.

The design of this first trial did not allow us to determine whether any one component of the therapeutic package was responsible for its effectiveness. Three other similar trials comparing family treatment for schizophrenia with other methods of management have now been published, and all show similar results in the short term (reviewed by Leff).[23] Furthermore, a two-year follow-up by Falloon's group[24] revealed a very similar advantage for the experimental group to that achieved by Leff's team over the same period of time. The next stage in this area of research is to attempt to tease out those elements in the family treatment of schizophrenia that are essential to its success, and such studies are in progress.

Conclusion

The development of a technique to assess emotional attitudes in family members has led to the fruitful expansion of an area of research. This has had a practical payoff in terms of the clinical management of schizophrenia, and a theoretical gain in terms of a deeper understanding of the reactivity of schizophrenic patients to their social environment. Such patients are sensitive not only to relatives' attitudes but also to the occurrence of life events, and the complex interactions between these environmental factors and maintenance neuroleptics have now been worked out in detail.[25] The success of this research approach to schizophrenia suggests that its application to depression could be equally fruitful, particularly as relatives' EE has already been shown to be linked to the outcome of depressive illnesses.[6,17]

References

1. Brown GW, Carstairs GM, Topping G: Post hospital adjustment of chronic mental patients. *Lancet* 2:685–689, 1958.

2. Brown GW, Rutter M: The measurement of family activities and relationships: A methodological study. *Hum. Relations* 19:241–263, 1966.

3. Vaughn CE, Leff JP: The measurement of Expressed Emotion in the families of psychiatric patients. *Br. J. Soc. Clin. Psychol* 15:157–165, 1976b.

4. Brown GW, Birley JLT, Wing JK: Influence of family life on the course of schizophrenic disorders: A replication. *Br. J. Psychiatry* 121:241–258, 1972.

5. Wing JK, Cooper JE, Sartorius N: *The measurement and classification of psychiatric symptoms: An instruction manual for the PSE and Catego System*, Cambridge University Press, London, 1974.

6. Vaughn CE, Leff JP: The influence of family and social factors on the course of psychiatric illness: A comparison of schizophrenic and depressed neurotic patients. *Br. J. Psychiatry* 129:125–137, 1976.

7. Vaughn CE et al.: Family factors in schizophrenic relapse. *Arch. Gen. Psychiatry* 41:1169–1177, 1984.

8. Jenkins JH et al.: Expressed Emotion in cross-cultural context: Familial responses to schizophrenic illness among Mexican-Americans. In Goldstein MS, Hand I, Hahlweg K (Eds.): *Treatment of Schizophrenia: Family Assessment and Intervention*, Springer, Berlin, 1986.

9. Leff J et al.: Influence of relatives' Expressed Emotion on the course of schizophrenia in Chandigarh. *Br. J. Psychiatry* 151:166–173, 1987.

10. Menon DK et al.: The distribution of Expressed Emotion components among relatives of schizophrenic patients in Aarhus and Chandigarh. *Br. J. Psychiatry* 151:160–165, 1987.

11. Warner R: *Recovery from Schizophrenia: Psychiatry and Political Economy*, Routledge & Kegan Paul, London, 1985.

12. World Health Organization: *Schizophrenia: An International Follow-up Study, Vol. II*, John Wiley & Sons, Chichester, 1979.

13. Leff JP, Vaughn C: The role of maintenance therapy and relatives Expressed Emotion in relapse of schizophrenia: a two-year follow-up. *Br. J. Psychiatry* 139:102–104, 1981.

14. Doane JA et al.: Parental communication deviance and affective style. *Arch. Gen. Psychiatry* 38:679–685, 1981.

15. Miklowitz DJ et al.: Interactional correlates of Expressed Emotion in the families of schizophrenics. *Br. J. Psychiatry* 144:482–487, 1984.

16. Szmuckler G et al.: Expressed Emotion in independent and family settings: A comparative study. *Br. J. Psychiatry* 151:174–178, 1987.

17. Hooley J, Orley J, Teasdale JD: Levels of Expressed Emotion and relapse in depressed patients. *Br. J. Psychiatry* 148:642–647, 1986.

18. Havstad LF: *Weight loss and weight loss maintenance as aspects of family emotional processes*. Ph.D. thesis. University of Southern California, Los Angeles, 1979.

19. Berkowitz R et al.: Educating relatives about schizophrenia. *Schizophr. Bull.* 10:418–430, 1984.

20. Berkowitz R, Kuipers L, Leff J: Keeping the patient well: Drug and social treatments of schizophrenic patients. *Psychopharmacol. Bull.* 17:89–90, 1981.

21. Leff JP et al.: A controlled trial of social intervention in the families of schizophrenic patients. *Br. J. Psychiatry* 141:121–134, 1982.

22. Leff JP et al.: A controlled trial of social intervention in the families of schizophrenic patients: Two-year follow-up. *Br. J. Psychiatry* 146:594–600, 1985.

23. Leff JP: Family treatment of schizophrenia. In Granville-Grossman K (Ed.): *Recent Advances in Clinical Psychiatry, No. 5*, Churchill Livingstone, London, 1985.

24. Falloon IRH et al.: Family management in the prevention of morbidity of schizophrenia: Clinical outcome of a two-year longitudinal study. *Arch. Gen. Psychiatry* 42:887, 1985.

25. Leff JP, Vaughn C: *Expressed Emotion in Families: Its Significance for Mental Illness*, Guilford, New York, 1985.

10

Social Skills Training for Schizophrenia
Ian R. H. Falloon

EDITOR'S NOTE

It should come as no surprise that competence in interpersonal skills is a significant determinant in the successful rehabilitation of all patients, especially those diagnosed as schizophrenic. To some degree, these patients may never have acquired such skills, and the lack of them may have contributed to their acute illnesses. In other cases, skills, once operative, may be lost in the course of the acute illness and its associated demoralization.

Psychotherapy per se often does not deal directly with the acquisition of social and occupational competence. Direct, planned teaching may be required. Assertiveness training is one form of such learning; the patient begins to understand how to assert himself with reduced timidity and anxiety in various situations. Role-playing is another approach to learning social skills.

Among the basic elements of social competence, one must consider the accurate perception and processing of cues, a minimally sufficient repertoire of social behavior, and adequate reinforcement for competent performance. Schizophrenic patients are particularly vulnerable to incorrect information perception and processing; many have not learned ordinary responses to specific social cues. Moreover, the abilities the patient has may be further compromised by the side-effects of major tranquilizing drugs.

Verbal instruction alone may be sufficient in many instances, particularly for such basic living skills as grooming, health care, budgeting, and leisure planning. More complex interactional skills require practice via role playing and then, with support, in real life situations. Involving the family in the patient's effort to adapt to the demands of the world can substantially reinforce the learning process.

Social Skills and Sustained Recovery

In recent years the focus of adult psychiatry has shifted from the sole treatment of acute psychopathology to a more holistic management of patients and their problems of community adjustment. Ranking high among the determinants of successful community adaptation is the patients' competence in interpersonal relationships. The establishment and maintenance of interpersonal competence are clearly key variables associated with the successful rehabilitation of persons who experience schizophrenia.[1,2]

With the advent of efficacious drug treatment for schizophrenia, there was considerable optimism that many of the social difficulties noted in persons with this disorder would dissipate once their psychotic symptoms were adequately controlled. Despite the fact that control of the florid delusions and hallucinations improves the social behavior that is associated with these cognitive distortions, medication has little impact on the deficits in social functioning that preceded the onset of schizophrenia. In other words, no amount of drug therapy or community support will enable patients to acquire the specific social skills that have not already been established in their repertoire, no more than drug therapy can enable them to perform a skilled job for which they have not received specific vocational training. For this reason, it is necessary to teach individuals the interpersonal skills they lack. Clearly, in the normal course of development such specific training is seldom required. Social competence is acquired throughout life, initially from family training and later through peer modeling. However, the onset of a handicapping disorder such as schizophrenia in the formative years of adolescence serves to restrict and retard the natural social learning experience, and it is not surprising that those who develop schizophrenia at a young age are the most handicapped in their interpersonal functioning.[3] A promising method for efficiently enhancing the social competence of young adults who have suffered one or more episodes of schizophrenia is known as social skills training.

Definition of Social Skills

There is no clear consensus about what constitutes socially skilled behavior, and attempts to define the particular characteristics of the skilled social performance have demonstrated wide variability. It is clear that many persons with an ungainly interpersonal style achieve superior results to those with a very fluent performance. Thus, at this stage of our knowledge it is probably unwise to attempt to operationalize criteria for social competence.

Rather, social skills may be conceptualized as those interpersonal transactions that enable people to maximize their ability to attain personal goals within their social milieu. These include abilities to give and receive information, to gain and sustain essential physical and material resources, and to engage in mutually supportive intimate relationships with other people.

Assessment of Social Skills

With the all-inclusive definition given above it is evident that the assessment of each patient's social skills must be highly individualized. The earliest attempts to assess social skills derived from social psychology.[4] These involved breaking down interpersonal interaction into the separate components of verbal and nonverbal expression, and then attempting to improve each microcomponent (e.g., eye contact, voice volume) in a series of steps. In assertion training, the focus is on assessing the appropriate expression of aggression in persons who persistently fail to achieve their goals because of excessive anxiety and timidity.[5] Recent approaches have tended to focus on the cognitive processes involved in effective problem-solving of potentially stressful social situations.[6] Thus, the assessment of social performance is highly dependent on a careful analysis of the patients' idiosyncratic strengths and weaknesses, their functional goals and aspirations, their motivation to change, and their environmental supports and stresses. After pinpointing the specific interpersonal situations that appear to prevent effective achievement of each person's functional goals or precipitate excessive environmental stress, more effective social performance can be sought. Although numerous self-report measures have been devised, the assessment of social skills invariably includes role-playing techniques in order to observe the patient's performance in a naturalistic simulation of the targeted interaction.[7,8]

The Elements of Social Competence

The competent performance in any social context involves several elements, including the accurate perception and processing of social cues, a minimally sufficient repertoire of social behavior, competent performance of the chosen social skill(s), and adequate reinforcement for competent performance. Patients who experience episodes of schizophrenia tend to show defects on one or more of these elements of interpersonal communication. Effective intervention must address each of these components in sequence.

Perception and Processing of Social Cues

Assessment. Much of the social skills training literature concerns enhancing the performance of appropriate social expression. However, a more basic deficit that is commonly overlooked is the ability to accurately perceive and interpret nonverbal and verbal information provided by other people in the social environment. The significance of this element is clear when one considers the gross sensory impairments of a blind or deaf person or the information-processing limitations of a person with a severe intellectual disability. More subtle disabilities accrue from averting the eyes from people while conversing with them, attempting to communicate in a noisy room, or being preoccupied by distracting thoughts.

Schizophrenia, in both the acute and subacute phases, is associated with a wide range of impairments in perception and information-processing.[9] In the acute phase of schizophrenia the patients' ability to interpret social cues may be severely distorted by delusional perception. Behavior that would commonly engender a positive connotation of friendship or acceptance, such as a smile, a head nod, a pat on the back, or a handshake, may be interpreted quite differently by floridly deluded persons. Such gestures may be considered to have a sinister, threatening, or special meaning that is idiosyncratic to the persons suffering from the delusion. The patients' subsequent social response to such cues is, therefore, likely to be considered inappropriate — at times bizarre — and lead to rejection and the breakdown of social relationships. Hallucinations and thought interference are probably less disruptive in terms of social relationships but when severe may disrupt the patients' flow of thoughts and lead to difficulties maintaining the fluency of social discourse.

During the subacute phase of schizophrenia, less severe cognitive impairments are evident, but deficits in attention and information-processing may appear. These defects increase the difficulty experienced in accurately summing up a social situation, as well as in deciding the optimal response in each specific context.[10]

While the difficulties in the reception and processing of social stimuli are specific to schizophrenia, persons who develop this disorder also share difficulties in this complex component of social functioning that are present in the general population. Many patients have not learned the sociocultural meaning of specific social cues. The use of touch and physical contact as a means of communication varies considerably across cultures, and even among different families in the same culture. Learning the cultural norms for such behavior may expedite assimilation into the mainstream of social activity. The social meaning of various body postures, facial expressions, or vocal intonations is not intuitive and, therefore, must be learned. The ability to accurately recognize such discriminating cues may greatly facilitate social interaction.

Persons who develop schizophrenia when young may experience a disruption in the process of learning the more subtle cues of adult social communication. Problems resulting from this disruption include persistently choosing the least receptive person with whom to engage in conversation, a behavior that results in repeated unexpected rebuffs, and being unable to recognize when a person has finished a sequence of conversation, a deficit that causes the patient to appear to frequently interrupt a group discussion.

During periods of depression or anxiety, patients may distort the meaning of social cues, placing more weight on negative or threatening cues and attending little to neutral or positive stimuli.

Intervention strategies. The optimal use of neuroleptic drugs is the treatment of choice for perceptual and information-processing deficits associated with psychotic thought disorders. This includes minimizing the secondary social performance deficits that accrue from the extrapyramidal side effects of many of these drugs. Cognitive deficits that remain in the subacute phases are less responsive to drugs. Attempts to enhance social skills in patients with residual thought disturbance can be effective when information is delivered simply and slowly, with repetition as necessary. Extraneous stimuli should be minimized.

Training in receiving and processing skills has been formalized in the program devised by Wallace.[11] It involves training patients to report accurately their perceptions of role-played social situations and to express how they would respond in each situation. They are taught to focus their attention on the relevant social cues and to adopt efficient cognitive problem-solving strategies. Prompting, instructions, modeling, and reinforcement are employed to shape these skills during practice sessions. Less intensive approaches have taught attentive "listening" skills, with greater emphasis on recognizing nonverbal cues.[12,13]

Repertoire of Social Responses

Assessment. The minimally sufficient repertoire of responses that is needed to sustain effective social role functioning in the community has yet to be determined. It is evident, however, that successful social adjustment necessitates a considerable range of appropriate social behavior. It includes skills associated with self-care, shopping, budgeting, health care, help-seeking, education, conversation, group participation, intimate relationships with family and friends, dating and sexual behavior, handling authority, and a range of general problem-solving functions. The relative importance of any of these domains varies from patient to patient according to personal goals and aspirations, premorbid social attainment, intellectual ability, and community supports. In clinical practice it is important to determine those domains in which each patient wishes to achieve competence, and those relevant skills that are deficient in his or her repertoire.

Common to all domains of social role functioning are certain basic skills of verbal and nonverbal communication. The appropriate expression of eye contact, body posture, facial expression, voice volume and tone, physical proximity, and touch may be as important as verbal expression in many interpersonal situations. The relative contributions of verbal and nonverbal components vary according to the specifics of the situation. For example, clear verbal content is crucial when giving a rendezvous address to a friend by telephone, whereas eye contact, facial expressions, physical proximity, and touch may play a major part in the effective expression of affection towards a lover. Therefore, it is not sufficient to merely possess adequate expressive features, but to deploy these elements in a highly flexible, adaptive style.

Schizophrenia has been specifically linked to difficulties in verbal and nonverbal expression. A relative lack of facial and vocal expression is considered characteristic, and inappropriate nonverbal expression is not uncommon. Side-effects of drugs may add to nonverbal deficits. Recent advances in drug therapies, however, have indicated that specific drugs may prove less detrimental to social behavior than others.[14] The limitations of a poverty of affect or inappropriate affect in terms of social functioning may be considerable, resulting in patients' being rejected and considered bizarre or even threatening by community members.

Intervention strategies. The focus of most social skills intervention programs has been that of training in an effective repertoire of social skills.[15-19] A variety of educational techniques has been employed. Many aspects of social behavior are adequately taught through verbal instructions alone. Handout notes and prompt cards are useful supplements to verbal instructions and discussions. Basic living skills such as grooming, health care, budgeting, and leisure planning can be taught using a classroom approach.[20-22]

On the other hand, more complex interactional skills, such as conversations or interviews, are usually taught through repeated practice of the skills, initially with supportive role-playing in the clinic followed by real-life practice in the natural environment. The demonstration or modeling of alternative responses — by the therapist, by use of videotape, or by other participants when training is conducted in a group—supplements verbal instructions and coaching. The sequences are kept brief and the coaching focuses, one at a time, on specific aspects of the overall response. Repeated rehearsal, with constructive performance feedback, enables the overall response to be shaped in a stepwise fashion until patients feel comfortable with their performances in real life. Videotaped feedback has been employed to enable the trainee to evaluate his or her own performance. However, the role of this technique in a person suffering from schizophrenia has not been fully evaluated, and it is not without detrimental effects, particularly with patients with poor self-images, who tend to see only the negative aspects of their appearance and performance.

Feedback is most effective when given in a supportive framework, with clear acknowledgment of the efforts of the patient and avoidance of harsh criticisms and confrontation. Training in a small cohesive group may provide such a setting. It has the additional advantage of offering a variety of models and partners for rehearsing in role-play and real-life contexts. Individuals with more profound social deficits may derive greater benefits from individual training, finding group settings too stressful.

Competent Performance of Social Behavior in Real Life

Assessment. Patients who possess an adequate repertoire of social skills may not necessarily employ their skills in a competent fashion in everyday life. In schizophrenia, perhaps the most common reason for inadequate performance in chronic patients is a lack of practice. Social behavior tends to atrophy in institutionalized patients. Activities such as shopping, problem-solving, asserting their rights, dating, and sexual behavior are usually discouraged. The thrust towards community-based programs, even for the management of the acute phase of the disorder, has helped to preserve the performance of appropriate social behavior. Understimulating social environments are not limited to hospital wards, however. A similar atrophy of social role behavior may be found in community settings and even in the patients' homes, if patients are encouraged to adopt a sick role and are actively discouraged from continuing to participate to the best of their abilities in work and social activities.

This performance loss is compounded by the often profound loss of self-confidence associated with the onset of schizophrenia. It can often result in the patients' appearing excessively apathetic and lacking in motivation to resume social roles. This demeanor may appear most strikingly in patients who were formerly sociable and functioned well. At times this picture may be consistent with that of reactive depression, a condition in which antidepressant drug treatment is seldom effective. Other patients display lifelong social inadequacy and tend to avoid social situations. It is often assumed that this schizoid tendency indicates that such patients are content in their social isolation. On the contrary, many are inhibited by high levels of anxiety associated with interpersonal performance and show the characteristic features of social phobics. They remain eager to join the mainstream of social discourse but are overwhelmed by fears of failure and rejection whenever they take faltering steps toward using their social skills.

It is evident that no single thread accounts for the lack of initiation of social behavior in real-life settings. Disuse, low self-esteem, and performance anxiety may all contribute, and they combine in a vicious cycle of increasing social withdrawal. The implications for treatment are clear and involve methods that aim to counter the specific variables underlying each patient's performance deficit.

Intervention strategies. The goal of achieving functionally beneficial changes in everyday social performance is crucial. Many approaches to social skills training have shown only a limited transfer into real-life use of the skills performed adequately in the clinical setting.[23] Specific strategies to assist this process of generalization must be included in the training approach. Such strategies include creating a training environment that closely approximates real life. Role-playing techniques used in social skills training attempt to replicate the contingencies found in the natural setting and avoid the use of fantasy. Simple props such as desks, chairs, and telephones serve to enhance realism. Better still, sessions may be conducted in the patient's home, workplace, or social habitat. This in vivo training may be preceded by rehearsal in the clinic.[24] Stein et al. have demonstrated the effectiveness of teaching a wide range of living skills entirely in the community.[25] Homework assignments are another strategy employed in most skills training programs. They involve setting specific social behavior to be practiced between sessions, usually based on skills practiced during the session. Friends, relatives, and other group members may be recruited to assist in this between-session practice. The results of homework efforts are evaluated at the beginning of the next session.[26]

Planning for the anticipated consequences of social performance, in order that patients can prepare themselves for both failure and unexpected success, is an often-neglected strategy. This problem-solving technique ensures that patients consider ways in which they can cope with their most feared consequences and also guarantees that they plan the basic steps associated with the social activity they are practicing. This may include maintaining punctuality, using public transport, budgeting, and keeping addresses and telephone numbers. Inadequate planning skills may result in major social handicaps for persons with excellent social skills.

Effective management of social anxiety may facilitate real-life performance. While preparatory role-played practice may help, perhaps the most effective method of reducing anxiety involves repeated performance in the natural setting.[27] Systematic desensitization has been employed successfully in patients with circumscribed social anxieties, such as eating in public or public speaking.[28] Deep muscular relaxation techniques can be adapted for unobtrusive use in social encounters.

For the chronic institutionalized patient who previously had an adequate repertoire of social skills that atrophied as a result of disuse, the most efficient intervention may be a program of systematic prompting and positive reinforcement of functionally relevant skills. This may be supplemented by role-playing practice. The same contingencies hold for patients who have been recently divorced or widowed and who may have to use interpersonal skills long forgotten, such as dating or joining social groups alone. Token economy methods, which provide systematic, individualized reinforcement in the hospital environment, have proven a highly effective strategy for enhancing the social skills of chronic patients and for providing successful social rehabilitation in the community.[29]

Reinforcement of Competent Performance

Successful social functioning depends on the sustained performance of social skills in a competent manner. The ability to persist in seeking jobs, friends, marital partners, financial resources, etc., may prove to be a considerable asset. In order to sustain such performance in the face of repeated rejection, extrinsic sources of reinforcement are crucial. Many patients blame themselves for a lack of success, even when their performances are impeccable. This lack of self-reinforcement readily extinguishes further attempts. In addition to self-reinforcement, patients should receive substantial support and encouragement from people in their immediate environment.

Patients are trained to accurately appraise the strengths and weaknesses of their social performance during role rehearsal and in reports of real-life encounters. Failed attempts are examined in terms of those elements that were competently performed, and those relevant aspects that could have been improved in future performances. Cognitive therapy approaches have been incorporated in social skills training, but to date there is limited evidence for their efficacy.

The supportive involvement of key persons in the patients' environments may have a major impact on the successful outcome of social skills training.[30] Family approaches that involve training the entire family group in communication and problem-solving skills have been effective in improving the social functioning of patients with schizophrenia.[31-32] These families have been trained to assist their impaired members in the acquisition of social skills in the community. For those patients not living with family members, supportive persons in the environment may be recruited to assist the patients in their quest for social competence.

References

1. Strauss JS, Carpenter WT: Prediction of outcome in schizophrenia: III. Five-year outcome and its predictors. *Arch. Gen. Psychiatry* 132:159, 1977.

2. Wing JK: Impairments in schizophrenia: A rational basis for social treatment. In Wirtho RD, Winokur G, Roff M (Eds.): *Life History Research in Psychopathology*, University of Minnesota Press, Minneapolis, Minn., 1975.

3. Goldstein MJ: Further data concerning the relation between premorbid adjustment and paranoid symptomatology. *Schizophr. Bull.* 4:236–243, 1978.

4. Argyle M, Trower P, Bryant B: Explorations in the treatment of personality disorders and neuroses by social skills training. *Br. J. Med. Psychol.* 47:63–72, 1974.

5. Wolpe J: *Psychotherapy by Reciprocal Inhibition*, Stanford University Press, Palo Alto, Calif., 1958.

6. Wallace CJ et al.: A review and critique of social skills training with schizophrenic patients. *Schizophr. Bull.* 6:42–63, 1980.

7. Liberman RP: Assessment of social skills. *Schizophr. Bull.* 8:62–83, 1982.

8. Hersen M, Bellack AS: Assessment of social skills. In Ciminero AR, Calhoun KS, Adams HE (Eds.): *Handbook for Behavioral Assessment*, John Wiley & Sons, New York, 1977.

9. Hemsley DR: Cognitive impairment in schizophrenia. In Burton A (Ed.): *The Pathology and Psychology of Cognition*, Methuen, London, 1982.

10. Spivak G, Platt JJ, Shure MB: *The Problem-Solving Approach to Adjustment*, Jossey-Bass, San Francisco, 1976.

11. Wallace CJ: The social skills training project of the Mental Health Clinical Research Center for the Study of Schizophrenia. In Curran JP, Monti PM (Eds.): *Social Skills Training: A Practical Handbook for Assessment and Treatment*, Guilford Press, New York, 1982.

12. Vitalo RL: Teaching improved interpersonal functioning as a preferred mode of treatment. *J. Clin. Psychol.* 22:166–171, 1971.

13. Falloon IRH, Lindley P, McDonald R: *Social Training: A Manual*, Psychological Treatment Section, Maudsley Hospital, London, 1974.

14. Falloon IRH, Watt DC, Shepherd M: The social outcome of patients in a trial of long-term continuation therapy in schizophrenia: Pimozide vs. fluphenazine. *Psychol. Med.* 8:265–274, 1978.

15. Doty DW: Role playing and incentives in the modification of the social interaction of chronic psychiatric patients. *J. Consult. Clin. Psychol.* 43:676–682, 1975.

16. Finch BE, Wallace CJ: Successful interpersonal skills training with schizophrenic patients. *J. Consult. Clin. Psychol.* 45:885–890, 1977.

17. Goldsmith JB, McFall RM: Development and evaluation of an interpersonal skill-training program for psychiatric inpatients. *J. Abn. Psychol.* 84:51–58, 1975.

18. Goldstein AP: *Structured Learning Therapy: Toward a Psychotherapy for the Poor*, Academic Press, New York, 1973.

19. Hersen M, Bellack AS: A multiple baseline analysis of social skills training in chronic schizophrenics. *J. Appl. Behav. Anal.* 9:239–246, 1976.

20. Lamb HR: An educational model for teaching living skills to long-term patients. *Hosp. Comm. Psychiatry* 27:875–877, 1976.

21. Liberman RP, King LW, DeRisi WJ: Behavior analysis and modification in community mental health. In Leitenberg H (Ed.): *Handbook of Behavior Therapy and Behavior Modification*, Prentice-Hall, Englewood Cliffs, N.J., 1976.

22. Ludwig AM: *Treating the Treatment Failures*, Grune and Stratton, New York, 1971.

23. Bellack AS, Hersen M, Turner SM: Generalization effects of social skills training in chronic schizophrenics: An experimental analysis. *Behav. Res. Therapy* 14:391–398, 1976.

24. Falloon IRH, Lloyd GG, Harpin RE: The treatment of social phobia: Real-life rehearsal and non-professional therapists. *J. Nerv. Ment. Dis.* 169:180–184, 1981.

25. Stein LI, Test MA, Marz AJ: Alternative to the hospital – A controlled study. *Am. J. Psychiatry* 132:149–162, 1975.

26. Falloon IRH et al.: Social skills training of outpatient groups: A controlled study of role rehearsal and homework. *Br. J. Psychiatry* 131:599–609, 1977.

27. Marks IM: Behavioral treatments of phobic and obsessive-compulsive disorders. In Hersen M, Eisler R, Miller P (Eds.): *Progress in Behavior Modification, Vol. 1*, Academic Press, New York, 1975.

28. Paul GL: *Insight versus Desensitization in Psychotherapy*, Stanford University Press, Palo Alto, Calif., 1966.

29. Paul GL, Lentz RJ: *Psychosocial Treatment of the Chronic Mental Patient*, Harvard University Press, Cambridge, Mass., 1977.

30. Falloon IRH: Interpersonal variables in behavioral group therapy. *Br. J. Med. Psychol.* 54:133–141, 1981.

31. Falloon IRH, Boyd JL, McGill CW: *Family Care of Schizophrenia: A Problem-Solving Approach to Mental Illness*, Guilford Press, New York, 1984.

32. Hogarty GE, Anderson CM, Reiss DJ, et al.: Family psycho-education, social skills training and maintenance chemotherapy in the aftercare treatment of schizophrenia. *Arch. Gen. Psychiatry* 43:633–642, 1986.

11

Maintenance Medication in Schizophrenia
Robert Linden, John M. Davis, and Joan Rubinstein

EDITOR'S NOTE

There appears to be overwhelming statistical evidence that antipsychotic drugs prevent relapses in schizophrenic patients. In one study of 374 schizophrenic patients following hospitalization and recovery, 73% of those who received placebo (without psychotherapy) had relapsed; 63% of those who received placebo (with psychotherapy) had relapsed; 33% of those receiving maintenance antipsychotic medication (without psychotherapy) had relapsed; and 26% of those on antipsychotic maintenance therapy (with psychotherapy) had relapsed.

The author focuses on the concept of rate of relapse. In the studies cited, the relapse rate varied from 7% to 14% per month and appeared to be reduced by maintenance on medication.

Who seems to need maintenance antipsychotic medication? Studies indicate that the higher the original treatment dose to bring the condition under control, the more likely a patient will be to relapse if the drug is terminated. Certain chronically ill patients may "burn out" and no longer need medication. Patients with acute, florid psychotic episodes, particularly in reaction to stressful life events, often do not need continued medication when improved, although studies of this problem are decidedly limited.

There is, of course, the well-known danger of tardive dyskinesia, requiring that patients on maintenance doses be carefully followed; the decision to place a patient on a maintenance regimen and continue it should be made with care and based on knowledge of the individual patient's illness and life situation, with due attention to psychological and environmental influences that can facilitate the patient's recovery and stability.

Introduction

In the years following the discovery of chlorpromazine's effectiveness as an antipsychotic agent, it became apparent that patients relapsed after they stopped taking their medication. Initially, a host of uncontrolled studies appeared, reporting the finding that maintenance medication decreased the frequency of relapse. Subsequently the methods of such studies were improved, and there have been 35 double-blind studies that have compared the relapse rates of patients on placebo and on maintenance medication. Of these studies, 33 have presented the number of patients who relapsed on placebo or on maintenance medication (Table 1).

Review of Double-Blind Studies

The earlier studies on maintenance medication were initiated early in the era of phenothiazines, when sophisticated methods for controlled investigation had not been completely worked out. These studies performed a pioneering function in the development of quantitative, double-blind research designs, but the methods used were not as refined as they have been in more recent studies. It is worth noting, however, that both the earlier studies and the more recent ones have yielded consistent results.

All the controlled studies of maintenance treatment of schizophrenia by antipsychotic drugs for more than one month are summarized in Table 1. These studies were carried out in a variety of settings: in private, state, and Veterans Administration hospitals; in inpatient and outpatient facilities; and in England, Europe, and the United States. After random assignment, in each of these studies one group of patients was maintained on neuroleptic medication and the other group was maintained on a "double-blind" identical placebo. The frequency with which each group relapsed was measured. While in many of these major studies chronic schizophrenic inpatients were used, there are also adequate data on schizophrenic outpatients.

In each of the studies, many more patients relapsed on placebo than on drug. Of a total of 3,609 patients studied, 20% relapsed on drug and 53% relapsed on placebo. Considered individually, every one of the studies has shown that more patients relapse on placebo than on maintenance medication. When the studies are combined by the appropriate statistical means,[33] this difference is statistically significant with a p-value of less than 10^{-100}. Thus there is overwhelming statistical evidence that the antipsychotic drugs prevent relapse in schizophrenia.

TABLE 1
Antipsychotic Prevention of Relapse

	No. of patients	Relapse on placebo (%)	Relapse on drug (%)	Difference in relapse rate (placebo-drug) (%)
Caffey et al.[1]	250	45	5	40
Prien and Cole[2]	762	42	16	26
Prien et al.[3]	325	56	20	36
Schiele[4]	80	60	3	57
Adelson and Epstein[5]	281	90	49	41
Morton[6]	40	70	25	45
Baro et al.[7]	26	100	0	100
Hershon et al.[8]	62	28	7	21
Rassidakis et al.[9]	84	58	34	24
Melnyk et al.[10]	40	50	0	50
Shawver et al.[11]	80	18	5	13
Freeman and Alson[12]	94	28	13	16
Whitaker and Hoy[13]	39	65	8	57
Garfield et al.[14]	27	31	11	20
Diamond and Marks[15]	40	70	25	45
Blackburn and Allen[16]	53	54	24	30
Gross and Reeves[17]	109	58	14	44
Englehardt et al.[18]	294	30	15	15
Leff and Wing[19]	30	83	33	50
Hogarty[20]	361	67	31	36
Troshinsky et al.[21]	43	63	4	59
Hirsch et al.[22]	74	66	8	58
Chien and Cole[23]	31	87	12	94
Gross[24]	61	65	34	31
Rifkin et al.[25]	62	68	7	61
Clark et al.[26]	35	78	27	51
Clark et al.[27]	19	70	43	27
Kinross-Wright and Charalampous[28]	40	70	5	65
Andrews et al.[29]	31	35	7	28
Wistedt[30]	38	63	38	25
Cheung[31]	28	62	13	48
Levine et al.[32] (P.O.)	33	59	33	26
Levine et al.[32] (I.M.)	34	30	18	12

Summary statistics, p less than 10^{-100}.
Source: Davis.[33]

Methodologic Factors

It is worthwhile to consider whether a constant error in study design might account for the consistent findings of efficacy of maintenance neuroleptics. One possible source of error is that side-effects might break the double blind for some patients. Most chronically ill patients, however, have developed tolerance to many of the side-effects of the drugs studied, so this short-coming would be relatively less important in the studies reviewed than in studies of acutely ill patients. The general methodologic problem of whether physicians or other evaluating personnel could have been biased by the patients' manifesting side-effects has been carefully investigated by several studies.

Paredes and associates[34] performed a double-blind study in which subjects were evaluated according to their degree of improvement and ranked accordingly. The subjects were also evaluated and ranked according to whether they exhibited side-effects. The correlation coefficient between presence or absence of side-effects and clinical improvement was essentially negligible ($r = 0.01$). Thus, it would seem that secondary clues from side-effects did not bias the results. Prien and Cole[2] performed essentially the same analysis and found no apparent relationship between occurrence of side-effects and clinical improvement in patients receiving high doses of chlorpromazine. Additionally, the Medical Research Council study conducted by Hirsch and associates[22] provided checks for biases and noted that questionnaires filled out when patients had completed the trial gave no indication that the community, ward nurses, general practitioners, or patients could detect who had been receiving active medication. Thus, none of the studies that have looked for bias due to side effects has found any evidence in that direction.

In this respect, it is worth noting that Adelson and Epstein[5] used active placebos with both sedative and anticholinergic properties and found essentially no greater efficacy with active placebo than with regular placebo. Thus, the empirical data that are available indicate that knowledge of side-effects does not account for the results reported. Additionally, the fact that these studies, which all produced similar findings, were carried out by a variety of different authors from different countries, using different designs in different settings, makes it unlikely that any constant error could have influenced the results.

Rate of Relapse With and Without Medication

Of particular interest to the question of maintenance medication is a study by Hogarty and Goldberg,[35] who studied 374 schizophrenic patients after recovery and discharge from the hospital. After an initial outpatient period during which they were stabilized on phenothiazine, the patients were divided into two groups: half were assigned to maintenance chlorpromazine, and half were assigned to placebo. Half of each group additionally received outpatient psychotherapy. At the end of one year, 73% of the placebo-without-psychotherapy group and 63% of the placebo-plus-psychotherapy group had relapsed. Only 33% of the drug-maintenance group and 26% of the drug-maintenance-plus-psychotherapy group had relapsed. If the patients in the drug-maintenance group who discontinued medication are excluded, the relapse rate for patients on medication for the 12-month period was only 16%. Measurement of variables relating to social functioning indicated that patients who received both drug and psychotherapy did better than those who received drug alone. Thus, it appears that while drugs prevent relapse, psychotherapy improves social functioning; in this sense, drugs and psychotherapy complement each other.

In analyzing the data from maintenance studies, Davis[33] suggested that, rather than thinking in terms of a fixed number of patients who will or will not relapse, it is more appropriate to think in terms of a rate of relapse. Specifically, we made the observation that the time course of relapse in a group of patients taken off medication is an exponential function similar to that seen with the radioactive half-life or the half-life of drugs in plasma. There is a constant rate of relapse, similar to the constant rate of decay seen with radioactive material or the constant rate of disappearance of a drug from plasma.

This can be illustrated by considering a hypothetical group of 100 patients with a relapse rate of 10% per month. In the first month, ten patients relapse and 90 remain in the study group; during the second month, 10% of 90, or nine patients, relapse and 81 patients remain; the next month, 10% of 81, or eight, relapse; and so forth, with 10% of the remaining patients relapsing each month. While the actual number of patients relapsing would decrease each month, the 10% rate of relapse remains constant. In this example, the "half-life" is about six months. At 12 months, or double the half-life, 25% of the original patients would remain unrelapsed, and at 18 months 12.5% would remain unrelapsed. In a statistical analysis of three studies (Caffey et al.[1], Prien and Cole,[2] Hogarty and Goldberg[35]), Davis found that the data were most consistent with a constant relapse rate. The data from these studies fit an exponential curve extremely well, with an r^2 in the neighborhood of 0.96.[36]

The literature conveys the impression that there is a substantial group of schizophrenic patients who will not relapse when off medication. It is often stated that approximately 50% of patients do not relapse when medication is discontinued and, therefore, maintenance medication is not indicated for a substantial number of patients. It should be noted that several studies from which the figure 50% has been culled have a follow-up period limited to four to six months.

Data from longer-term studies indicate that while 50% of patients have not relapsed by four to six months, when followed for 12 to 18 months this group continued to relapse at a constant rate. Apparently, patients are not at a greater risk for relapse in the first few months off medication, and they do not become progressively less at risk the longer they remain without a relapse. Instead, the risk of relapse remains constant. In the three studies under consideration, the relapse rate varies from 7% to 14% per month. Given that a comparable group was maintained on medication, it can be estimated that neuroleptics reduce the rate of relapse by a factor of 2.5 to 5.

The above considerations are of interest with respect to patients who have not relapsed after a considerable time off medication. Empirically, the relapse rate in the Hogarty and Goldberg[35] study is constant up to 18 months and then appears to decrease. If some patients in the study do not suffer from a recurrent form of illness, they will never relapse, and the relapse rate will drop to zero after all the patients with the potential for relapse do so. On the basis of these considerations, Hogarty et al.[36] sought to examine the relapse rate of patients who had not had a relapse for two years or longer. As only a few patients in the original placebo group had not experienced a relapse, a statistical study was not possible. However, Hogarty did follow up the larger group of patients who had been on medication and had not relapsed for two years. Antipsychotic medication was discontinued in these patients, and relapses occurred in an exponential fashion, with a relapse rate quite similar to that of the initial placebo group. Apparently, while relapse was prevented for a considerable length of time by neuroleptics, when medication was discontinued the patients relapsed at a rate similar to that of patients initially taken off neuroleptics after only two months of maintenance medication.

Clinical Issues in Maintenance Therapy

For what types of schizophrenic disorder is maintenance medication indicated? Evidence pertinent to maintenance antipsychotic medication in inpatients was provided by Prien and associates.[3] These investigators combined two NIMH studies of maintenance phenothiazines and found that the patients' history of medication (i.e., the dose levels at which the patients previously had had a therapeutic response) presented a reasonably good prediction of relapse (see Table 2). The higher the treatment dose, the more likely were the patients to relapse when medication was stopped. This is intuitively sensible, because it is reasonable to suppose that patients' dose levels were determined empirically. That is, patients may be maintained on high doses as a consequence of increased symptoms resulting from an attempt by their physician to lower their dosage.

These studies also revealed a less marked tendency for very chronically ill patients to require lower dosages. This suggests that the schizophrenic pro-

TABLE 2
Previous Dose as a Predictor of Relapse

Prestudy dose level	Total No. of patients	Patients relapsed	
		N	Percent
No medication	30	2	7
Under 300 mg	99	23	23
300–500 mg	91	47	52
500 mg	81	53	65

Data from Prien et al.[3]

cess may "burn out" in some very chronically ill patients. Such patients may have definitely needed drugs years ago but may have changed with time and aging. All patients should be reexamined periodically to determine whether they really need maintenance medication. On occasion, patients should have their drugs discontinued or their dosage lowered so that it can be determined empirically whether the neuroleptic treatment is indeed necessary or if a lower dose would suffice.

Although tardive dyskinesia occurs in outpatients who receive relatively short-term treatment, the incidence of tardive dyskinesia is highest in elderly state-hospital patients who have been receiving high doses of medication for many years. It follows that the greatest attention should be directed toward measures for preventing tardive dyskinesia in state hospitals. In the more controlled situation of the state hospital, relapse can be very quickly treated, since the patient is under continuous observation by nursing staff and physicians. Therefore, efforts should be made to reduce the dose or to discontinue medication and see if relapse occurs. Medication can easily be reinstituted when necessary, but because tardive dyskinesia represents a sufficiently serious problem, every effort should be made to use the lowest effective dose in the hospital situation. In the outpatient situation, much more judgment is required to balance possible benefits against possible risks.

Brief Psychotic Episode

So-called reactive schizophrenic patients, who may have one florid psychotic episode with a fairly quick remission during adolescence, may constitute a special population from the standpoint of maintenance. To my knowledge, "reactive" psychoses (brief psychotic disorders, schizophreniform psychosis) have not been studied with respect to maintenance antipsychotics. There is no firm knowledge concerning whether maintenance medication is indicated for these patients. A review of studies on the natural history of reactive psychosis by such workers as Stephens and Astrup[37-40] suggests that the prognosis of these patients may be fairly good; i.e., many of these patients might not relapse without medication. Therefore, for first-episode "reactive" schizophrenic patients or those with hysterical psychosis, it might be reasonable to use short-term maintenance treatment to ensure that the patients have a solid recovery from the first episode but to avoid long-term maintenance.

In sum, considerations of the patient's chronicity and drug history (including responsiveness to various dosages and episodes of relapse following changes in dose level) are relevant in deciding issues regarding inpatient maintenance medication. From a common sense perspective, evidence that the patient was initially helped by antipsychotic treatment would be another important variable or indication, as would the potential consequences to the patient of another relapse. It is important to recognize that for outpatients relapses are a relatively serious event because a wide variety of social variables become involved: the patient's adjustment to his family, job, and social situation may be seriously compromised. A deterioration of the patient's functioning after discontinuance of medication may result in serious work or family problems that place the patient under even greater stress. In addition, the development of psychotic behavior may create serious social repercussions that may harm his later attempts to readjust to his social setting.

Long-Acting Antipsychotics

Of seven studies comparing fluphenazine depot to the oral formulation, two studies found the depot form superior to an oral antipsychotic and five studies found the depot and oral forms equivalent. It may be that there was less compliance with oral medication in the first two studies. In any case, the depot intramuscular form should be considered for patients who do not show an optimal response to oral medication or are suspected of poor compliance as evidenced by frequent relapses. The different pharmacokinetics of an intramuscular injection, by which the "first-pass effect" of metabolism in the liver is avoided, may be of further benefit to some patients. The two depot formulations of fluphenazine are quite similar, and only marginal differences have been found; but from the five studies that directly compare fluphenazine deconoate to fluphenazine enanthate, it appears that the deconoate form is somewhat more potent, is slightly longer acting, and has slightly fewer side-effects. Thus, the deconoate formulation is probably to be preferred as a long-acting depot fluphenazine.[41,42]

There are two depot formulations marketed in the United States, haloperidol decanoate and fluphenazine decanoate. They have been shown to be therapeutically equivalent. As mentioned above, we performed a plasma level study of fluphenazine decanoate and showed high plasma levels in the few hours after an injection, but then showed steady low levels for the next 14 days. We speculate that this dose dumping phenomenon (high plasma levels in the hours after the injections) is responsible for the extrapyramidal side effects that occur after each injection in some patients. Haloperidol decanoate does not have the dose dumping effects and haloperidol plasma levels are essentially constant during its four-week dosage interval. It is interesting to note that of the six studies which compared haloperidol decanoate with fluphenazine decanoate, five found that haloperidol was associated with less extrapyramidal side effects and/or low use of antiparkinsonian drugs, a finding consistent with the above speculation.[43-48]

Conclusion

A review of 33 controlled studies on the use of maintenance antipsychotic medication reveals that, of 3,609 patients studied, 53% relapsed on placebo and 20% relapsed on drugs. Maintenance medication clearly prevented relapse in a substantial number of patients, and the percentage of relapses in the drug-treated groups was less than half that observed in the control groups. Maintenance antipsychotics are indicated for prophylactic purposes in schizophrenic patients at risk for relapse. The decision to continue on a drug for an extended period should be arrived at clinically for each patient on the basis of a knowledge of his illness and life situation. It seems reasonable to treat most patients on medication for three months to one year after a psychotic episode, to be certain that they have recovered from their present illness. Over longer periods, the use of long-term maintenance drugs should be individualized.

References

1. Caffey EM, Diamond LS, Frank TV, et al.: Discontinuation or reduction of chemotherapy in chronic schizophrenics. *J. Chronic Dis.* 17:347–358, 1964.

2. Prien RF, Cole JO: High dose chlorpromazine therapy in chronic schizophrenia. Report of National Institute of Mental Health Psychopharmacology Research Branch Collaborative Study Group. *Arch. Gen. Psychiatry* 18:482–495, 1968.

3. Prien RF, Cole JO, Belkin NF: Relapse in chronic schizophrenics following abrupt withdrawal of tranquilizing medication. *Br. J. Psychiatry* 115:679–686, 1969.

4. Schiele BC: Loxapine succinete: A controlled double-blind study in chronic schizophrenia. *Dis. Nerv. Syst.* 36:361–364, 1975.

5. Adelson D, Epstein LJ: A study of phenothiazines in male and female chronically ill schizophrenic patients. *J. Nerv. Ment. Dis.* 134:543–554, 1962.

6. Morton MR: A study of withdrawal of chlorpromazine or trifluoperazine in chronic schizophrenia. *Am. J. Psychiatry* 124:1585–1588, 1968.

7. Baro F, Brugmans J, Dom R, van Lommel R: Maintenance therapy of chronic psychotic patients with a weekly oral dose of R 16 341. *J. Clin. Pharmacol.* 10:330–341, 1970.

8. Hershon HI, Kennedy PF, McGuire RJ: Persistence of extrapyramidal disorders and psychiatric relapse after withdrawal of long-term phenothiazine therapy. *Br. J. Psychiatry* 120:41–50, 1972.

9. Rassidakis NC, Kondakis X, Papanastassiou A, et al.: Withdrawal of antipsychotic drugs from chronic psychiatric patients. *Bull. Menninger Clin.* 34:216–222, 1970.

10. Melnyk WT, Worthington AG, Laverty SG: Abrupt withdrawal of chlorpromazine and thioridazine from schizophrenic inpatients. *Can. Psychiatr. Assoc. J.* 11:410–413, 1966.

11. Shawver JR, Gorham DR, Leskin LW, Good WW, Kabnick DE: Comparison of chlorpromazine and reserpine in maintenance drug therapy. *Dis. Nerv. Syst.* 20:452–457, 1959.

12. Freeman LS, Alson E: Prolonged withdrawal of chlorpromazine in chronic patients. *Dis. Nerv. Syst.* 23:522–525, 1962.

13. Whitaker CB, Hoy RM: Withdrawal of perphenazine in chronic schizophrenia. *Br. J. Psychiatry* 109:422–427, 1959.

14. Garfield SL, Gershon S. Sletten I, Newbaver H, Fenel E: Withdrawal of ataractic medication in schizophrenic patients. *Dis. Nerv. Syst.* 27:321–325, 1966.

15. Diamond LS, Marks JB: Discontinuance of tranquilizers among chronic schizophrenic patients receiving maintenance dosage. *J. Nerv. Ment. Dis.* 131:247–251, 1960.

16. Blackburn H, Allen J: Behavioral effects of interrupting and resuming tranquilizing medication among schizophrenics. *J. Nerv. Ment. Dis.* 133:303–307, 1961.

17. Gross M, Reeves WP: Relapse after withdrawal of ataractic drugs in mental patients in transition. In Greenblatt M (Ed.): *Mental Patients in Transition,* Charles C Thomas, Publisher, Springfield Ill., 1961, pp. 313–321.

18. Engelhardt DM, Rosen B, Freedman D, Margolis R: Phenothiazines in the prevention of psychiatric hospitalization. *Arch. Gen. Psychiatry* 16:98–99, 1967.

19. Leff JP, Wing JK: Trial of maintenance therapy in schizophrenics. *Br. Med. J.* 2:599–604, 1971.

20. Hogarty GE, Ulrich RF: Temporal effects of drug and placebo in delaying relapse in schizophrenic outpatients. *Arch. Gen. Psychiatry* 34:297–301, 1977.

21. Troshinksy CH, Aaronson HG, Stone RK: Maintenance phenothiazine in the aftercare of schizophrenic patients. *Pa. Psychiatr. Q.* 2:11–15, 1962.

22. Hirsch SR, Gaind R, Rohde PD, et al.: Outpatient maintenance of chronic schizophrenic patients with long-acting fluphenazine: Double-blind placebo trial. *Br. Med. J.* 1:633–637, 1973.

23. Chien CP, Cole JO: Drugs and rehabilitation in schizophrenia. In Greenblatt

M (Ed.): *Drugs in Combination with Other Therapies,* Grune & Stratton, New York, 1975, pp. 13–14.

24. Gross HS: A double-blind comparison of once-a-day pimozide, trifluoperazine, and placebo in the maintenance care of chronic schizophrenics. *Curr. Ther. Res.* 16:696–705, 1975.

25. Rifkin A, Quitkin F, Klein DF: Fluphenazine decanoate, oral fluphenazine and placebo in treatment of remitted schizophrenics. *Arch. Gen. Psychiatry* 34:1215–1219, 1977.

26. Clark ML, Huber W, Hill D, Wood F, Costiloe JP: Pimozide in chronic outpatients. *Dis. Nerv. Syst.* 36:137–141, 1975.

27. Clark ML, Huber W, Serafetinides EA, Colmore JP: Pimozide (oral): A tolerance study. *Clin. Trial J. (Suppl.)* 2:25–32, 1971.

28. Kinross-Wright J, Charalampous KD: A controlled study of a very long acting phenothiazine preparation. *Int. J. Neuropsychiatry* 1:66–70, 1965.

29. Andrews P, Hall JN, Snaith RP: A controlled trial of phenothiazine withdrawal in chronic schizophrenic patients. *Br. J. Psychiatry* 128:451–455, 1976.

30. Wistedt B: Withdrawal of long-acting neuroleptics in schizophrenic outpatients. *Acta Univ. Upsalinses:* 391–397, 1981.

31. Cheung HK: Schizophrenics fully remitted on neuroleptics for 3–5 years. *Br. J. Psychiatry* 138:490–494, 1981.

32. Levine J, Schooler N, Serene F, Escobar J, Gelenberg A, Mandel H, Somer R, Steinbook R: Discontinuation of oral and depot fluphenazine in schizophrenic patients after one year of continuous medication. In Cattabeni E (Ed.): *Long-Term Effects on Neuroleptics,* Raven Press, New York, 1980, pp. 483–484.

33. Davis JM: Maintenance therapy in psychiatry: I. Schizophrenia. *Am. J. Psychiatry* 132:1237–1245, 1975.

34. Paredes A, Baumgold J, Pugh LA, et al.: Clinical judgment in the assessment of psychopharmacological effects. *J. Nerv. Ment. Dis.* 142:153–160, 1966.

35. Hogarty GE, Goldberg SC: Drugs and sociotherapy in the aftercare of schizophrenic patients: One-year relapse rates. *Arch. Gen. Psychiatry* 28:54–62, 1973.

36. Hogarty GE, Ulrich RF, Mussare F, Aristigueta N: Drug discontinuation among long term, successfully maintained schizophrenic outpatients. *Dis. Nerv. Syst.* 37:494–500, 1976.

37. Stephens JH: Long-term course and prognosis of schizophrenia. *Semin. Psychiatry* 2:464–485, 1970.

38. Stephens JH, Astrup C: Prognosis in "process" and "non-process" schizophrenia. *Am. J. Psychiatry* 119:945–953, 1963.

39. Astrup C, Fossum A, Hoomboe R: *Prognosis in Functional Psychoses,* Charles C Thomas, Publisher, Springfield, Ill., 1962.

40. Astrup C, Noreik K: *Functional Psychoses: Diagnosis and Prognostic Models,* Charles C Thomas, Publisher, Springfield, Ill., 1966.

41. Kane J, Quitkin F, Rifkin A, Klein DF: Comparison of the incidence and severity of extrapyramidal side effects with fluphenazine enanthate and fluphenazine decanoate. *Am. J. Psychiatry* 135:1539–1542, 1978.

42. Van Pragg HM, Dols LCW: Fluphenazine enanthate and fluphenazine decanoate: A comparison of their duration of action and motor side effects. *Am. J. Psychiatry* 130:801–804, 1973.

43. Chouinard G, Annable L, Campbell W, Boisvert D, and Bradwejn J: A double-blind, controlled clinical trial of haloperidol decanoate and fluphenazine decanoate in the maintenance treatment of schizophrenia. *Psychopharm. Bull.* 20(1):108–109, 1984.

44. Kissling W, Moller HJ, Walter K, Wittman B, Krueger R, and Trenk D: Double-blind comparison of haloperidol decanoate effectiveness, side-effects, dosage and serum levels during a six months' treatment for relapse prevention. *Pharmacopsychiat.* 18:240–245, 1985.

45. McCreadie RG, McKane JP, Robinson ADT, Wiles DH, and Stirling GS: Depot neuroleptics as maintenance therapy in chronic schizophrenic in-patients. *Intl. Clin. Psychopharm.* 1(Suppl. 1):13–14, 1986.

46. Meco G, et al: Aloperidolo decanoato: studio in doppio cieco versus flufenazina decanoato nei disordini schizofreniformi e nella schizofrenia cronica. In *Recenti progessi in terapia neuropsicofarmacologica*, DeMaio D and Longo VD, eds. Liviana Press: Padova. Pp. 141–146, 1985.

47. Wistedt, B: A comparative trial of haloperidol decanoate and fluphenazine decanoate in chronic schizophrenic patients. *Intl. Clin. Psychopharm.* 1(Supp.1): 15–23, 1986.

48. Cookson JC, Kennedy NM, and Gribbon D: Weight gain and prolactin levels in patients on long-term antipsychotic medication: a double-blind comparative trial of haloperidol decanoate and fluphenazine decanoate. *Intl. Clin. Psychopharm.* 1(Suppl.1):41–51, 1986.

Additional Reading

Clark ML, Ramsey HR, Ragland RE, Rahhal DK, Serafetinides EA, Costiloe JP: Chlorpromazine in chronic schizophrenia: Behavioral dose-response relationships. *Psychopharmacologia* 18:260–270, 1970.

Clark ML, Ramsey HR, Rahhal DK, Serafetinides EA, Wood FD, Costiloe JP: Chlorpromazine in chronic schizophrenia: The effect of age and hospitalization on behavioral dose-response relationships. *Arch. Gen. Psychiatry* 27:479–483, 1972.

Donlon P, Meadow A, Tupin J, Wahby M: High vs. standard dosage fluphenazine HCl in acute schizophrenia. *J. Clin. Psychiatry* 39:800–804, 1978.

Hogarty GE, Schooler NR, Ulrich R, Mussare F, Ferro P, Herron E: Fluphenazine and social therapy in the aftercare of schizophrenic patients. *Arch. Gen. Psychiatry* 36:1283–1294, 1979.

Langfeld G: The prognosis in schizophrenia. *Acta Psychiatr. Neurol. Scand. (Suppl.)* 110:7–66, 1956.

Levine J, Schooler N, Cassano G: The role of depot neuroleptics in the treatment of schizophrenic patients. *Psychol. Med.* 9:383–386, 1978.

Prien RF, Levine J, Cole JO: High dose trifluoperazine therapy in chronic schizophrenia. *Am. J. Psychiatry* 126:305–313, 1969.

Prien RF, Levine J, Switalski RW: Discontinuation of chemotherapy for chronic schizophrenics. *Hosp. Commun. Psychiatry* 22:4–7, 1971.

Rifkin A, Quitkin F, Rabinet C, Klein DF: Fluphenazine decanoate, oral fluphenazine and placebo in the treatment of remitted schizophrenics: I. Relapse rates after one year. *Arch. Gen. Psychiatry* 34:43–47, 1977.

Schooler NR, Levine J: Fluphenazine and fluphenazine HCl in the treatment of schizophrenic patients. In *Proceedings of the Meeting of the C.I.N.P.,* Vol. II, Pergamon Press, Oxford, 1978, p. 418.

Valient GE: Prospective prediction of schizophrenic remission. *Arch. Gen. Psychiatry* 11:509–518, 1964.

Valient GE: The prediction of recovery in schizophrenia. *J. Nerv. Ment. Dis.* 133:534–543, 1962.

12

Psychodynamic and Psychotherapeutic Considerations of Self-Mutilation

Don R. Lipsitt

EDITOR'S NOTE

Self-mutilation is not a common problem among psychiatric patients, but when it occurs it can be baffling and difficult to control. The characteristic evolution of such a self-destructive act begins with a building up of tension, a sense of hopelessness, and relief gained by the self-mutilation accompanied by an insensitivity to pain. Psychotic thinking frequently precedes the act, but this often clears immediately thereafter. Long-standing sexual conflicts are common in such patients.

Although many self-mutilative patients are diagnosed as schizophrenic, many also fall into other diagnostic categories — transsexualism, characterologic disorders, even psychoneuroses. More violent forms of this behavior seem to occur among men. Wrist-cutting and slashing seem to occur more often among young women with low self-image, compulsive and impulsive traits, a tendency to manipulate the environment by their actions, and a history of marked sexual conflict and early disturbances in the parent-child relationship.

Factitious disorders, bizarre and not well understood, may involve self-mutilation as a way to permit the individual to assume the role of patient; curiously such patients are often willing to experience risky and painful medical diagnostic procedures in search of an answer to their self-induced symptoms. These patients differ from malingerers, who may mutilate themselves for some clearcut gain — financial compensation, avoidance of responsibility, escape from legal punishment — but who will do whatever they can to avoid painful or potentially dangerous diagnostic procedures.

In this chapter the author reviews some of the proposed psychodynamic explanations for self-mutilation. Among the more prominent issues involved are masochistic gratification; the wish to survive as a whole by sacrificing a part of the bodily self; the need to exert control and mastery; religious preoccupations and delusions linked to psychotic pathology; parental deprivation with a high history of family violence and abuse; a search for the physical contact so lacking in a nonnurturing home environment; and sexual conflicts.

Treatment is aimed at the management of the general psychopathologic state of the patient and also at the self-mutilative behavior per se. Long-term psychotherapy, with intermittent hospitalization during times of high risk, is suggested. One must be wary of the negative influences of staff countertransference in hospital settings, however, and be careful to avoid the hospital setting aggravating rather than amelio-rating the self-mutilative behavior. Family therapy and group therapy are often indicated as well.

Introduction

Self-mutilation, for other than suicidal purposes, has remained a cultural and psychological curiosity. *National Geographic* devotees are familiar enough with a multitude of bodily deformations, scarifications, piercings, and mutilations specific to one or another tribe. Even historical accounts of castration for religious (ancient priests) or protective (eunuchs in a harem) reasons make some kind of "sense." But more "meaningless" socially deviant acts have attracted the attention of psychiatrists for decades. How does one render comprehensible the acts of a van Gogh severing an ear,[1] an intention-al wrist-slasher without suicidal intent,[2,3] acts of autoenucleation,[4-5] auto-castration,[6-7] autocannibalism,[8] other self-amputations,[9-10] or the self-induc-tion of trauma or disease for no other apparent purpose than to achieve patient status?[11] Textbooks in psychiatry have been notably deficient in their coverage of the topic of self-mutilation. Only in recent years, through clini-cal observation and psychodynamic formulation, has thoughtful attention been paid to such behavioral abnormality.

What follows is a case example; a review of clinical descriptions of self-mutilative behavior (exclusive of suicide attempts); efforts to understand and explain such behavior; and suggestions for diagnosis, classification, and treatment of patients with tendencies to disfigure or maim themselves.

A Case of Autocastration

A well-educated 47-year-old single man, previously capable as a banker and lawyer, was brought by ambulance to a hospital emergency room from his hotel room. He had attracted attention because of noise and sounds of "scuffling," though he was found alone, with blood-soaked towels applied to his groin after he had severed his penis with a Swiss army knife; he had also partially detached the scrotum and testicles. It was later learned that he had "won the struggle" by resisting the voice instructing him in this action and had prevented completion of the act by hurling his knife across the room. Surprisingly, in the emergency room he was entirely lucid, free of psychotic thought, paradoxically more anxiety-free than the staff who attended him, free of pain, and able to provide an accurate chronological history and description of the psychotic thinking that had preceded and accompanied the act. He characterized his affect before the act as "uptight" and not suicidal or violent.

The patient described previous psychiatric history, including hospitalizations, some experimentation when younger with LSD, a long-term homosexual relationship recently dissolved, and an enduring intellectual interest in philosophy and religion. His experimentation with LSD was in pursuit of "psychoreligious experiences" and a greater wish to integrate and "unify" various Eastern and Western cosmic theories. He recalled delusions of grandeur in which he, as the Messiah, would save the world. Found in his hotel room were several pages of clearly written doodles, neologisms, and word-play showing marked fragmentation of thought focused around matters of "unism," "unisex," etc. Words and his own name were cut up (with lines) to form and re-form new words. He later described at length his sexual conflicts since adolescence, his lifelong wish to "not be different," and his social affiliation with cultist groups espousing oneness, unity, abolition of individual differences, and the like. Following relatively successful surgical restoration and reimplantation, the patient requested therapy to better understand his behavior and "not be crazy anymore."

Clinical Descriptions of Self-mutilative Behavior

This case shares some of the characteristics observed in other reported cases of self-mutilation: the building tension before the act, with a sense of no other solution; feelings of loss before and a sense of relief after the act; insensitivity to pain accompanying the act; the long-standing presence of sexual conflict; and an awareness of psychotic thinking just preceding and at the time of the event, usually clearing subsequently. While a few cases[12] of combined self-mutilation and assaultiveness by men have been described, several accounts of wrist-slashing and self-cutting by women have not been characterized as otherwise assaultive, impulsive, or suicidal.[13-15] Self-amputation, self-castration, self-enucleation, and autocannabilism would appear to be special cases of self-mutilation, suggesting a more violent resolution of conflict, with a likelihood of more symbolic (psychological) meaning to the act and perhaps, at least in the case of autocannibalism, a suggestion of organic impairment, as in Lesch-Nyhan disease and other examples accompanied by mental retardation.[16]

Violent (psychotic) self-mutilation. From 1900 to 1979, only 44 cases of self-castration (removal of the testes, excluding amputation of the penis) had been reported in the English literature.[17] Such acts were believed to reflect an abnormal attitude toward the genitals, a tendency to regard the genitals as exercising influence over the whole organism, an abnormal integration of the body image that permits mutilation, a sense of intactness and relief thereafter, and a strong conscious motivation.[18]

Until 1954, the literature suggested that all cases of autocastration occurred in psychotic delusional individuals, usually schizophrenics. With increasing clinical interest in transsexualism, however, several cases of autocastration have been described in individuals thought to have gender-identity dysphoria and personality disorder, rather than psychosis.[17,19,20] Such patients were men with strong feminine identifications, an absent or uninvolved father during formative years, a positive relationship with a dominant mother, and physical repudiation of the male genitalia.[17,21] Transsexuals are thought to exclude the penis and testes from their body image and to be less violent and more planful in their autocastrations than schizophrenics.[17] A case of autocastration in a 44-year-old secret transvestite was described as nonpsychotic behavior gratifying an unconscious wish and solving an unconscious conflict.[22] Though the literature contains rare cases described as nonpsychotic,[23] the *Comprehensive Textbook of Psychiatry*[24] describes extreme forms of self-mutilation occurring primarily in adult schizophrenics, and case reports in the literature seem to support this.[4,25]

Autocannibalism has been rarely described, but has invariably accompanied grossly psychotic behavior. One patient burned parts of the body to prove ability to withstand pain and physical damage, then ate the distal and middle phalanges of the index finger.[8] This and another case[26] are notable for their association with psychotic identifications with Christ and presumed conflicts over fears of being killed or castrated.

The themes of maintaining control over one's destiny and sacrificing a part to preserve the whole (life) appear frequently in cases of all degrees of self-mutilation. Religious preoccupation has been described.[27,28] Not infrequently, drug abuse or alcohol intoxification is an accompanying finding in severe self-mutilation.

Nonpsychotic ("manipulative") mutilators. A category of self-mutilators has been described as generally nonpsychotic and nonsuicidal. These are the wrist-cutters and slashers, usually young, attractive women with personality disorders and extensive interpersonal problems.[2,13-15,29] Thought disorder was a much less frequent finding than feelings of inadequacy and poor self-image, with evidence of both compulsive and impulsive traits. While the behavior of these persons has been described as manipulative, designed to seek an active response from the environment, the self-cutting act also served the purpose of reducing unbearable tension. The slashing would occur with sometimes slight provocation, and would be accompanied by pleasure and insensitivity to pain. Commonly, there is evidence of marked sexual conflict and early disturbances in parent-child relationships, with open displays of sexuality and aggression. Grunebaum and Klerman have written that "the patient reports, usually inarticulately, the onset of vague feelings of discomfort—a mixture of loneliness, anxiety, resentment, and sexual tension—she does not relate them to the change in her interpersonal relations and often does not or cannot verbalize the extent of her tension to her doctor or other members of the staff."[13] Most patients studied did not experience pain, reported relief of tension, or felt reassured that life was not empty or unreal.

Self-mutilation of factitious disorder. In some ways, the self-mutilation accompanying factitious disorder is more bizarre, and less well understood, than the other forms of self-mutilation described above.

According to *DSM-III*, those who feign or induce illness do so consciously and with no other motivation than to assume the role of patient, usually in the hospital setting. A fairly extensive literature on factitious illness[11,30,31] reveals a broad spectrum of behaviors used to achieve this objective: surreptitious ingestion of drugs such as insulin, thyroid extract, or anticoagulants, injection of bacterial substances into the skin or veins; tampering with surgical incisions; insertion of foreign objects into body orifices; skin excoriation; thermometer manipulation; and falsification of medical history and simulation of symptoms. While some of these deceptions may be relatively benign in and of themselves, the invasive and surgical procedures sometimes used to clarify the true diagnosis may themselves carry relatively high risk. One of the curiosities of this condition is the patient's receptivity—in fact, invitation—to surgical explorations, cardiac catheterization, even amputation, and other potentially dangerous and painful procedures. An extreme form of factitious disorder—Munchausen's syndrome—is seen largely in males; is characterized by compulsive reenactment of illness, with admissions to hospitals in a broad geographical area; and is usually characterized by more elaborate, bizarre, dramatic, but plausible stories and "evidence" of illness.

While patients with factitious disorder seem more diagnostically heterogeneous than other self-mutilative patients, characteristics of sexual conflict, poor interpersonal relations, tumultuous early histories, and a high tolerance for pain are common to both groups. It is necessary to recognize the personality diagnosis in factitious disorder and to distinguish it from malingering and dissociative states observed in somatoform disorders.

Malingering and somatoform disorders. Self-mutilation with an apparent motive of financial gain, exemption from responsibility or escape from legal punishment generally characterizes the true malingerer, though the label is often used casually and pejoratively. Furthermore, true malingerers usually tend to be docile, cooperative, and compliant but, unlike those with factitious disorder, will try to avoid painful invasive or surgical procedures.

Patients with somatoform disorders, in which mind and body interact in unconscious ways, are also often wrongly accused by medical personnel of malingering. Evidence of psychogenic pain, conversion disorder, or hypochondriasis, even when accompanied by conditions that appear self-induced (e.g., skin excoriation), distinguishes them from consciously imitated or self-induced illness.[32]

Neurotic Habits

A whole spectrum of mild dermatologic conditions — including nail-biting, hair-plucking, skin maceration from sucking, squeezing, and picking of skin blemishes, scars, and scabs — do not fall under the rubric of severe psychopathology of either psychotic or factitious disorder. Usually such behavior has neurotic antecedents, which can be understood and often stopped or modified through psychotherapeutic or behavioral intervention. When the compulsive nature of such habits becomes extreme, as in trichotillomania — which may include head, pubic, and axillary hair — a reconsideration of the diagnosis may be indicated.[33,34]

Theories of Self-mutilation

Almost all efforts to understand pathologic self-mutilative behavior have invoked similar concepts.[29,35-38] Many writers have described the conflict over sexuality leading to physical and emotional tension, with self-mutilation a form of tension reduction and pleasure. This is compatible with psychoanalytic theories that describe neurosis as essentially a buildup of sexual tension, relieved by relaxation.

In the case of self-mutilation, relaxation is achieved through self-destructive means; the masochistic component of achieving gratification has been noted in virtually all cases of such behavior. Wilhelm Reich's discussion of masochism[39] refers to "the ultimate power of life [as] tension with the prospect of relaxation (or pleasure)," the desperation of self-destruction as "the last and only possibility of relaxation." This applies to total as well as "partial" or "focal" suicide, terms used by Karl Menninger[40] and others[41] to explain self-mutilative behavior.

Building on the biological explanation of sacrifice of the part to preserve the whole, Fenichel described the phenomenon of autotomy, wherein a lizard can detach a part of its tail when endangered by predators.[42] In much the same way, psychoanalytic theorists have posited high levels of castration anxiety prompting individuals to sacrifice bodily parts or integrity to avoid the symbolic threat of total annihilation. Self-mutilation, in this context, is thus seen as a wish for survival rather than fulfillment of a suicidal wish. Accompanying such sacrifice is the expiation of guilt, a punishment imposed upon the self for forbidden (usually sexual) fantasies and impulses.

A theoretical extension of such psychoanalytic formulations exists in the hypothesis that self-mutilators, under extreme levels of anxiety, often express their need for control and mastery of themselves by performing their own predictable amputations.[43] Patients with factitious disorder, such as Munchausen's syndrome, may similarly maintain control over the need for punishment by manipulating a physician or surgeon into performing needless procedures.

The correlation of self-mutilatory acts with religious preoccupation and delusions is of special clinical interest. Many psychotic self-mutilations are accompanied by the biblical talion law of "an eye for an eye" or "if thy right hand offend thee, cut it off." Again, Fenichel has described the association of the two:

The attempt to get rid of pressure from the superego is the aim of all self-destruction. . . . The analysis of ascetic pride regularly exhibits the idea of self-sacrifice for the purpose of regaining participation in omnipotence, the pride signifying the triumph over having achieved this participation. "I sacrifice myself for the great cause, and thus the greatness of the cause falls on me." That is what priests do who castrate themselves in order to dedicate themselves to God. Their self-castration is a means of entering into the great protecting union.[42]

A number of writers have described the experience of depersonalization, the "preverbal" traumata[14] of a tumultuous childhood, apparent dissociative episodes among wrist-cutters and more psychotic self-mutilators,[44] a primitive need to reassure oneself of existence by seeing and feeling one's own blood and perhaps experiencing pain while being reassured of mastery, control, and survival.[45] Carroll et al.[46] have noted the frequency of reports of parental deprivation in the childhood histories of self-mutilating patients. Their study suggests that separation anxiety and threats of abandonment often trigger episodes of self-mutilation. They also found a high incidence of family violence and disharmony in parental and child-parent relationships, including physical or sexual abuse.

Carroll and associates theorized that "parental hostility fosters development of a punitive superego that, under stress, overwhelms ego defenses and triggers self-mutilation." The sense of calm, relief, and decreased tension following self-mutilation was described as promoting a reintegration of ego defenses. These researchers further stated that "the lack of maternal handling in early childhood reported by self-mutilating patients also suggests a preconflictual component. Self-mutilators may come to associate physical abuse with contact that satisfies the need for physical touching and attention; the need for contact may override the unpleasant sense of pain or the self-mutilators may associate pain with need satisfaction and thus not experience it as pain."

Annie Reich's efforts to explain pathologic forms of self-esteem regulation[47] are consistent with Carroll's notion that "narcissistic patients who have been deprived of gratifications required for the development of a cohesive self may exhibit such behavior."[46] In describing the child's response to pregenital and genital emotional traumata, Reich said that the child's primitive feelings of pleasure and unquestioned security were shattered, destroying the infantile feelings of power over one's object world and one's own body. The resultant feelings of helplessness, anxiety, and rage led to primitive attempts to transform the sexual body narcissism into something nonsexual and nonobjectionable. Having lost his (normal) childhood omnipotence, the adult patient who has a pathologic imbalance of self-esteem turns vehement aggression upon the deprecated (castrated) self in an effort to undo feelings of insufficiency. Such efforts to restore self-esteem are particularly seen in patients with factitious disorders and especially in Munchausen's patients who fabricate lofty impostured professional identities.

In the case of self-cutting, Siomopoulos[48] has described this as an impulse neurosis, pointing out the diagnostic inconsistencies in the literature on this topic. Self-cutters had been referred to as persons with severe character disorders or borderline states, schizophrenics, sociopaths, and persons with inadequate or emotionally unstable personalities, thought to represent inconsistencies in diagnostic criteria rather than changes or differences in illness patterns. Siomopoulos equates self-cutting, which may occur on any part of the body, with another form of "self-abuse" — namely, masturbation — suggesting that the tension state prior to the act of cutting and the relief and relaxation following are common features of the "struggle over doing it or not doing it." In his clinical cases, Siomopoulos observed that self-cutting followed the renunciation of long-standing masturbatory practice during adolescence, and supports his theory with Stekel's description of scratching of the skin and Fenichel's description of similar activities as "masturbatory equivalents." He supports the finding of others of a lack of maternal handling during infancy and sees the self-cutting as "a self-stimulating act intended to make up for the lack of outside stimulation experienced early in the lives of these patients." Supporting his classification of self-cutting as an impulse neurosis, the author states that "self-cutting appears to be a compromise formation, a distorted instinctual gratification, or else a simultaneous expression of two opposing forces, one of which is aiming at gratification of an instinctual impulse while the other tends to defend the self against it."

The case example of autocastration described early in this chapter exhibits the various elements described in most theoretical formulations: sexual conflict and "struggle," grandiose psychoreligious fantasies, relaxation following the sacrifice of a body part, an actual struggle for control (against the voice directing the man to amputate his penis), a masochistic solution to sadistic impulses following a major loss (of a homosexual lover), and temporary psychotic suspension of reality testing.

Diagnostic Classification, Management, and Treatment

The dilemma of diagnostic classification of self-mutilators reflected in psychiatric literature led Pattison and Kahan[49] to propose that the "deliberate self-harm syndrome" be established (in *DSM-IV*) as a separate diagnostic classification. A description of this syndrome is based on an analysis of 56 published index cases. Their description of the prototype model of the deliberate self-harm syndrome includes onset in late adolescence: numerous episodes of self-harm; various types of self-harm behavior; low lethality; continuation of the behavior over many years; four predominant psychological symptoms (despair, anxiety, anger, cognitive constriction); predisposing factors of lack of social support, homosexuality (men), drug and alcohol abuse, and suicidal ideation (women); and associated depression and psychosis, although more frequently with borderline or histrionic personality disorders. The psychodynamic hypothesis offered by these authors is that "deliberate self-harm represents a 'masochistic surrender' response when the person experiences an intolerable crisis in rapprochement-phase relationships with others, as described by Mahler and associates in the development of young children. Thus deliberate self-harm may occur frequently in fixated personality development (borderline, histrionic) or during acute regression in more mature character structures." Though Pattison and Kahan make no reference to the self-mutilative behavior of patients with factitious disorder, their theoretical formulation and description of clinical features are applicable. The deliberate self-harm syndrome thus is characterized as an impulse disorder by (1) failure to resist an impulse; (2) increasing tension before commission of the act; and (3) experience of pleasure, gratification, or release during commission of the act.

What are the implications of this designation for management and treatment of self-mutilators? For the most part, if the deliberate self-harm syndrome is a chronic condition related to character disorder in which the episodes of self-harm are impulsive and of low lethality, then long-term psychotherapeutic treatment with intermittent management of target symptoms would seem most appropriate. The pregenital and preverbal nature of personality disturbance described by some would suggest a need for containment, limit-setting, and a "holding environment" utilized in the treatment of severe borderline and narcissistic disorders. Intermittent hospitalization may be necessary when regression requires the increased intensity and security of such treatment parameters.[38]

However, the definitive diagnosis of the deliberate self-harm syndrome does not carry with it the high-risk implications of other self-destructive forms of behavior and may generally be managed more predictably on an outpatient basis. Indeed, it is part of appropriate treatment to properly identify the patient with Munchausen's syndrome or another factitious disorder, for example, whose illness is often exacerbated and the risk increased by hospitalization. Except in cases in which a self-induced "illness" (e.g., sepsis, electrolyte imbalance, anticoagulation, etc.) requires medical correction, proper psychiatric care is rarely, if ever, possible in the general hospital setting; patients with factitious disorder, in particular, must be receptive to and motivated for ongoing outpatient psychotherapeutic intervention for any benefit to accrue.

Graff and Mallin[14] suggest that because slashing is rooted in the preverbal life of the patient, nonverbal means of providing comfort, satisfying dependency needs, and providing tangible (nonverbal) evidence of being cared for are essential; these, it is suggested, are most readily available in the protective atmosphere of a psychiatric hospital. Grunebaum and Klerman,[13] while endorsing the use of hospitalization to develop a therapeutic alliance, emphasize the nodal points in treatment that can give rise to intrastaff conflict, with occasional heightening of the risks of acting-out behavior; "while the hazards of suicide during the termination phase are always present, our experience suggests that too prolonged hospitalization and too ready response to the patient's regressive and self-destructive symptoms are the greater hazard."

Implications of the study by Grunebaum and Klerman, as well as reports of the potential for staff-patient friction and acting-out in relation to patients with factitious disorder, are strong testimony to the need for clarification of staff reactions and countertransference attitudes. The need for non-punitive acceptance, calm limit-setting, and offers of protective and appropriate treatment will help greatly to decrease the potential for further acts of self-harm.

The prevalence of personality disorder in patients with deliberate self-harm syndrome makes a strong case for involvement of the family in treatment efforts as well as the use of group therapy. Patients whose self-mutilation is related to drug use, alcohol, mental retardation, psychosis, or depression must obviously be treated symptomatically, often with a combination of psychopharmacology, psychotherapy, and hospitalization; self-mutilation related to organic illness or mental retardation may require physical restraint in addition to other modalities. Recent reports suggest benefits from behavioral[51,52] and pharmacologic[53] approaches to certain types of self-harm syndromes, especially those related to mental retardation[54] and certain character disorders.[55] As in successful suicide, the risk in acts of "partial suicide" (i.e., self-mutilation) appears higher in males than females, with the more bizarre forms of behavior disorder found largely in men.

Finally, the overwhelming impression that self-mutilative behavior is related to parental and child-parent disharmony has broad implications for preventive psychiatry,[56] public health, and epidemiologic approaches to family well-being if the disastrous consequences of character disorders are to be avoided.

References

1. Lubin A: Vincent Van Gogh's ear. *Psychoanal. Q.* 30:351–384, 1961.

2. Pao P: The syndrome of delicate self-cutting. *Br. J. Med. Psychol.* 42:195–206, 1969.

3. Clendenin WW, Murphy GE: Wrist cutting: New epidemiological findings. *Arch. Gen. Psychiatry* 25:465–469, 1971.

4. MacLean G, Robertson BM: Self-enucleation and psychosis: Report of two cases and discussion. *Arch. Gen. Psychiatry* 33:242–249, 1976.

5. Eisenhauer CL: Self-inflicted ocular removal by two psychiatric inpatients. *Hosp. Community Psychiatry* 36:189–191, 1985.

6. Pabis R, Mirza MA, Tozman S: A case of autocastration. *Am. J. Psychiatry* 137:626–627, 1980.

7. Conacher GN et al.: Autocastration in Ontario Federal Penitentiary (letter). *Br. J. Psychiatry* 150:565–566, 1987.

8. Mintz IL: Autocannibalism. *Am. J. Psychiatry* 120:1017, 1964.

9. Tenzer JA, Orozco H: Traumatic glossectomy: Report of a case. *Oral Surg.* 30:182–184, 1970.

10. Loons PM et al.: Self-amputation of the female breast. *Psychosomatics* 27:667–668, 1986.

11. Lipsitt DR: The enigma of factitious illness. In *Health and Science Annual*, 1982, Encyclopedia Britannica, Chicago, 1982.

12. Bach-y-Rita G: Habitual violence and self-mutilation. *Am. J. Psychiatry* 131:1018–1020, 1974.

13. Grunebaum HU, Klerman GL: Wrist slashing. *Am. J. Psychiatry* 124:527–534, 1967.

14. Graff H, Mallin R: The syndrome of the wrist cutter. *Am. J. Psychiatry* 124:36–42, 1967.

15. Rosenthal RJ, Rinzler C, Wallsh R, et al.: Wrist-cutting syndrome: The meaning of a gesture. *Am. J. Psychiatry* 128:1363–1368, 1972.

16. Singh S et al.: A case of Lesch-Nyhan syndrome with delayed onset of self-mutilation: search for abnormal biochemical, immunological and cell growth characteristics in fibroblasts and neurotransmitters in urine. *Adv. Exp. Med. Biol.* 195 (Part A): 205–210, 1986.

17. Haberman MA, Michael RP: Autocastration in transsexualism. *Am. J. Psychiatry* 136:347–348, 1979.

18. Hemphill RE: A case of genital self-mutilation. *Br. J. Med. Psychol.* 24:291–295, 1951.

19. Lowy J, DePriest M: Three cases of genital self-surgery and their relationship in transsexualism. *J. Sex. Research* 12:283–294, 1976.

20. Lowy FH, Kolivakis TL: Autocastration by a male transsexual. *Can. Psychiatr. Assoc. J.* 16:399–404, 1971.

21. Blacker KH, Wong N: Four cases of autocastration. *Arch. Gen. Psychiatry* 8:169–176, 1963.

22. Esman AH: A case of self-castration. *J. Nerv. Ment. Dis.* 120:79–82, 1954.

23. Cleveland SE: Three cases of self-castration. *J. Nerv. Ment. Dis.* 123:386–391, 1956.

24. Kaplan HI, Freedman AM, Sadock BJ: *Comprehensive Textbook of Psychiatry*, Third Edition, Volume 1, Williams & Wilkins, Baltimore, 1976, p. 1025.

25. Michael KD, Beck R: Self-amputation of the tongue. *Int. J. Psychoanal. Psychother.* 2:93–99, 1973.

26. Betts WC: Autocannibalism. *Am. J. Psychiatry* 120:1017, 1964.

27. Kushner AW: Two cases of autocastration due to religious delusions. *Br. J. Med. Psychol.* 40:293–298, 1967.

28. Shore D, Anderson DJ, Cutler NR: Reduction of self-mutilation in hospitalized schizophrenics. *Am. J. Psychiatry* 135:1406–1407, 1978.

29. Novotnoy P: Self-cutting. *Bull. Menninger Clin.* 36:505–514, 1972.

30. Aduan RP, Fauci AS, Dale DC, Herzberg JH, Wolff SM: Factitious fever and self-induced infection. *Ann. Intern. Med.* 90:230–242, 1979.

31. Reich P, Gottfried LA: Factitious disorders in a teaching hospital. *Ann. Intern. Med.* 99:240–247, 1983.

32. American Psychiatric Association: *Diagnostic and Statistical Manual of Mental Disorders*, Third Edition (DSM-III), A.P.A., Washington, D.C., 1980.

33. Waisman M: Pickers, pluckers and impostors: A panorama of cutaneous self-mutilation. *Postgrad. Med.* 38:620–630, 1965.

34. Stinnett J, Hollender M: Compulsive self-mutilation. *J. Nerv. Mental Dis.* 150:371–375, 1970.

35. Podvoll EM: Self-mutilation within a hospital setting: A study of identity and social compliance. *Br. J. Med. Psychol.* 42:213–221, 1969.

36. Gardner AR, Gardner AJ: Self-mutilation, obsessionality and narcissism. *Br. J. Psychiatry* 127:127–132, 1975.

37. Lester D: Self-mutilating behavior. *Psychol. Bull.* 78:119–128, 1975.

38. Roy A: Self-mutilation. *Br. J. Med. Psychol.* 51:201–203, 1978.

39. Reich W: *Character Analysis*, Farrar, Strauss and Cudahy, New York, 1949, pp. 289–290.

40. Menninger KA: *Man Against Himself*, Harcourt, Brace and Co., New York, 1938.

41. Rosen DH, Hoffman AM: Focal suicide: Self-enucleation by two young psychotic individuals. *Am. J. Psychiatry* 128:123–126, 1972.

42. Fenichel O: *The Psychoanalytic Theory of Neurosis*, Norton, New York, 1945, pp. 77, 364.

43. Dubovsky SL: "Experimental" self-mutilation. *Am. J. Psychiatry* 135:1240–1241, 1978.

44. Waltzer H: Depersonalization and self-destruction. *Am. J. Psychiatry* 125:399–401, 1968.

45. Kafka JS: The body as transitional object: A psychoanalytic study of self-mutilating patients. *Br. J. Med. Psychol.* 42:207–212, 1969.

46. Carroll J, Schaffer C, Spensley J, Abramowitz SI: Family experiences of self-mutilating patients. *Am. J. Psychiatry* 137:852–853, 1980.

47. Reich A: Pathologic forms of self-esteem regulation. *Psychoanal. Study Child* 15:215–232, 1960.

48. Siomopoulos V: Repeated self-cutting: An impulse neurosis. *Am. J. Psychother.* 28:85–94, 1974.

49. Pattison EM, Kahan J: The deliberate self-harm syndrome. *Am. J. Psychiatry* 140:867–872, 1983.

50. Silver D: Psychodynamics and psychotherapeutic management of the self-destructive character-disordered patient. *Psychiatr. Clin. North Am.* 8:357–375, 1985.

51. Heidorn SD et al.: Generalization and maintenance of the reduction of self-injurious behavior maintained by two types of reinforcement. *Behav. Res. Ther.* 22:581–586, 1984.

52. Kaminer Y et al.: The stress inoculation training management of self-mutilating behavior: a case study. *J. Behav. Ther. Exp. Psychiatry* 18:289–292, 1987.

53. Szymanski L et al.: Naltrexone in treatment of self-injurious behavior: a clinical study. *Res. Dev. Disabil.* 8:179–190, 1987.

54. Mikkelsen EJ: Low dose haloperidol for stereotypic self-injurious behavior in the mentally retarded (letter). *NEJM* 315:3989, 1986.

55. Primeau F, Fontaine R: Obsessive-compulsive disorder with self-mutilation: a subgroup responsive to pharmacotherapy. *Can. J. Psychiatry* 32:699–701, 1987.

56. Green AH: Self-destructive behavior in battered children. *Am. J. Psychiatry* 135:579–582, 1978.

13

The Violent Patient:
Assessment and Management
John R. Lion

EDITOR'S NOTE

Violence is not a diagnosis. Aggressive behavior can occur in any number of diagnostic settings and in persons who do not qualify for any psychiatric diagnosis at all.

In practice, the clinician may be called on to determine whether a patient who imagines himself as violent or entertains aggressive fantasies toward someone is a serious risk or not.

In assessing a patient's potential for violence, the history of previous episodes of aggressive behavior should be studied. The less intact the patient's reality testing is — if, for instance, he hears voices commanding him to kill someone — the higher the risk. Drug abuse, particularly with barbiturates and amphetamines, is associated with violent behavior. The patient who has a specific victim in mind and manifests overtly homicidal ideation should be promptly hospitalized until the situation can be clarified and resolved.

One should always inquire about the availability of weapons and consult with available family members to fill in the necessary facts. The doctor's intuitive feelings are important clues to potential violence, even if he errs on the side of being too conservative. Certain psychodynamic factors are also important to consider: a history of having been abused as a child; helplessness and insults to masculinity in men; serious object loss; specific sexual abnormalities. The possibility of organic factors should also be considered, such as epilepsy or senility; evaluation should include sleep EEG and a thorough neurological review.

The management of the violent patient often requires a combined psychopharmacologic and psychotherapeutic approach, and should be based on an understanding of the nature and setting of the aggressive behavior. Certain principles prevail. For example, it is important not to increase the patient's sense of helplessness and of being out of control since this may intensify his rage and belligerence. Hence it is often better to engage in a one-to-one confrontation and certainly to avoid having a number of people hold the patient down. Similarly it is best to avoid overmedicating, particularly in paranoid patients.

In using medications, one should never overlook the importance of psychological

163

management. The psychotherapist should attempt to help such patients recognize their emotions, such as rage, more accurately and to elaborate upon fantasy as a way to translate their tendency to act impulsively and immediately to provocation into a greater ability to use foresight and anticipate the consequences of their behavior. During in-hospital care, staff should be conscious of countertransference attitudes and actions that may accentuate rather than relieve a patient's violent tendencies.

Introduction

When psychiatrists think about "violent patients" they have treated, they usually remember hospitalized psychotic persons such as those with paranoid schizophrenia or patients who have used hallucinogens and are aggressive and belligerent. Some clinicians may recollect patients with severe behavior disorders seen in an outpatient clinic or within a jail or forensic facility. Violence may be associated with many clinical syndromes in psychiatry. There is no such diagnosis as "violent patient"; violence can be seen in manic-depressive illness, agitated depression, intermittent explosive disorders, alcoholism, or sexual paraphilia. The point to be made is that aggression is a symptom that cuts across many diagnostic entities. The clinician confronted with "a violent patient" needs to consider whether the violence is a manifestation of the subculture, an affective disease process, an incipient psychosis, a character disorder, a disorder of impulse control, an attention-deficit disorder, an organic mental disorder, or any of a variety of other illnesses that have complex behavioral characteristics.

Definitions of Violence

Formal definitions of violence vary. The American Psychiatric Task Force on Clinical Aspects of the Violent Individual has defined a violent patient as one who "acts or has acted in such a way to produce physical harm or destruction."[1] That Task Force report acknowledges that there are people who fantasize harm but are not properly defined as "violent" because, from the behavioral standpoint, the harm has not been committed. This has important clinical implications. Psychiatrists may see persons who have homicidal ideation or are afraid of "going out of control." In such instances, the clinician must not only assess the patient's risk but also consider the identification of a potential victim. The latter has assumed medicolegal significance following the recent Tarasoff Decision in California, wherein the Supreme Court found that a psychiatrist has a duty to issue a warning when he encounters a patient who threatens violence to someone.[2] Thus, the psychiatrist who confronts such a patient must decide whether the patient is simply fantasizing violence or is truly dangerous. Many homicidal patients "cry for help"[3] in the same way suicidal patients do—a fact often not appreciated by clinicians, who tend to repudiate violent patients and are frightened by them. In fact, one of the biggest obstacles to the assessment of violent patients is the physician's own denial.[3] Many clinicians deal with aggressive patients dispositionally and send them to state hospitals or place them in the hands of law-enforcement agencies. Strong countertransference forces shape this process and often lead to the clinician's misperception of dangerousness because he projects his own fears and anxieties onto a violent patient, seeing him as more ominous than he really is. In fact, the patient may wish help in controlling his aggressive urges.[4]

Assessing a Patient's Violence

There are different ways in which a violent patient may present clinically. When he has already acted in an aggressive fashion, he is often brought by law-enforcement officers to an emergency room. In an emergency room of a general hospital or psychiatric facility, patients may describe fears of acting on aggressive impulses and may verbalize diffuse anxieties of "running amuck" or more specific concerns that they will hurt a particular person. When the complaint is vague and diffuse, it often cloaks the identity of a true victim about whom the patient has many ambivalent feelings; that ambivalence itself is protective and spares the patient the pain of realizing the rage he has at someone upon whom he is dependent as well as at the dependency itself. Patients with more specifically directed violent urges have often been pathologically enmeshed in violence before. This is commonly seen in child abuse, spouse battering, and a variety of other dyadic relationships involving pathological interactions between two persons.

From the standpoint of assessment, the clinician must ascertain the mental status and determine whether the patient's reality testing is intact. Thus, a patient who hears voices telling him to kill is a significant risk to society. A severely depressed patient should not be considered unlikely to commit homicide, since some patients who are suicidal will kill others first to "spare them pain"; such situations are not uncommon and have been described in one population of homicidal patients.[5]

The homicidal or suicidal patient must be asked whether he has thought about doing harm to a specific person or to himself. A history of drug use, such as alcoholism, or the use of hallucinogens or inhalants (glue sniffing), increase risk.[6] Barbiturate abuse has been reported to be associated with violent behavior.[7] Paranoid psychoses may result from the use of amphetamines, and homicide has been associated with the abuse of such drugs.[8] Overt homicidal ideation and the availability of a potential victim always signal the need for hospitalization until the situation can be resolved; it is a mistake to see the patient alone without assessing the overt or covert provocation of another person, and potential victims usually welcome the chance to present their point of view. The clinician needs to recall that the perpetrators and victims of most homicides are persons who already know each other, not strangers. Thus it is mandatory to inquire about the family, since it is likely that the patient's anger stems from conflict there. When violent patients are candidly told by the examiner that he wishes to see the spouse or parent, they usually urge him to do so. Interviews with victims or families should not be done in secret. Joint interviews or sessions are usually most productive for diagnostic purposes and clearly show the interactions of members.

The clinician needs to inquire about the availability of weapons. The use of the automobile should also be assessed, since a car can be a weapon and its misuse often signals risk on the highway — particularly if the patient is prone to drink.[9] The patient should be asked about traffic violations and convictions.

Other questions are requisite but often not asked. The clinician should inquire how violent the patient has ever been, what is the most violent thing he has ever done and whether he has ever had legal difficulties or arrests resulting from violence. These are rather unsavory queries that may evoke disconcerting answers for the interviewer.

To summarize, risk of violence increases with a history of previous violence, the availability of a weapon, the availability of a potential victim, the existence of a pathological relationship with that person, and the use of a toxic agent that can lead to the disinhibition of violent urges and impulses.

Other Clues to Potential Violence

The way the clinician feels about a patient plays a strong role in the assessment of every psychiatric illness, and the situation is no different in the case of violence. If patients appear indifferent to others and generate within the interviewer a sense of distrust and alienation, risk should be considered higher. Other patients may evoke warmer feelings and attitudes of alliance and trust that make them less of a risk. Those who work with violent patients have found that "softer" data — such as their value systems and their beliefs about life, friends, animals, and heroes, their ideals, and their capacity for friends—are better prognostic indicators for "dangerousness" than any psychological scale or test.[10] In fact, no existing scales or tests are currently thought to be prospectively useful for violence; and in any event, the clinician seeing the patient in an acute setting is unlikely to have time or presence of mind to administer pencil-and-paper tests. The degree of introspectiveness a patient is capable of and the dystonic nature of his anger are variables to be assessed. Usually, the patients who are violent do not enjoy the rage but perceive it as dysphoric and want controls established. They thus welcome relief if they are reassured that help will be furnished them and that they will not be allowed to go out of control. The situation is analogous to a suicidal patient who really asks for controls, frightened that he may well harm himself in the process of decompensation.

There is literature dealing with childhood traits implicated with violence in later life. Neuropathic traits—such as enuresis, pyromania, and cruelty to animals—have been associated with violence but are not predictive of it.[11] Such a discovery might make the clinician examine more seriously the patient's propensity toward aggression—particularly when coupled with a history of school suspensions because of temper outbursts in childhood and adolescence. Severe parental deprivation and brutalization or child abuse is a frequent finding in a violent patient. It is well known that violence begets violence so that the patient learns to react to frustration with aggression.[12] From the psychodynamic standpoint, helplessness and insults to masculinity are key factors in the susceptibility to rage in men. For example, when self-esteem is tenuous, patients may react in an all-or-none fashion to a simple insult and become enraged, particularly when drinking. As a general dynamic principle, violence occurs most frequently among persons who are most insecure and need to strongly defend inner weaknesses.

Object loss is an important factor and often the precipitant to violence. Death, alienation from a lover, or loss of job can result in violence and rage rather than sadness.

Another consideration for the clinician is the patient's attitudes toward sexuality. Rage and anger at women may lead to sadistic fantasies that become realized in deviant behavior or rape, which has as its aim more the humiliation and injury of women than orgiastic satisfaction.[13] Fear of adult genital sexuality is the dynamic in pedophiliac behavior. The clinician may be asked to comment upon whether a pedophiliac may launch into violent behavior. This is a very difficult question to answer on the basis of one interview, as is the general issue of sexuality. In theory, under the provocation of frustration by any child they approach, such patients may become aggressive. This is difficult to predict, however, and in-depth assessment is necessary, together with psychological testing. These patients need to be seen several times. Other sexual paraphilias, such as exhibitionism and voyeurism, are generally associated with passive persons and less frequently lead to violent behavior.[13]

Organic Etiologic Factors

Violence is a behavior that has organic determinants as well as psychodynamic ones. Thus, neurologic dysfunction is important to consider. There are a number of anatomical structures in the brain that have been implicated in both the expression of aggression and its inhibition in man. The limbic system, hippocampus, and amygdala have been experimentally manipulated both to induce rage and to pacify animals and man.[14] Electrical stimulation of these areas in humans has been shown to lead to violent behavior, while natural diseases (such as epilepsy or cerebral neoplasms) can also result in temper outbursts. Brain dysfunction may manifest itself in mood lability, paroxsymal temper outbursts, and episodic violence. A wide range of organic dysfunctions have as their common denominator a propensity toward impulsivity and aggressiveness. Children with mental retardation or attention-deficit disorders, patients with temporal-lobe disease processes, and geriatric patients with senile dementias are examples. Neuropsychiatric assessment should proceed along the lines of that done for a mentally retarded child. Thus, the clinician should inquire about head injury, anoxia in childhood, convulsions, trauma, or any events that may have predisposed the patient to subtle organic impairment.

Some patients with violent outbursts and "temper" have very sudden outbursts of rage followed immediately by remorse. Phenomenologically, these outbursts have the flavoring of epilepsy, with altered states of consciousness or such other prodromal events as micropsia or gustatory or olfactory sensations. These patients may also complain of rage "building up" in their bodies and they may also talk about postictal-like complaints of sleepiness or drowsiness following the angry outbursts. There is a considerable amount of literature on aggression and temporal-lobe epilepsy;[15] the current thinking about this association is that violence may be the manifestation of the interictal component or the postictal phase[16] of the disease process rather than the epileptic discharge itself. That is, patients with psychomotor epilepsy may become violent after an epileptic outburst when they are restrained, and they may show temper outbursts in a generalized irritability between epileptic discharges. The "intermittent explosive disorder" described in *DSM-III*, represents a new conceptualization of the old term "explosive personality," which was described in *DSM-II*.[17] The Intermittent Explosive Disorder takes into account central-nervous-system aspects of dysfunction. Organic factors play a role in "minimal brain dysfunction" syndromes, formally referred to in *DSM-III* as "attention deficit disorders." Some literature indicates that certain of these children may grow up to demonstrate intermittent explosive disorders—or at least show the same aggressiveness and impulsivity that characterized their personality and behavior in childhood or adolescence.[18]

If the psychiatrist considers organic dysfunction, he may wish to refer the patient to a neurologist for a sleep EEG study. Sleep EEG is particularly important, since the incidence of interictal abnormalities with temporal-lobe disease processes is very low and a good sleep tracing is desirable.[19] Referral to a neurologist is also indicated for assessment of cortical function in the parietal, temporal, or frontal lobe. Psychological tests for organicity, such as the Reitan-Halstead battery, may determine visual-motor impairment indicative of central-nervous-system dysfunction.

There are certain small groups of patients who may present with "epileptoid" types of violence in association with minimal alcohol intake. This was called "pathological intoxication" in *DSM-II* and has been reconceptualized as "idiosyncratic alcohol intoxication" in *DSM-III*.[20] Basically, the term is thought to refer to a process that may reflect the activation of temporal-lobe epilepsy by small amounts of alcohol, although some workers have conceptualized the disorder in more psychodynamic terms. These patients often present with a history of "blackouts," amnestic episodes with violence. Diagnosis is often difficult, but organicity should be considered.

Psychological Testing

Additional diagnostic clarification of the patient's propensity for violence can be obtained from careful psychological testing projective. Projective tests, such as the TAT or Rorschach, are useful to ascertain the level of paranoia and projection as well as the level of depression and danger.

A word should be said about the prediction of dangerousness.[21] A large amount of literature supports the clinical concern that such predictions of a patient's risk will result in false positives—i.e., that the predictor, in assessing a group of patients, will label some as more dangerous than they really are and hence possibly retain them within the hospital or jail. Humility is called for in this venture, and mental health professionals need to bear in mind that the criminal justice system evaluates parole and probation candidates in every prison; this task is tantamount to the "prediction" of dangerousness in that those carrying out these evaluations ascertain risk through the most subjective means.

Intervention in Acute Episodes

The need for intervention by the clinician in the case of a violent patient depends on the setting. Patients are often brought into the emergency room by policemen, and the immediate task is to quiet the patient and restore order. Sometimes this can be accomplished with a simple one-to-one confrontation, since the patient's violence is often directly proportional to the number of people holding him down. However, the clinician should use some intuition and feel comfortable; thus, if he senses that the patient will not quiet down when faced alone, suitable help should be present during the interview. The patient should be told that he is frightening, and the clinician can be candid about his own concerns for safety as he attempts to understand what brought the patient in during the critical period. The patient can be offered some oral medication. The amount of medication should usually be small since one of the dynamics is helplessness and the patient is afraid of losing control. He thus does not wish to be "knocked out," and he can be told that the medication he is receiving may not be enough and that a second or supplemental dose may have to be given. This is preferable to overwhelming him with a drug.

Paranoid patients are particularly sensitive to oversedation and react more favorably if small amounts of a drug are chosen. Too often, patients are admitted in a highly agitated state and immediately given a large dose of parenteral medication, a tactic that often exacerbates violence rather than controlling it. When a patient is offered medication, he should be told exactly what the drug is and be allowed to express his feelings about it. A useful medication in emergency rooms for alcoholic or geriatric patients who are mildly agitated is 5 or 10 mg of the benzodiazepine diazepam (Valium). This is well absorbed by the oral route of administration. More agitated and psychotic patients will require antipsychotic drugs. In my opinion, the drug of choice is haloperidol (Haldol), which produces few cardiovascular effects, such as hypotension. Small amounts of this drug (5 or 10 mg) can be given sequentially every 30 minutes until quiescence ensues; usually two or three injections are sufficient.[22]

The Use of Restraint

The process and strategy of physically restraining patients should be carried out swiftly and humanely. Rarely is it a rehearsed procedure. Clinicians who frequently come in contact with violent patients ought to have strategies worked out with security staff so that order can be promptly restored.[23,24] There is a variety of restraint techniques, including leather cuffs, sheet restraints, and camisoles and jackets. Use of them is unavoidable despite the stigma attached to the devices; effective use depends on a written policy and a rehearsed strategy.[24] Use of a seclusion room likewise demands a written policy.[23] Seclusion rooms usually contain only a mattress. Sometimes, unfortunately, they are makeshift affairs containing items of danger, such as oxygen jets or light fixtures, which an agitated patient can destroy or injure himself with. Some thought must be given to the design of the room; it should be free of proturberances and be away from the mainstream of patient interaction. An observation window is requisite. Regular clinical checks by nursing staff should document the rationale for continued retention in seclusion. Often, restraint and maintenance in the psychiatric ward are preferable to the isolation of seclusion and ultimately lead to greater calmness.

The role of security personnel in emergency-room and crisis-clinic settings is of paramount importance. These persons should be carefully chosen and should have some training in psychiatry. They should be viewed as members of the team rather than perceived in an adversary relationship as members of the police force who are called on to do the "dirty work" of subjugating violent patients. Generally speaking, any patient entering an emergency-room facility and requiring parenteral medication and/or physical restraints needs to be hospitalized.

Some toxic syndromes, such as PCP psychosis with violence, are reported to worsen with the use of antipsychotic drugs. Some workers have suggested that antianxiety agents, such as diazepam, are more useful.[25]

Psychopharmacologic Management of Hospitalized Patients

With respect to hospitalized patients who are psychotic, any antipsychotic drug is useful for the control of belligerence and aggressiveness, since no single drug of this class is specific for aggression.[26] For example, haloperidol (Haldol) may be useful for some patients, molindone (Moban) for others, and trifluoperazine (Stelazine) for still others. The aim is to control the underlying psychopathologic state with the hope that the aggression abates secondarily. Lithium is the drug of choice for manic patients who show belligerence and combativeness as part of the manic picture,[27] although in some cases an antipsychotic drug may have to be used during the early phases until the lithium takes effect. If the patient is agitated and shows combativeness or hostility as a function of a severe agitated depression, an antidepressant with sedative properties, such as amitriptyline (Elavil), may be useful. Catatonically excited patients may respond to ECT, with a reduction in the aggression secondary to the resolution of the psychosis.

Personality Disorders and Violent Behavior

There are many personality disorders that may show aggressiveness as a function of character pathology.[28] The antisocial personality, by definition, most typically demonstrates hostility and a history of criminal activity. The passive-aggressive personality is more obstructionistic but may also show hostile outbursts and irritability. Paranoid personalities may show lability and mood swings, together with suspiciousness and mistrust. Borderline personalities may show lability and aggressiveness, and the latter may be quickly internalized or just as easily externalized; such patients may become as self-destructive as they are angry, and the introversion may be swift and related only to the availability of the object of their anger. The narcissistic personality may show anger as a function of the need for approval and the frustration thereof, while the compulsive personality may demonstrate anger as a function of some interference either with perfectionism or with acknowledgment of that trait. The histrionic personality is also capable of demonstrating lability of mood and hostile feelings over time.

In summary, many patients with personality disorders have inherent problems with the expression or control of aggressiveness. Patients with personality disorders are treated with great difficulty.[28] If these persons show target symptoms of anxiety that cause them to become combative and belligerent as a function of their general hypervigilance, benzodiazepines may be useful, although some of these patients tend to abuse such drugs. Paranoid patients sometimes respond to small amounts of diazepam (Valium) or chlordiazepoxide (Librium), while borderline patients may respond to these drugs or to small amounts of an antipsychotic drug. Again, the intent is to take the edge off anxiety while retaining the hypervigilance so critical to these patients. It is important to avoid inducing subtle side-effects, such as akathisia or sedation, because patients will not take drugs if these symptoms appear. One tactic to use with labile paranoid patients is to give them a very small amount of, say, lorazepam (Ativan) and instruct them to take 1 mg of the drug if they find their anger building up. For example, they can be instructed to remove themselves from the work situation, go to the bathroom, take the drug, and resume work in approximately 10 minutes, when some effect will be noticeable and will reduce the overresponsiveness that characterizes their interaction with superiors.

Violence and Epilepsy

Patients with epileptic types of violence or those found to have an intermittent explosive disorder or actual psychomotor epilepsy may benefit from anticonvulsants.[29] Phenytoin sodium (Dilantin) may be useful for these patients, although a more recent drug of choice is carbamazepine (Tegretol).[30] The advantage of the anticonvulsants is that blood levels give an index of therapeutic efficacy. Blood levels can be used to titrate the therapeutic range. Also, compliance can be monitored. The rationale for using anticonvulsants may be the discovery of brain dysfunction through laboratory tests, such as the EEG or psychometrics, or it can be on purely clinical grounds. Quite often, the clinician will find only weak data to support his decision to use the drug. For example, there may be historical data to indicate "minimal brain dysfunction" and some dysrhythmia on EEG examination, but the violence is typically paroxysmal and episodic and the temper outbursts so "epileptoid" that sufficient justification for the use of a drug exists.

Other Medication Approaches

Central-nervous-system stimulants, such as dextroamphetamine (Dexedrine) or methylphenidate (Ritalin), have traditionally been used to control the belligerence and hyperactivity associated with the attention-deficit disorders.[31] Recent literature indicates that these drugs, while used primarily with children, may be useful in adolescents and young adults, although the agents are still "experimental" and not specifically indicated by the FDA for use in older patients. Unfortunately, adolescents who show impulsivity, lability of mood and affect, and aggressiveness are often precisely those who might be prone to misuse or abuse the drugs of the CNS-activating class. Hence, trust becomes important and the family should be involved. Depending on where the clinician resides, permission may be obtained from the state agency licensing these drugs for use.

Hormonal agents, such as medroxyprogesterone acetate (Provera), have been used experimentally to control sexual aggressiveness.[32] The rationale for use is the drugs' lowering of serum testosterone. They produce a dramatic reduction in heightened sexual drive. These drugs have been used in compulsive masturbators and in many paraphilias, and they are, in my opinion, the drugs of choice for rape behavior. Unfortunately, medroxyprogesterone has not been licensed for use by the FDA, and experimental protocols have to be devised to be used by the clinician in an institutional setting.

Disulfiram may be used to treat alcoholics who are prone to violence in association with drinking.

Problems in Managing Medication

The use of medications to treat aggressive patients is not a simple matter and often arises out of desperation, so choices are compromised and continuity and rationale impaired.[33] For example, an aggressive patient may be placed on one drug in the emergency room and then treated with another upon transfer to the hospital unit. Then, because staff are frightened of him, the drug he gets is seen as "not working" after only a few days and he is placed on another, only to be switched again after a conference. The expression is frequently heard that a violent patient has "been on everything" when in fact he has received minimal to moderate amounts of varying pharmacologic agents for inadequate lengths of time. Patients should systematically be tried on one drug in an orderly fashion; that drug should be slowly titrated upward to establish clinical limits until there is evidence of toxicity or inefficacy. The drug should be used for an adequate length of time and the reason for discontinuation carefully spelled out on the chart. It is useful to have a flow sheet for each patient, with headings indicating the maximum amount of the drug used and the extent of time the patient received the drug.

Surgical Management

Various surgical treatments have been advocated for epileptoid aggressive behavior that is unresponsive to anticonvulsant regimens. For example, amygdalectomy[34] is a stereotactic procedure in which selective lesions are made in a limbic-system structure to produce some degree of pacification. The results of such clinical efforts have been controversial although there is some evidence to indicate that aggressiveness that is clearly related to amygdala dysfunction can be lessened with the careful use of such techniques. However, long-term follow-up studies are difficult, and the entire area has been clouded by controversies surrounding psychosurgery.

Psychotherapy

Psychotherapeutic considerations for aggressive patients are of importance. Basically, the goal of psychotherapy is to deal with the patient whose behavior usually comes on so quickly that there is little opportunity for reflection. Thus, the initial task of treatment is to make the patient realize when he is angry and to get him to recognize the rage within him. This is often best accomplished by instructing the patient to identify the somatic accompaniments of his anger. The patient should be able to tell that a tightened chest and clenched fists indicate that he is angry; such realization is a prelude to the intellectual appreciation of an angry state and the ultimate articulation of it.

Another important issue in the psychotherapy of violent and impulsive patients is elaboration of fantasy. Many of these characterologically disordered patients who "fly off the handle" appear to have diminished fantasy lives and react to stimuli with an immediate physical response. These patients are unable to meditate on the consequences of their acts and must be trained to understand the outcomes of violent behavior.[35] Generally speaking, the above-mentioned strategies, together with insight-oriented psychotherapy, lead to depression as a patient comes to grips with vulnerabilities and his inability to use old patterns of coping with helplessness by using force. This depression is very real and can assume suicidal proportions.

Some workers have described group therapy as a valuable tool for enhancing fantasy and the somatic awareness of aggression.[36] Individual psychotherapy generally focuses more on the intrapsychic determinants of rage, which include issues of self-esteem and sexual identity. As mentioned before, many patients who are violent have experienced violence in childhood, and a review of the rage induced by punitive parents becomes a poignant issue in individual psychotherapy. Violent ideation is often evoked by the intimacy of the psychotherapeutic relationship and the developing transference.

Countertransference issues are important. Clinicians themselves may become apprehensive of a violent patient and displace that fear onto him; the patient is then seen as malevolent. Or the clinician covertly avoids acknowledgment of anger because of difficulties he himself has with the subject or with the expression of hostilities. Collegial consultation may be desirable when the therapist finds himself frightened of a patient. Group dynamics may also contain countertransference issues — as is seen in a hospital ward setting where nursing staff personnel repudiate a patient and place him in seclusion, using heavier and heavier dosages of medication in order to distance themselves from the patient. The patient, becoming more and more alienated, becomes increasingly aggressive. This vicious cycle can be broken by deemphasizing medication and making an effort to bring the patient out of seclusion to interact with the staff.

Hospital Management and Mismanagement

Another factor operative within hospital settings may contribute to aggression, and that is the failure to record, document, or discuss patient assault. When patients do assault other patients or staff, staff often expend energies in the management of the particular incident and do not pause to review the matter in staff conferences or even in a patient group meeting. Assaults are often underreported in incident forms because staff becomes inured to such assaults, particularly in a forensic setting or chronic hospital setting.[37] Or staff may feel that to report an assault is to admit a clinical error in management.

Assaults within psychiatric hospitals reflect a variety of factors, including hospital leadership, staffing patterns, the mix of patients, crowding, and the clinical experience of physicians and nurses. A review of serious incidents should be made regularly, and attempts should be made to ascertain patterns. Did the assault occur at night? Did it occur during a particular nursing shift? Who were the personnel on that shift? Did the same patient hit many other patients? Is there a "victim" patient?

In state hospitals, there is usually a small group of chronically hostile patients who have been residents of the facility for many years and are more or less notorious. Sometimes these are psychotic persons with brain damage who remain in seclusion for long periods and are taking excessive amounts of medication. Strong fears permeate the milieu about these patients, and attempts should be made to ascertain the basis for these fears. Was this patient really "dangerous"? Or is he just so perceived because he makes threats all the time? Has medication really reduced the frequency of violent outbursts? The last question can be answered only if the base rate of outbursts is known. Thus, some data need to be gathered.

Preventive Strategies

The process of reducing impulsivity and lability is initially facilitated by giving the patient a place to call when he feels he is going out of control. Optimally, this should be the therapist's number. While the opportunity of calling a therapist may obviously be misused, genuine crises may give the clinician an excellent chance to observe the patient in a state of rage and to perceive the dynamics firsthand. Thought and affective disorders persist over weeks and months and are easily seen by the clinician. In contrast, violent patients are often seen "interbehaviorally"—between episodes of psychopathology—so that they appear normal in the office and later tell the physician about their violent outbursts. Clinicians working with violent patients are often at a disadvantage in that they always hear about a temper outburst after it is over and even then, secondhand, from a relative. This handicap may be overcome by more direct contact with the patient during moments of stress, as inconvenient as the arrangement may be for the therapist. A phone call may avert a violent outburst.

Family therapy is important for violent patients and for their potential victims. A number of workers have looked at violent relationships and describe a family constellation of dynamics.[38] For example, some parents covertly sanction violent behavior by their children while overtly condemning it. The subtleties are best brought to life when all members of the family come together.[39]

References

1. American Psychiatric Association. *Clinical Aspects of the Violent Individual*, Task Force Report #8, APA, Washington, DC, July 1974.

2. Roth LH, Meisel A: Dangerousness, confidentiality and the duty to warn. *Am. J. Psychiatry* 134:508–511, 1977.

3. Lion JR: *Evaluation and Management of the Violent Patient*, Charles C Thomas, Springfield, Ill., 1972.

4. Lion JR, Pasternack SA: Countertransference reactions to violent patients. *Am. J. Psychiatry* 130:207–210, 1973.

5. West DJ: *Murder Followed by Suicide*, Harvard University Press, Cambridge, Mass., 1967.

6. Peterson RC, Stillman RC: *Phencyclidine (PCP Abuse): An Appraisal*, NIDA Research Monograph 21, DHEW, U.S. Govt. Print. Office, Washington, DC, 1978.

7. Tinklenberg JR, Woodrow KM: Drug use among assaultive and sexual offenders. In Frazier SH (ed): *Human Aggression: Proceedings of the 1972 Annual Meeting of the Association for Research in Nervous and Mental Disease*, Williams & Wilkins, Baltimore, 1973.

8. Ellinwood EH: Assault and homicide associated with amphetamine abuse. *Am. J. Psychiatry* 127:1170–1175, 1971.

9. Selzer ML, Rogers JE, Kern S: Fatal accidents: The role of psychopathology, social stress and acute disturbances. *Am. J. Psychiatry* 124:1028–1036, 1968.

10. Kozol H: The diagnosis of dangerousness. In Pasternack SA (ed): *Violence and Victims*, Spectrum Publications, New York, 1975.

11. Hellman DS, Blackman N: Enuresis, firesetting and cruelty to animals. A triad predictive of adult crime. *Am. J. Psychiatry* 122:1431–1435, 1966.

12. Green AH: The child abuse syndrome and the treatment of abusing parents. In Pasternack S A (ed): *Violence and Victims*, Spectrum Publications, New York, 1975.

13. Cohen ML, Grofalo R, Boucher R, Seghorn T: The psychology of rapists. In Pasternack SA (ed): *Violence and Victims*, Spectrum Publications, New York, 1975.

14. Mark VH, Ervin FR: *Violence and the Brain*, Harper & Row, New York, 1970.

15. Benson FD, Blumer D: *Psychiatric Aspects of Neurologic Diseases*, Grune and Stratton, New York, 1975.

16. Rodin EA: Psychomotor epilepsy and aggressive behavior. *Arch. Gen. Psychiatry* 28:210–213, 1973.

17. Monroe RR: *Episodic Behavior Disorders: A Psychodynamic and Neurophysiologic Analysis*, Harvard University Press, Cambridge, Mass., 1970.

18. Menkes MM, Rowe JS, Menkes JH: A twenty-five year follow-up study on the hyperkinetic child with minimal brain dysfunction. *Pediatrics* 39:393-399, 1967.

19. Ervin RF: Brain disorders. IV: Associated with convulsions (epilepsy). In Freedman A, Kaplan M (eds): *Comprehensive Textbook of Psychiatry*, Williams and Wilkins, Baltimore, 1967.

20. Bach-y-Rita G, Lion JR, Ervin FR: Pathological intoxication: Clinical and electroencephalographic studies. *Am. J. Psychiatry* 127:698-703, 1971.

21. Monahan J: *The Clinical Prediction of Violent Behavior*. Crime and Delinquency Issues Monograph, NIMH, DHHS Publ. No (ADM): 81-921, 1981.

22. Donlon PT, Hopkin J, Tupin JP: Efficacy and safety of rapid neuroleptization with injectable haloperidol. *Am. J. Psychiatry* 136:273-278, 1979.

23. Gutheil TC: Observations on the theoretical bases for seclusion of the psychiatric inpatient. *Am. J. Psychiatry* 135:325-328, 1978.

24. Rosen H, DiGiacomo JN: The role of physical restraint in the treatment of psychiatric illness. *J. Clin. Psychiatry* 32:228-232, 1978.

25. Peterson RC, Stillman RC: *Phencyclidine (PCP Abuse): An Appraisal*, NIDA Research Monograph 21, DHEW, U.S. Govt. Print. Office, Washington, DC, 1978.

26. Lion JR: Conceptual issues in the use of drugs for the treatment of aggression in man. *J. Nerv. Ment. Dis.* 160:76-82, 1975.

27. Sheard M: Lithium in the treatment of aggression. *J. Nerv. Ment. Dis.* 160:108-118, 1975.

28. Lion JR: *Personality Disorders: Diagnosis and Management*, Williams and Wilkins, Baltimore, 1974.

29. Monroe RR: Anticonvulsants in the treatment of aggression. *J. Nerv. Ment. Dis.* 160:119-126, 1974.

30. *International Drug Therapy Newsletter* 14:29-31, October, 1979.

31. Allen RP, Safer D, Covi L: Effects of psychostimulants on aggression. *J. Nerv. Ment. Dis.* 160:138-145, 1975.

32. Money J: Use of an androgen depleting hormone in the treatment of male sex offenders. *J. Sex. Res.* 6:165-172, 1970.

33. Lion JR: *The Art of Medicating Psychiatric Patients*, Williams & Wilkins, Baltimore, 1978.

34. Sweet WH, Ervin FR, Mark VH: The relationship of violent behavior to focal cerebral disease. In Garattini S, Siggs EG (eds): *Aggressive Behavior,* John Wiley & Sons, New York, 1969.

35. Lion JR: The role of depression in the treatment of aggressive personality disorders. *Am. J. Psychiatry* 129:347-349, 1972.

36. Lion JR et al,: A group approach with violent outpatients. *Int. J. Group Psychother.* 27:67-74, 1977.

37. Lion JR, Snyder W, Merrill G: Underreporting of assaults in a mental hospital. *Hosp. Commun. Psychiatry* 32:497-498, 1981.

38. Symonds M: The psychodynamics of violence-prone marriages. *Am. J. Psychoanal.* 38:213-222, 1978.

39. Harbin HT: Episodic dyscontrol and family dynamics. *Am. J. Psychiatry* 134:1113-1116, 1977.

14

The Psychiatrist as Victim:

The Recognition and Management of the Homicidal Patient

Bruce L. Danto

EDITOR'S NOTE

Few events are more distressing to physicians than to learn of the murder of a psychiatrist. Always the question arises—could it have been predicted? Could it have been prevented? Some information and certain guidelines are available.

There is not much literature on the subject. What there is indicates that the age and sex of therapists who have been victims of patient assault are not relevant factors. The risk of being a target of violence does seem greater among less experienced psychiatrists, those who see a large number of patients, and, most clearly, those who deny and fail to appraise the potential for violence in such patients.

Using case illustrations, the author demonstrates how lack of communication, assuming a passive stance, overlooking clues in the patient's verbalizations and behavior, failing to take a careful past history of violence, and not knowing how to defuse the dangerous patient are among the elements that seem to increase the possibility of the therapist's being attacked—and perhaps killed—by a patient with psychotic delusions who cannot release himself from terror and rage in some other way.

Although patients with paranoid symptoms obviously represent the greatest threat, one must not overlook the potential for violence in the suicidally depressed patient as well.

Introduction

In 1981 alone, three psychiatrists were murdered, most likely by patients under their care. Although most of us carry out our practices without living under the shadow of being potential homicide victims, we can usually recall at least one situation in our own experience involving a patient who we thought might be a risk, because of either threats made against us or some form of assaultive behavior. A few of us probably have known a psychiatrist who was murdered. This prospect is one of the most terrifying complications of psychiatric practice, one which, however infrequent, nonetheless demands that we consider some of the strategies that can be employed to identify such patients and to be able to manage the situation effectively if such a crisis confronts us.

The Literature on Violent Patients

In Ekblom's[1] review of the literature on violent acts by psychiatric patients between 1889 and 1970 he emphasized the scarcity of adequate studies. Kolle felt that patient attacks on staff members usually resulted from provocative behavior on the psychiatric staff's part.[2] Kalogerakis attempted to identify the psychodynamic and sociological influences in a series of violent patients.[3]

In a questionnaire sampling of 184 psychiatrists, psychologists, and social workers in 1972, Whitman et al. received 101 responses, 53 from psychiatrists.[4] These physicians saw a total of 3810 patients that year, 416 of whom were perceived to represent some assaultive threat. The age or sex of the therapists did not seem relevant. The risk of violence or threats, however, did increase in proportion to the number of patients each psychotherapist saw. About 10% of patients in all kinds of treatment were seen to represent a threat of violence.

In 1975, Madden et al.[5] conducted a survey of 155 psychiatrists who held full- or part-time appointments with the University of Maryland School of Medicine. Of that group, 48 had been assaulted by patients—for a combined total of 68 separate assaults. Most of the clinicians were in their younger years or early phases of training when assaulted. Most of the assaultive patients were in active psychiatric treatment. Most of the therapist-victims continued to treat their patients after the attack. The mode of assault took many forms. Several therapists had heavy objects thrown at them, such as ashtrays; one psychiatrist was shot in the chest; another experienced a nasal fracture; most were slapped or struck with the patient's hand or fist. By and large, the majority of patients were diagnosed as schizophrenic, ranging from paranoid to catatonic; a smaller number had borderline or personality disorders. The rest were depressed, alcoholic, or hyperactive, or had some type of adjustment reaction.

In this review, about 55% of the psychiatrists anticipated the attack and 53% felt that they themselves had been in some way provocative—e.g., by making comments or interpretations unfavorable to their patients, such as refusing to meet a patient's request, forcing a patient to take medication, setting either too many or not enough limits on the patient's behavior, failing to deal with transference reactions or homosexual panic, or being too insistent that the patient be confronted with upsetting material. Some therapists felt that if they had backed off, the assault might not have occurred. Others openly acknowledged having felt dislike for the patient and conveyed this to him. In one case, the therapist felt he had expressed his dislike by not acting on a request to write a letter—a request that had been made of him five times.

Some felt that assaults arose from permitting the patient to act out aggressive feelings during the treatment hour. Others thought that they had been too seductive, and that an assault was the patient's way of protecting himself against a degree of physical and emotional proximity he could not tolerate. Some believed that too much kindness toward the patient was an attempt by the therapist to deny or veil intense dislike of the patient.

Not surprisingly, the setting—e.g., a prison, the forensic unit of a state hospital, or an emergency room—seemed to increase the risk of assault.

Madden and his group found that denial of danger by the psychiatrist played a vital role in how he handled assaultive patients, enhancing the risk of attack. One therapist, for example, had been threatened many times by one particular patient and still failed to take any action whatsoever. One psychiatrist who was killed had been attempting to disarm a patient.

In another study, Sherwyn Woods has dealt with a special group of potentially and actually violent patients.[6] These were heterosexual men for whom violence was an ego defense against intense psychic pain and loss of self-esteem. The crisis was provoked by conflicts over dependency and power, or lack of power, often symbolized by homosexual feelings or acts that were felt by the patients as proof of their dreaded homosexuality. Woods calls this state "pseudohomosexual panic." The act of violence is meant to ward off such feelings by serving as a demonstration of power, strength, and competitive victory through aggression. The process gives rise to or reinforces a denial of underlying passivity. It makes the patient feel manly because, he believes, he is in control. Woods cautions against injudicious interpretations of latent homosexuality since these can increase fear, at times to the point of panic.

Illustrative Case Histories

The following three case examples are drawn from my own practice and are meant to highlight several key points — that when a psychiatrist is murdered, this tragedy may often be due to a failure to correctly elicit and appraise a patient's past history of violence and be guided by such information, and lack of skill, experience, and alertness to spot the crisis and handle it effectively no matter how frightened the psychiatrist may be.

Case no. 1. Pat, a 31-year-old single white man, had been diagnosed as suffering from a schizophrenic reaction, paranoid type, at the age of 16. He had been admitted then to a well-known private psychiatric institution in the East. His admitting psychiatrist asked him what he thought about his future, and Pat said, "Well, I don't know. Get me a gun, and I'll shoot people's heads off." His psychiatrist wrote immediately after that comment, "Patient lacking in insight." Was he? He killed another psychiatrist in a suburban area near Detroit in the summer of 1981. What happened between that psychiatrist, Dr. T., and Pat is worth examining.

Pat had been Dr. T.'s outpatient for four years. Dr. T., born and reared in the Middle East, had great difficulty speaking English. He saw Pat four times a year and on an occasional emergency basis because Pat was frequently depressed, had made several suicide attempts, and hallucinated auditorily. He relied on medication as control for Pat. For reasons never clarified, Dr. T.'s customary treatment hour consisted of answering telephone calls, sometimes lasting 25 minutes, writing notes about his previous appointment, and talking to Pat (or any patient) for about 10 minutes. He had prescribed Navane 5 mg *q.i.d*, and when Pat was especially agitated, he added Stelazine 5 mg *t.i.d*.

Before he killed Dr. T., Pat had been struggling with a mounting urge to kill himself. He felt great psychic pain and thought there was no future or purpose to his life. To his surprise, he obtained a license to purchase a firearm despite his psychiatric history and unfamiliarity with guns. Four days later, after unsuccessfully trying to kill himself, he called his psychiatrist for an emergency appointment. As usual, the psychiatrist was writing notes about his previous appointment. He did not look at Pat once; otherwise he would have seen Pat enter his office wearing hip-hugging "cutoffs," with his gun protruding prominently out of his pocket. The other pocket bulged with bullets.

Pat interrupted Dr. T.'s note-writing and announced that he wanted to kill himself. Instead of looking up or assuring Pat he did not want him to do that, he kept writing, asked how he would do it, and turned his back on Pat while reaching for a textbook. Pat did not answer except to ask if he could use Dr. T.'s bathroom. Without giving up his apparent fascination with his note-writing, Dr. T. agreed. Pat exited, checked his gun in the bathroom, and heard voices urging him to kill Dr. T. "It doesn't matter anymore," the voices said. "You had better do it now." He re-entered Dr. T.'s office, fired at him five times, reloaded, and then shot the probably now-dead psychiatrist two more times. Ironically, three of the shots were in the back of Dr. T.'s head. Pat had fulfilled his earlier prophecy: "Get me a gun, and I'll shoot people's heads off!"

Case no. 2. Dr. H. had completed his psychiatric residency training in a well-known research type of psychiatric facility in Michigan. His entry into the training program had followed several years of general medical practice in a small city, about 60 miles from his training locations. After graduation he returned to his own community and practiced general psychiatry in a general hospital and office for three to four years.

Dr. H. admitted Bill, a 28-year-old single white man, for 10 days in April 1975, and readmitted him for another 10 days 11 days after his discharge from his first admission to the psychiatric unit of a small general hospital. Dr. H. had diagnosed him as suffering from a paranoid state. Bill presented a history of feeling he had been poisoned and believed that someone must have hated him deeply to have done such a terrible thing. He requested a total-body x-ray from his psychiatrist. Just four weeks before his first psychiatric admission, he had been admitted to another hospital with the same complaints and had been given a work-up by a urologist with no significant results. Following that admission, Bill became more agitated.

In January, 1975, he had had a craniotomy at still another hospital following a subdural hematoma arising from a bar fight. It was also known that Bill, a gigantic man who often fought in bars, had a significant history of alcoholism.

All radiologic, blood chemistry, and neurological studies were normal. Bill remained suspicious and doubtful and was obsessed with the idea that he was about to die from arsenic poisoning. He attributed his sexual impotency to this obsession.

A probate court commitment petition had been granted with the first admission under the care of Dr. H., but admission to the general hospital instead of to a state hospital was permitted because Bill's father was a well-known city official. His commitment petition had read that he was behaving in a bizarre manner and was considered dangerous to himself and others. However, despite his commitment to the general hospital and despite receiving Thorazine, Dilantin, and phenobarbital, he signed himself out against medical advice. For reasons unclear to me after my review of all those records, Dr. H. commented in his discharge summary that Bill had shown some improvement in his orientation and behavior. It was apparent that the psychiatrist did not see from the records how dangerous Bill actually was.

In July, 1975, a psychiatrist in Detroit cleared Bill and said he did not require admission to a hospital. This was after Bill had threatened another person with an unloaded rifle; he then proceeded to Dr. H.'s home. At midnight he used his unloaded rifle as a battering ram and broke in through the French doors of Dr. H.'s bedroom. Dr. H. grabbed for a pearl-handled knife on his nightstand. As Bill and he grappled, Bill reached for some large slivers of heavy glass from the door he had smashed in. Dr. H. called the sheriff's department for help. Over the next 12 minutes the dispatcher was forced to listen to Dr. H.'s screams as he was stabbed 14 times by Bill. Dr. H.'s wife leaped out through the battered French doors as Bill also stabbed her twice with large, long sections of glass. She escaped and lived. Dr. H. died while moaning over the phone.

Bill was captured by a deputy as he walked to his own car, his clothes covered with Dr. H.'s blood.

I evaluated him for the prosecution and found him incompetent to stand trial, as did some other forensic psychiatrists. Finally, in 1981, Bill was convicted of second-degree murder of Dr. H. and the attempted murder of Dr. H.'s wife. Bill had told bar buddies that he planned to kill Dr. H. because he felt the doctor had poisoned him with arsenic and caused his impotency.

Case no. 3. Linda, a 28-year-old single black woman, was the mother of two children. She had been appointed to the police department of a small city in Michigan when the affirmative-action programs encouraged police departments to hire members of racial and religious minority groups as well as women. She had served with her department for four years and was charged with felonious assault when she shot her partner in an argument over who would drive their patrol car. Her chauvinistic partner had demanded to drive, and she shot him in the leg. He then shot her in the chest. Both recovered. She was acquitted on the basis of a self-defense that utilized both racism and sexism as legal issues. The department was forced to rehire her but was permitted to insist she be graduated from a police academy out of town before she could be recertified. She failed in her efforts because she could not obtain passing grades.

Her attorney filed a worker's compensation petition, sent her to me for a psychiatric forensic evaluation, and asked me to treat her as well. I diagnosed her as a schizophrenic, paranoid type. I was aware of her antiwhite sentiments and felt that since I was an active police officer as well as a psychiatrist, there would be some common bond. It was a near-fatal mistake.

A week after she had missed her fourth appointment (she had said very little during the first three), I received a phone call. She said, "When's my damned appointment?" I assured her soothingly that I was happy to hear from her because I had been unsuccessful in reaching her by phone since her missed appointment, and said that I would see her that day if she could make it in from her own city. She mumbled that she could. Four hours later she called again, making the same angry demand. By this time I was sure she was actively psychotic, confused, and hearing voices. I calmly assured her that I would meet her at 5 p.m. I called another deputy and asked if he could sit in the waiting room from 5:10 onward because I was concerned about a disturbed former police officer and wanted his backup. I had no secretary then. He assured me I could count on him. Then I called her attorney (who was also black) and asked him to call me at 5:15 p.m. because if I could not calm her down by then, I wanted to count on him to talk to her, to help calm her obviously agitated state. Both parties agreed to my requests, but both failed either to appear or to call. After her arrival and until she left, I was totally alone. I had an off-duty 38-caliber handgun in my belt, out of view, under my vest.

When she arrived, she was stone-faced and was insulting toward me. I did not exist. Her mechanical movements were hostile. She cocked her head like a bird listening to the movements of a worm. She was hearing voices. Her opening statement was, "Okay, you fat bastard, I'm ready for you!"

I could see that she needed more space than my small waiting room afforded in terms of body "buffer zone." I backed up slowly, invited her into the larger examination room, and commented, "It seems you're pretty upset. I'm glad you're here. I feel you need to talk to me."

She proceeded swiftly to the chair farthest from me. I knew she needed a seating arrangement that was not physically intimate and had arranged for that herself. Displaying dead eyes and a gaze as if I were not there, she placed her large, flat purse on her lap, opened the flap, and inserted her right hand. I suspected she had a handgun there. My hand was nearly touching my own gun.

I had a decision to make. I had several quick fantasies of a shootout between us. I saw headlines about a psychiatrist/police officer shooting it out with a patient and former police officer. I decided to defuse her the best way I could and to use lethal force only if I had no other alternative. I would pull my off-duty gun only if I saw her right arm muscles begin to move or if she withdrew a gun and pointed it at me. While observing her, I kept up a running commentary because she simply was not talking. I felt that staring at her would accomplish nothing and might aggravate her feeling of isolation and estrangement. There was no one else to call. My own outside resources had failed me.

What I said went something like this: "I am most distressed to see you so upset and hardly able to talk. I can see where you need me to help you come down from your mood. I think, when you called me for an appointment, you were asking me for help. The best way for you to come out of this is to talk out your feelings. I sense that you are hearing voices, which must be pretty frightening to you. It looks like they might tell you to do things you don't want to do. All I want is for you to hang on and keep control so I can help you. This is the right place to talk it out. We can work out a way of helping you keep control so you don't have to feel so angry."

It began to work. Soon I observed her looking at me as if she saw me. Her right arm relaxed and, after a short time, she withdrew it without a weapon in her hand. I kept verbally rewarding her for seeing me and keeping control of herself. I told her I was delighted that her mood of anger was lifting. It was apparent that I was free from apparent danger. She smiled appropriately, with a suggestion of warmth. As the hour ended, she was more relaxed, as was I. I told her that I was glad she had kept the appointment and that I felt she might be more comfortable if we could arrange hospitalization and prescribe the right amount of medication for her. She agreed. I informed her I would be contacting her family to make arrangements, and she agreed again.

Later, through her attorney and her family, she was admitted to another hospital under the care of another psychiatrist who was also black. I reasoned the wisdom of that decision on the basis that I had no business treating her with her condition and feelings against whites. I had made a near-fatal error in assuming I could handle her problem.

She left the hospital after a few days and was committed to a state hospital. That was the last I saw of her.

Defusing her seemed to have been relatively easy after I had drained off some of my own anxiety through fantasies, which helped me to see my options for managing her. I chose the only sensible option—defusing her and bringing her in for a safe landing, so to speak. I allowed distance between us, talked to her softly and without provocation or anger, and did not challenge her sense of power in holding her gun. I did not demand its surrender or try to physically disarm her. My weapon was not pulled defensively, and I stayed with the best way of coping with her: communication, supportive statements, encouragement to maintain control, and reward for appropriate behavior.

My defusement technique was based on my years of work as a part-time police officer and forensic psychiatrist who has worked in jails and prisons and as an emergency-room psychiatrist and city physician. This was not the first close call or confrontation with a potentially violent and armed patient. I have never had to pull a weapon defensively except once, in breaking through a door to bring out a barricaded gunman who may or may not have been armed.

Principles of Preventive Management

It should be apparent, from the literature and from these case illustrations, that patients who demonstrate paranoid type of schizophrenic reactions or persons with prominent paranoid symptoms or traits are probably the most dangerous to the psychiatrist.

The psychiatrist must always exercise care in obtaining a detailed history regarding violent behavior, ownership or use of firearms or other lethal weapons, previous psychiatric hospitalizations, arrests for violent behavior, and aggressive types of fantasies. As the psychiatrist initiates treatment with a psychotic patient, he must focus his attention on psychotic transference feelings toward him from the patient. He must also observe his own behavior: Is he too intimate with the patient? Does he have too much physical contact? He must avoid being overly solicitous or critical of his patient. Furthermore, he must not procrastinate in fulfilling reasonable requests from patients for some action on his part, such as writing a letter. He must not remain silent when his patient is angry and agitated. He must be firm but sensitive and able to establish reasonable limits. Talking out feelings is an absolute must; encouragement to act out angry feelings for a person barely able to establish control over violent feelings poses a risk that defies description. Talking softly, gently disapproving of violent alternatives, and offering to hold a weapon for a patient and giving him a receipt are effective techniques. Such a receipt can include a clause stating that the patient agrees he cannot have his weapon back until both he and the psychiatrist concur. If the psychiatrist is too uncomfortable about holding the patient's weapon, a relative or other responsible party must be found and asked to participate in making the same kind of receipt contract.

When dealing with the violent or angry patient, the psychiatrist must establish and maintain eye contact at all times. He must know what feelings are expressed in his patient's eyes and must watch the hands for signs of fist formation or fingering of some heavy object or weapon. Had Dr. T. seen the gun sticking out of Pat's pocket, he would have requested that it be turned over for safekeeping and Pat would have been relieved. It would have meant that Dr. T. was the effective rescuer that Pat needed him to be.

If such rescue fails or the psychiatrist practices denial about a risk of violence, the patient may attack him with rage. He feels abandoned by the psychiatrist because he was not rescued from his own rage.

Physical disarming may work in the movies but seldom is effective in psychiatric office practice. Supporting the patient in his agreement to let the therapist keep a weapon for him during his emotional upheaval has been effective. It has the additional value of letting the patient feel that he is participating as an equal in his own control. When this happens, the psychiatrist can congratulate his patient on his good judgment, control, and emotional growth. That is what the patient desperately needs from his psychiatrist at the time.

Calling others for help may inflame the patient. If they are available and do arrive, they may be provocative toward the patient and worsen the management problems for the psychiatrist. Pleading with the armed patient who portends assault is one of the most common reactions of a frightened victim, who will reason that there is a spouse or children who need his life to continue. It often fails, for to the frustrated patient, who knows only losses in his life at the time of his rage, murder may look attractive because it makes him feel more powerful than his psychiatrist and he can avenge his own deficiencies and failures in love by depriving the psychiatrist's family of their loved one.

If the psychiatrist finds himself in a situation where his patient is holding a firearm on him in his office, he can, in spite of his terror, say something that might help save his life. In a quiet voice he could say, "You have the power. I respect that in the gun you are holding on me. I know you're upset, and so am I. I think it would be easier for me to help you if I didn't have to stare at that gun. Could we make a deal? Would you mind just letting it rest on the seat or table next to you while we talk? When I don't have to worry about it going off—something I feel you don't want either—we can relax a little more and find a way of helping you. I will make no effort to reach for your gun. I think we'd both feel better talking this out and finding an easier and more comfortable way of helping you deal with your situation."

It should be obvious that this approach can draw the patient into an agreement. It is unprovocative and noninflammatory. It offers help and invites the patient to enter an agreement by which he, too, is responsible for achieving control. And once he lowers his gun or weapon, he is demonstrating his willingness to submit to the reasonable limit-setting of the psychiatrist. It will be easier to enlist his cooperation later in permitting the psychiatrist to hold his gun for him.

Once the threat of violence has receded, regardless of whether the patient has gone home or been admitted to a hospital, the psychiatrist should call the patient, thank him for being so cooperative, and tell him how pleased he is that they could work out a rational solution that was better than one involving violence. This kind of human gesture and antiviolence message should be communicated to the violent patient. This is how he can be assisted to develop other options for dealing with fear, isolation, and imagined threat.

I believe that the psychiatrist must find ways, through verbal communication and by playing the right ego-role model, to help his violent patient reconstitute his otherwise fragile ego. As he accepts the psychiatrist's suggestions about coping with conflict in nonviolent ways, the patient can dilute his own dangerousness and inner feelings of helplessness. The psychiatrist profits most by encouraging his patient to share in the search for control. The patient feels better when he has made that important decision not to be violent toward his rescuer and special psychological resource. This process must be realized before other measures can be brought into play.

Other measures, of course, require the psychiatrist to make a decision about appropriate psychotropic medication after the crisis. Along with this, hospitalization is often a consideration—as well, perhaps, as further in-depth medical, neurological, or psychological studies. Again, emphasis must be placed on the fact that the crisis of impending violence must be handled first.

Summary

It seems that the psychiatrist who is most likely to find himself the target of a homicidal patient is one who does not pay sufficient attention to the interpersonal dynamics of the treatment situation and relies too heavily on psychotropic medication. He is often insensitive, unobservant, provocative, power-oriented, and unable to share power with his patients. He has often been made a transference object by a psychotic patient and has failed to comprehend and manage that transference effectively. In some instances, he may have overlooked the potential for violence in depressed patients, failing to appreciate that the distance between an urge to commit suicide and one to commit murder can sometimes be very short indeed. There is, of course, always the completely unforeseeable accident—the psychiatrist-victim who has barely had any contact with the homicidal patient before the murder takes place. But denying the potential danger when recognizable signs have presented themselves and failing to rise to the occasion affirmatively to reach the patient too often set the stage for tragedy.

References

1. Ekblom B: *Acts of Violence by Patients in Mental Hospitals*, Scandinavian University Books, Uppsala, 1970.

2. *Ibid.*, p. 10.

3. Kalogerakis MG: The assaultive psychotic patient. *Psychiatr. Q.* 45:372–381, 1971.

4. Coping with assault — A test for the therapist. *Psychiatric News*, July 2, 1975, p. 7.

5. Madden DJ, Lion JR, Penna MW: Assaults on psychiatrists by patients. *Am. J. Psychiatry* 133:422–425, 1976.

6. Woods SM: Violence: Psychotherapy of pseudohomosexual panic. *Arch. Gen. Psychiatry* 27:255–258, 1972.

15

Dangerousness as a Criterion for Involuntary Commitment
Robert L. Sadoff

EDITOR'S NOTE

Changes in social philosophy have brought about significant changes in legislation and judicial rulings that affect psychiatric patients. One of the recent shifts of this nature is the gradual departure from the traditional concept of society having the right and obligation to act to care for those who cannot care for themselves to a more "police power doctrine" whereby a person's right to freedom takes precedence over all other needs except for the safety of society. Hence the emergence of "dangerousness" — to others or to oneself — as the primary grounds for involuntary hospitalization.

The result of this trend is confusion. Many people who are severely ill and in need of care but unwilling to be hospitalized cannot be forced to that alternative. Dangerousness itself defies definition. How does a violent act differ from a violent intent? If a patient is committed for being dangerous, what is being treated? The illness can be alleviated, but this may or may not affect the risk of future aggression. When is the patient who has been hospitalized because of violent behavior no longer a menace? Who should make that decision?

The matter of whether violent behavior can be reliably predicted is a seriously controversial one, yet psychiatrists are called on to testify in such matters and, in practice, they are even confronted with the legal demand to reveal violent intentions expressed by patients in violation of ordinary confidentiality.

In an age in which violence has become a national and international concern, it is no surprise that this issue has seriously touched the professional lives of psychiatrists in a most central way.

Introduction

The *parens patriae* rule for involuntary hospitalization, according to which the state acted as a good parent taking care of its citizens who were unable to take care of themselves, has given way in most jurisdictions to the police power doctrine. Formerly, patients were committed to the hospital if they were mentally ill and in need of hospitalization. Initially, the petition was signed by one physician; this later was changed in most states to a two-physician commitment. The reasoning was that one physician could be a friend of the family, and the patient could be put in the hospital "for his own good" at the request of the family. The purpose of a second independent physician was to insure that such collusion did not occur. However, in many jurisdictions, the two psychiatrists would examine the patient together and there would not be a truly independent examination. It was soon determined that in the criteria for hospitalization, the phrase "in need of hospitalization" was unconstitutionally vague, and the newer concept of mentally ill and "dangerous" was instituted, especially in the case of *Lessard v. Schmidt.*[1]

Defining "Dangerousness"

In most jurisdictions the concept is undefined, with the determination of dangerousness left up to the examining psychiatrist. Also, in most jurisdictions the concept includes danger of harm to oneself as well as danger of harm to others. In some jurisdictions there is a time limitation imposed; in Pennsylvania,[2] for example, there is a 30-day limit for the examination following the dangerous behavior, as well as for the prediction that such dangerous behavior would continue if the patient were not hospitalized within the next 30 days. The danger includes danger to others and three types of danger to one's self:

1. Danger of suicide.
2. Danger of self-destructive acts of a physical, aggressive nature.
3. Danger of neglect which would lead to physical harm to the patient.

All of these dangers, of course, are related to and caused by the person's mental illness.

The concept of dangerousness continued to be justified by mental health attorneys, who argued by referring to John Stuart Mill's claim: "The only purpose for which power can be rightfully exercised over any member of a civilized community, against his will, is to prevent harm to others. His own good, either physical or moral, is not a sufficient warrant."[3]

Thus, there are now people who are severely mentally ill but not "dangerous" by vague standards, who are not hospitalizable against their will. Some of these people are referred to with such labels as the "vent men" or "bag ladies." These are people who have no homes or no places of stable residence and either live on the heat vents near large buildings or travel in the urban areas carrying their possessions in shopping bags. However, since they are dangerous to no one (except, perhaps, to themselves through neglect), they are not commitable. Society has learned to tolerate those who are different as long as they are not violent.

In using the concept of "dangerousness" as a criterion for involuntary hospitalization, several authors have attempted to define the word "dangerous." Kozol et al.[4] defined dangerousness as "a potential for inflicting serious bodily harm on another." With that definition it appears that under proper clinical conditions, everyone would be dangerous to a certain extent.

Goldzband[5] considers that dangerousness is "the quality of an individual or a situation leading to the potential or actuation of harm to an individual, community or social order. It is inherent in this definition that dangerousness is not necessarily destructive, although frequently seen as such by specific individuals or social orders threatened by such a quality." This definition appears to be limited to the sociological rather than the intrapsychic.

Heller[6] gives us a complex intrapsychic definition as follows: "Dangerousness, then, may be viewed as either a transient or a lasting state of impairment of certain ego functions . . . secondary to a variety of constitutional, organic, psychologic, developmental or environmental factors, and resulting in a recognizable deterioration of the specific functions of judgment, self-observation and the capacity to defend against anxiety or tension." This is a fine psychodynamic definition of dangerousness, but does not appear to be sufficiently comprehensive for use in testimony for involuntary commitment.

Problems of Dangerousness as a Criterion

Some of the problems of using dangerousness as a criterion for involuntary commitment are the following:

First, we do not have treatment for dangerousness. We may treat people or illnesses but not dangerousness. Thus though a person who is committed as both mentally ill and dangerous may be treated and his mental illness may improve or go into remission, his potential for dangerousness may be as high as it was previously. This is so because all dangerous behavior is not necessarily related to the mental illness of the individual who is considered to be dangerous.

Thus, in the case of *State v. Davee*[7] the judge would not discharge Mr. Davee even though he was no longer mentally ill and could not benefit from traditional treatment within the hospital. The judge considered that Davee was still sufficiently dangerous to require treatment. In that case, in order to keep Davee in the hospital, the Supreme Court of Missouri had to redefine "treatment" to include observation and containment rather than the use of medication or psychotherapy.

It appears, then, that this is one of the serious problems of utilizing dangerousness as a criterion for commitment. People may maintain their potential for violent behavior while their mental illness goes into remission. The hospital will then be left with a number of people who are only "dangerous" but not mentally ill and not in need of hospitalization.

A second problem regarding the use of dangerousness as a criterion for involuntary commitment is the need to be able to predict when a person is no longer dangerous as he is about to be discharged. Psychiatrists have sufficient difficulty in predicting that a person is going to become violent under certain conditions; it is more difficult to predict that a person no longer has the potential for violent behavior when he is discharged.[8] The difficulty lies in the environment within the hospital where the patient may feel secure and not express the behavior which led him to the hospital in the first place. How will the psychiatrist know, based on his observations of the patient in a protected environment of the hospital, whether that patient will become violent if he is discharged into an open community?

A third difficulty arises when the predictive elements of dangerousness include an overt act on the part of the patient. Some researchers have expressed belief that psychiatrists cannot predict dangerousness or violent behavior in an individual unless that person has in the past expressed violent behavior under certain clinical conditions. Others have determined that threats of harm without an overt act may be significant and sufficient cause for hospitalization on the basis of dangerousness. The case of *Mathew v. Nelson*[9] adequately displays this apparent conflict. Most of the expert witnesses who testified in that case stated that it did not matter whether a person committed an overt act or not; the psychiatrist had no expertise in the prediction of dangerousness.

The Question of the Psychiatrist as Expert in Predictions

A corollary difficulty with respect to the use of dangerousness as a criterion for hospitalization lies in the development of psychiatrists who claim an expertise in such predictions. Because psychiatrists have testified that a particular individual is both mentally ill and dangerous, the courts have come to believe that psychiatrists have developed a particular expertise in this regard. Thus, psychiatrists may be held to a standard of care which includes their ability to make such predictions when, in fact, most psychiatrists acknowledge that they have no such ability.

Attorneys such as Ennis and Litwack have concluded that psychiatrists cannot predict future violent behavior any better than the average lay person.[10] In a series of studies, Steadman and Cocozza have determined that psychiatrists have no expertise in the prediction of dangerousness or future violent behavior.[11] Despite these studies and most psychiatrists' own beliefs, the criterion of dangerousness continues, and psychiatrists continue to testify that certain individuals are both mentally ill and dangerous in order to effectuate their commitment to the hospital.

If a psychiatrist is deemed to be an expert in the prediction of dangerousness, he is then also deemed to be an expert in the prediction of non-dangerousness in particular individuals. Thus, if a patient is prematurely discharged from the hospital—i.e., leaves the hospital and then goes into the community and kills himself or injures or kills someone else—the psychiatrist will be criticized for having failed in his ability to predict such behavior. Often the psychiatrist and/or the hospital will be sued by the family of the patient or by the family of the victim if homicide is involved. The claim will be that the psychiatrist "should have known" that the patient was still "dangerous" and should not have been discharged from the hospital into the community.

On the other hand, the psychiatrist treating the patient in the hospital is under pressure by attorneys from the mental health bar who are insisting on "least restrictive alternative" and less than maximum security provisions. The psychiatrist in this case must be the one to make the decision about adequate treatment and adequate security regarding his patient. Most psychiatrists would prefer to act conservatively in this regard and keep the patient in the hospital longer in order to avoid a tragedy. Some have recommended that if the judge has the responsibility for committing a patient and thereby depriving him of his liberty, it should be the judge who restores liberty to the patient and makes the decision about discharge with the help of the treating psychiatrist. However, some psychiatrists are reluctant to call upon the judge for such decisions because they feel this is a medical decision and not a judicial one. In difficult cases, however, it may be prudent to utilize the immunity of the court in helping the psychiatrist make a decision that would not be wise for him to make alone.

Another difficulty that has arisen as a result of the psychiatrist being seen as an expert in the prediction of dangerousness in his patient is the so-called "Tarasoff phenomenon." In the Tarasoff case[12] the Supreme Court of California decided that the treating psychiatrist or psychologist has a special duty to third parties who may be injured by the violent behavior of their

patient. The court indicated that the psychiatrist or psychologist has a duty
to warn the third party if his patient specifically threatens to harm the other
person. That is, the psychiatrist must breach the confidentiality of the
doctor-patient relationship in order to preserve the life or safety of the third
person. This concept was upheld in New Jersey in the case of *McIntosh v.
Milano.*[13]

The American Psychiatric Association argued in an amicus brief that the
California Supreme Court reached its decision erroneously based on the
belief that psychiatrists could predict dangerousness or violence in their
patients. The court gave the opinion that even though psychiatrists may not
be experts in predicting violence, they certainly are aware of the potential
harm a patient can cause if the patient threatens to harm the third person
and the psychiatrist believes that the patient is serious in his violent
intent.

Dangerousness: A Critical Overview

In commenting on the link between mental illness and dangerousness,
Shah[14] notes with some concern: "It is somewhat difficult to discern how
this link between mental illness and dangerous behavior came about and
why it continues to be maintained with such enduring zeal with regard to the
entire group of persons officially defined as mentally ill." He concludes
that, in part, the linking of dangerousness with mental illness enables society to utilize preventive detention against certain groups of individuals,
namely the mentally ill (e.g., *State v. Davee*). Possibly this link has arisen
and has been maintained out of the generally held myth that all mentally ill
persons are not dangerous but all dangerous ones are mentally ill.

In arguing against the use of dangerousness as a criterion in commitment
proceedings, Peszke[15] argues that such commitment procedures utilizing
dangerousness as a criterion could be harmful, leading to "an upsurge in
belligerent behavior among mentally ill persons who want attention and
realize they must appear 'dangerous' to obtain it." Peszke feels that from a
medical viewpoint it may be necessary at times to commit nondangerous
persons for treatment. If this is not done, he states, this criterion of dangerousness would lead to a "denial of needed treatment for many persons
whose mental illness makes them withdraw and are otherwise non-aggres-
sive." He states the obvious conclusion raised by a number of clinicians: "It
does not strike me as reasonable or responsible that, for the purpose of
treatment, individuals who are mentally ill and whose form of illness is
expressed in belligerent activity will be treated and those who are withdrawn
and catatonic will be neglected."

John Monahan,[16] who has conducted research studies in the prediction of dangerousness, concludes that utilizing dangerousness as a criterion for commitment will lead to a greater number of commitments, since psychiatrists who make such predictions usually err on the side of conservatism; they predict that people will be dangerous who may not be so in order to include those who are. Laves,[17] an attorney, supports this conclusion when she notes that "the dearth of psychiatric research into the question of dangerousness has led to extreme subjectivity in its definition by professionals and to overprediction of its occurrence." Finally, she concludes that psychiatrists should "abdicate the role of expert in legal proceedings of this nature, since they can by no means aid petitioners for commitment in the production of proof beyond a reasonable doubt or by a preponderance of the evidence."

Shah[18] is quite concerned about the use of dangerousness that is poorly defined and asks the following questions:

1. What kinds of behavior are sufficiently threatening to society to be officially defined as dangerous?
2. With what degree of certainty can one say that an individual will in the future engage in dangerous behavior and, if so, over what period of time?

Appropriate Conditions for Predicting Dangerousness

Psychiatrists, as clinicians, can aid the court in making certain predictions about behavior in particular patients. They are able (as are many others including correctional officers, mental health aides, police officers and others) to predict when a particular person is going to explode or become imminently violent. One does not need to be a psychiatrist, however, to make such a prediction, and that type of prediction would not be relevant to commitment proceedings.

The second area where clinicians may be helpful to the court in making such predictions is if the prediction is limited to clinical conditions. That is to say, in the case of a patient who is labeled paranoid schizophrenic, and who has in the past under certain clinical conditions become violent, a psychiatrist can reasonably predict that that person under those same clinical conditions will become violent again. The conditions may include his stopping his medication, drinking alcohol to excess, having his word challenged in a bar, which then leads to a fight. The psychiatrist may also be able to predict that a particular male who has had numerous bouts of violent behavior with his wife when she challenged him or spoke up to him would in the future—under the same clinical conditions—again become violent.

To go beyond the obvious clinical conditions under which people can become violent is to enter the world of speculation. It does not behoove the clinician, the psychiatrist, to speculate in the court that a particular individual being evaluated for possible commitment could become violent or dangerous, unless clinical evidence exists to support such a conclusion.

John MacDonald[19] has written extensively on homicidal threats or the threat to kill and has offered clinical guidelines in assessing individuals with such potential. Bernard Rubin[20] has written on the "prediction of dangerousness in mentally ill criminals" and has offered specific guidelines and criteria, including past history, biological considerations, and psychodynamic aspects, which are helpful especially in criminals but may not translate to commitment of non-criminal individuals.

John Monahan[21] has written on prediction research and the emergency commitment of dangerous, mentally ill persons and concludes that there is a qualitative difference between predictions of violence made in the community for the purpose of short-term emergency commitment, and those reported for longer-term institutionalized patients and prisoners. He believes that research on the failure to predict violence "accurately in the latter situation cannot reasonably be extrapolated to a similar conclusion in short term emergency commitment cases."

Summary

It would seem that dangerousness has invaded the criteria for involuntary hospitalization under the police power of the state to protect the citizens. Police power is only one criterion for commitment, and *parens patriae* should not be abandoned totally in favor of police power and dangerousness. Psychiatrists have been called upon to make such predictions about violent behavior and dangerousness and have done so without proper consideration of the inherent dangers and the speculation that accompanies such unscientific predictions. Following an extensive study of this issue, the American Psychiatric Association's Task Force on Clinical Aspects of the Violent Individual prepared a report in July 1974 and concludes, "It has been noted that 'dangerousness' is neither a psychiatric nor a medical diagnosis, but involves issues of legal judgment and definition, as well as issues of social policy. Psychiatric expertise in the prediction of 'dangerousness' is not established, and clinicians should avoid 'conclusory' judgments in this regard."[22]

References

1. Lessard v. Schmidt, 349 F. Supp. 1078 (wis. 1972).

2. Act 143 taken from Senate Bill 1025, The General Assembly of Pa. Printers 1601, Sess. 1975.

3. Mill, J. S. on Liberty, quoted in: M. A. Peszke, "Is Dangerousness an Issue for Physicians in Emergency Commitment?" *Am. J. Psychiatr.* 132:825–828, 1975.

4. Kozol, H. L., Boucher, R. J., Garofalo, R. F.: The Diagnosis and Treatment of Dangerousness, *Crime and Delinquency* 18:371–392, 1972.

5. Goldzband, M. G.: "Dangerousness," *Bull. Am. Acad. Psychiatry and Law* 1:238–144, December 1973.

6. Heller, M. S.: "Dangerousness, Diagnosis and Disposition," Proceedings of Fourth Judicial Sentencing Institute, Crime Commission of Philadelphia, June 1968.

7. State v. Davee, 558 S. W. 2d 335.

8. Sadoff, R. L.: "Indications for Involuntary Hospitalization: Dangerousness or Mental Illness?" *Law and Mental Health Professions*, W. E. Barton, C. J. Sanborn, (eds.) International University Press, New York, 1978.

9. U. S. Exrel. Mathew v. Nelson, 461F. Supp. 7707 (1978).

10. Ennis, B., Litwack, T.: "Psychiatry and the Presumption of Expertise: Flipping Coins in the Courtroom," *California Law Review* 62:694–752, 1974.

11. Steadman, H., Cocozza, J: *Career of the Criminally Insane: Excessive Social Control of Deviants*, Lexington, Mass. Lexington Books, 1974.

12. Tarasoff v. Regents of the University of California, 529P. 2d 553.

13. McIntosh v. Milano, 168 N.J. Super, 466 (Law Div. 1979).

14. Shah, S. A.: "Dangerousness and Civil Commitment of the Mentally Ill: Some Public Policy Considerations," *Am. J. Psychiatr.* 132:502–505, 1975.

15. Peszke, M. A.: "Is Dangerousness an Issue for Physicians in Emergency Commitment?" *Am. J. Psychiatr.* 132:825–828, 1975.

16. Monahan, J.: "Prediction Research and the Emergency Commitment of Dangerous Mentally Ill Persons: A Reconsideration," *Am. J. Psychiatr.* 132:2, February 1978.

17. Laves, R. G.: "The Prediction of 'Dangerousness' as a Criterion for Involuntary Civil Commitment: Constitutional Considerations," *J. Psychiatr. & Law* 3:291–326, Fall 1975.

18. Shah, S. A.: *op. cit.*

19. MacDonald, J. M.: "Homicidal Threats," *Am. J. Psychiatr.* 124:4 October 1967, p. 475.

20. Rubin, B.: "Prediction of Dangerousness in Mentally Ill Criminals," *Arch. Gen. Psychiatr.* 27:397, September 1972.

21. Monahan, J.: *op. cit.*

22. American Psychiatric Association Task Force Report VIII, Clinical Aspects of the Violent Individual, July 1974, p. 33.

16

Civil Rights of Hospitalized Mental Patients:

Evolution of Court Rulings

Michael L. Perlin

EDITOR'S NOTE

The landmark case of *Wyatt v. Stickney* established certain broad principles with regard to the rights of institutionalized patients. Since then, numerous decisions have been rendered to more specifically define what those rights are and how they must be protected. For example, whereas *Wyatt* held that patients have an unrestricted right to visitation with an attorney, an Illinois federal court subsequently held that monitoring such visitations invaded the patient's right to privacy and confidentiality. Other issues dealt with have included the right to see visitors, the right to vote, freedom from reprisals for exercising constitutional rights, protection against undue seizure of assets, the right to publish a newsletter, and freedom from censorship of mail.

Broader issues have also been approached. One court determined that "control, repression, restriction, and overuse of tranquillizing medications were so pervasive . . . as to infringe on [the patient's] right of liberty in the least restrictive alternative." Dividing the potential deprivations of freedom into minor and major categories, the court then set up specific recourse for patients faced with either prospect.

Work programs are often therapeutically valuable. When, after a ruling that all patient workers had to be compensated according to the Fair Labor Standards Act, a number of state work programs were abolished, it was apparent that the patients suffered. Subsequent litigation has led to a set of guidelines that must be met with regard to patient work programs: individualized assignments must be integrated into each patient's treatment plan under the supervision of qualified staff, and the patients should be compensated at the same rate that the institution would have to pay nonpatients for the same work.

200

Although legal determination of patients' rights began in the setting of government facilities, it is obvious that private facilities will no longer be insulated from future civil rights challenges. Even whole systems, such as the Veterans' Administration, have come under court scrutiny.

To paraphrase the court statement in one recent case, the law must insure not only that patients receive adequate medical care, but they must be treated appropriately as human beings as well.

Extending the *Wyatt v. Stickney* Decision

While the most heralded United States Supreme Court decisions and much of the familiar literature dealing with the law in regard to mental patients' rights have dealt with the right to treatment[1] and the right to refuse treatment,[2] it is clear that, as the law develops, counsel representing institutionalized persons have become more sensitive to other important issues relating to daily institutional life "as a realization that filing omnibus [right to] treatment/conditions suits is not [always] a sufficient remedy"[3] for handling these problems.[4]

Several reasons account for this. First, many of the issues brought into the treatment rubric in the line of cases, beginning with the landmark decision in *Wyatt v. Stickney*[5] have needed further attention, scrutiny, explanation, and elaboration in subsequent litigation to give them contemporaneous meaning. Second, many of the problems faced by institutionalized persons are more complex than simple "treatment" language might indicate. Third, whereas *Wyatt* and its progeny were state hospital cases, different strategies might be necessary for dealing with institutional problems raised by reason of hospitalization in private, local, or federal facilities.

Although the first generation of treatment decisions simply tracked the *Wyatt* standards,[6] subsequent cases gave specific life to its listed individual rights. For example, *Wyatt* had stated that "Patients shall have the same rights to visitation . . . as patients at other public hospitals [except where specially restricted by a qualified mental health professional formulating the patient's particular treatment plan]."[7] A later federal case from Wisconsin specifically struck down a hospital policy that limited the rights of patients to allocate available visiting hours among particular individuals, on the grounds that the policy bore no rational relationship to either the security needs of the hospital or an "adequate therapy program."[8] Where *Wyatt* held that "Patients shall have an unrestricted right to visitation with attorneys,"[9] a federal court in Illinois found a cause of action stated in a case alleging a psychiatric hospital doctor and nurse monitored a patient's conversations with her attorney on the theory that such conversations were "private and [might] be privileged."[10] Finally, while *Wyatt* ordered that "Patients shall have an unrestricted right to send sealed mail,"[11] a second federal case from Wisconsin permanently enjoined hospital directors from censoring and interfering with patients' mail in any way (save for contraband inspections in the patients' presence).[12]

Clarification of Rights of Institutionalized Patients

Other post-*Wyatt* psychiatric hospital rights cases have fleshed out institutional rights in other face-specific contexts. A New Jersey court held that residency at a state facility does not per se render one ineligible to vote,[13] a federal court in that state ruled that patients have the right to be free from reprisals for exercising their constitutional rights,[14] a federal court in Pennsylvania decided that the state cannot simply seize patients' assets without notice or hearing,[15] and a Connecticut district court held that the First Amendment gives patients the right to have a newsletter distributed.[16] Non-hospital institutional cases involving pretrial detainees and/or prisoners have elaborated upon *Wyatt* in cases involving the use of telephones,[17] the wearing of one's own clothing,[18] and the right to exercise.[19] It goes without saying that hospitalized persons will be seen by the courts as having at least as many rights as those involved in the criminal process.[20]

Other litigation, however, has moved appreciably further than these largely one-issue cases to explore the limits of the "institutional rights" concept. After the court entered its first set of *Wyatt*-esque orders in the Lima State Hospital *Davis* litigation in an Ohio federal district court,[21] patients' lawyers returned to court to seek further relief. In addition to ruling on such issues as the hospital's fingerprinting practices, the need for counsel at hospital staffings, and literature censorship,[22] the court dealt with "first impression" issues, such as permissibility of hospital security measures and the application of the due process clause to disciplinary proceedings. The articulation of these issues in *Davis* reflected the importance of non-treatment issues to a hospital population.

Limits on So-Called Hospital Security Measures

On the issue of security, the Ohio court found that the measures employed by the hospital—emphasizing "control, repression, restriction, and overuse of tranquilizing medicine"[23]—were "so pervasive and oppressive as to infringe upon the plaintiffs' constitutional right to liberty in the least restrictive alternative."[24] Consequently, the court ordered an alteration in the hospital's administrative structure so that its security chief would be directly responsible to the clinical director on all matters "which affect patient treatment."[25] Thus, even though the issue was couched as a "liberty" (rather than as a "treatment") issue, the court underscored the need to have the clinical director—the official in charge of all treatment matters—as the ultimate supervisor of the security chief.

Addressing the question of the applicability of the due process clause to disciplinary hearings, the court, relying on cases involving prisoners, found that such procedural safeguards are implicated when disciplinary action restricts liberty entitlements and deprives a patient of the same right to treatment in the least restrictive alternative setting.[26] The court thus divided potential deprivations into categories of the relatively minor (e.g., loss of yard or commissary privileges) and the relatively serious (e.g., seclusion, placement in restraints, or transfer to a more secure ward).[27] For minor deprivations, minimum due process safeguards would include a prehearing notice, a hearing before an individual other than the complainant, and a written statement of the grounds for removal of the privilege.[28] For more serious deprivations, safeguards would include 24-hour written notice, the right to call witnesses and introduce evidence at a hearing before an impartial factfinder, the right to written fact-findings and a recitation of the evidence relied upon for the decision, and a right to assistance at the hearing if the patient is "illiterate or the issues complex."[29]

Thus, the court clearly expanded institutional rights far beyond the boundaries contemplated in *Wyatt*. Parenthetically, although it is arguable that the U.S. Supreme Court's *Youngberg v. Romeo* decision may have subtly cut back to some extent on the breadth of the "least restrictive alternative" concept by its unsolicited use of the phrase "reasonably nonrestrictive confinement conditions,"[30] the analysis engaged in by the *Davis* court has not been challenged since the latter decision.

The Need for Qualified Staff

In addition, a more recent opinion in the same *Davis* litigation builds on another aspect of *Wyatt*: the requirement that there be a "trained and qualified staff."[31] In reviewing uncontradicted testimony that essential in-service training was seriously deficient,[32] the court ruled that, in order for the right to treatment to be fulfilled, defendants had to provide comprehensive staff training programs that include orientation, induction training, in-service training, continuing education, the use of staff consultants, and systematic exit interviews.[33] Again, this ruling goes well beyond the scope of the original *Wyatt* case and gives life to one of the treatment requisites in a common-sense way beyond mere hortatory language, in a context likely to be embraced by hospital staff as well as by patients and their lawyers.

Work Programs in Institutions

One case study of special interest concerns the question of institutional work, an issue which has been antipodally characterized as "work therapy" or "institutional peonage."[34] Preliminarily, compulsory noncompensated work programs were proscribed by the Thirteenth Amendment,[35] the Eighth Amendment,[36] and, in *Wyatt*, by reason of the constitutional right to treatment.[37] Subsequently, however, it was held that the Federal Labor Standards Act[38] applied to all patient workers in nonfederal mental hospitals even if the work done was therapeutic, "[S]o long as the institution derives any consequential economic benefit."[39] The court, however, ordered the Secretary of Labor to "implement reasonable enforcement efforts."[40] State responses to that decision — *Souder v. Brennan* — ranged from acquiescence to total abolition of all programs.[41] Where programs were abolished, however, it soon became clear that patients were psychologically and emotionally adversely affected,[42] and were deprived of a significant vehicle by which "to secure release from the facility."[43]

In less than a year and a half after the *Souder* order became operative, however, the U.S. Supreme Court — in a case which, on its face, had nothing to do with mental patients — held that those sections of the Federal Labor Standards Act that extended minimum wage protection to all state employees were unconstitutional.[44] As these amendments had formed the underpinning of *Souder*, the Department of Labor chose to no longer "enforce the regulations promulgated pursuant to the *Souder* mandate."[45]

This, however, did not end the institutional work litigation. In yet another facet of the *Davis* litigation, the court held that, while the right to treatment did not compel the state to provide all patients with an opportunity to participate in therapeutic and compensated work programs, countertherapeutic work assignments violated that right. The court further stated that, to the extent that work programs were to be operated, a set of specific standards must be met. These include individualized assignments integrated into the patients' treatment plans performed under the supervision of appropriately qualified staff and for which the patients are compensated at the same rate that the institution would have to pay an outsider for comparable work.[46] *Davis*, thus, became the first post-*Wyatt* case to significantly expand the contours of the law in this area.

These concepts, however, were taken one step further in the New Jersey case of *Schindenwolf v. Klein*,[47] in which the plaintiffs, state hospital residents, argued that they were entitled to the right to participate in compensated, therapeutic, voluntary work programs, based on their right to treatment in the least restrictive setting,[48] the very argument rejected in *Davis*. The case was ultimately settled under the following terms: the state agreed to involve in employment and vocational rehabilitation services at least 25% of all hospital patients, to explore and utilize vocational rehabilitation services in the community, to implement the *Davis* decree regarding procedural requirements, to develop comprehensive plans for hospital employment/vocational programming, to expand sheltered workshops, to initiate affirmative action programs, and to compensate patients doing institutional work in accordance with state and federal minimum wage laws.[49]

It is not yet clear if *Schindenwolf* will have a major national impact. However, at the least, it stands for the propositions that: (1) courts will go beyond notions of treatment based simply on a medical model to vindicate economic rights of patients, and (2) a seemingly insurmountable legal defeat — the gutting of the *Souder* decision in light of the Supreme Court's ruling that struck down the pertinent wage act sections — can be overcome if familiar problems were approached in unfamiliar ways, relying on treatment concepts as well as economic principles.

Extending the Law to Private and Federal Institutions

It is also worth considering the other side of the coin of "other" institutional rights; that is, the rights of patients in "other" institutions than those run by the state or its subdivisions. While the earliest litigation concerned itself solely with state institutions and/or state systems, subsequent cases have suggested that, to some extent at least, the legal principles in question may apply equally to persons institutionalized in private facilities or in federally operated hospitals. Thus, the classification of a hospital cannot be used as an artificial barrier to insulate it from patients' allegations that their constitutional rights have been violated.

In a civil rights case brought against a private New York hospital for allegedly unlawful hospitalization, the federal court rejected the hospital's motion to dismiss the case, ruling that, under New York law, the private hospital performed a public function, thus constituting state action, a prerequisite for the maintenance of such a civil rights suit.[50] Because the private facility — New York Hospital — was "expressly included among the institutions . . . authorized by statute to participate in the governmental function of caring for the mentally disabled,"[51] and especially in light of "the considerable historical tradition of state involvement with involuntary civil commitment,"[52] and the state's "extensive regulation of those private agencies engaged in providing mental health services,"[53] a "public function" was performed, and state action found.[54] Although follow-up litigation has been limited,[55] it is likely that private facilities will be less insulated from future civil rights challenges in matters involving psychiatric hospitalization and the state process.[56]

Perhaps of more significance is recent litigation assaulting a citadel traditionally considered impervious to legal attack—the Veterans' Administration's hospital system. The case *Falter v. Veterans' Administration*,[57] began as part of an effort to have the New Jersey Patient's Bill of Rights[58]—state legislation—implemented at a V.A. facility in that state. The V.A. refused, contending that it was a federal facility and thus immune from state law.[59]

A group of patients then sued facility administrators and the V.A., seeking relief from violations of several "other" institutional rights, including visitation policies, mail and telephone use, freedom from reprisals, access to one's own clothes, and the right to exercise,[60] many of the issues addressed in the early *Wyatt* opinions. Additionally, the plaintiffs asked the court to order the V.A. to promulgate a "V.A. patients' bill of rights" so as to "provide patients and staff with . . . information, regarding their respective rights, duties, and powers, necessary to guide their actions."[61] Importantly, in addition to the usual array of constitutional and statutory arguments, the plaintiffs also sued under the equal protection clause. Veterans at the Lyons Hospital, they argued, were deprived of "numerous rights, privileges and freedoms" not denied to patients at other facilities under the V.A.'s control and supervision.[62]

When the defendants moved to dismiss the action, the court ruled that, if proven, the plaintiffs' constitutional claims under the equal protection clause would be a sufficient basis upon which it could structure relief.[63] At that posture of the case, if the plaintiffs' allegations were correct, they would demonstrate that "patients are treated in a substantially different manner at Lyons from the way that patients were treated at other V.A. hospitals.[64] Each one of the plaintiffs' substantive constitutional claims thus survived the defendants' attack, and the case was scheduled for trial.[65]

The significance of the *Falter* case should be clear. First, it demonstrates that no hospital system is impregnable where constitutional violations are alleged. Secondly, it reiterates the importance, as discussed above, of the "other" institutional rights to institutionalized patients. Thirdly, it acknowledges that an administrative "Bill of Rights" may be an essential tool of hospital rights enforcement. Finally, it extends the focus of the court's acceptable inquiry beyond the specific institution in question to an entire system to see if patients in the complaining institution have, in the court's words, "fewer perquisites"[66] than patients elsewhere in the same system.

Treating Patients as Human Beings

In summary, cases involving "other" institutional rights — medical, social, civil, and economic[67] — will probably increase in number in the coming years as courts continue to explore matters beyond either the adequacy or the unwanted imposition of medical treatment. Especially telling may be the court's dictum in *Falter*: "When I say that [patients] are treated differently, I am not referring to the substance of their medical or psychiatric treatment, I am referring to how they are treated as human beings."[68] It is likely that this inquiry — "how are they treated as human beings" — will be the subject of much future litigation.

References

1. See, *e.g.*, *Youngberg v. Romeo 457 U.S. 307* (1982); 4 App., *Task Panel Reports Submitted to the President's Commission on Mental Health* (1978).

2. See, *e.g.*, *Mills v. Rogers, 457 U.S. 291* (1982); Plotkin, "Limiting the Therapeutic Orgy: Mental Patients' Right to Refuse Treatment," 72 *Northwestern L. Rev.* 461 (1977).

3. Perlin, "Other Rights of Residents in Institutions," in 2 Friedman, ed., *Legal Rights of Mentally Disabled Persons* 1009, 1011 (P.L.I. ed. 1979) (hereinafter "Other Rights").

4. See also, e.g., Brakel, "Legal Problems of People in Mental and Penal Institutions: An Exploratory Study," [1978] *Am. Bar Found. Res. J.* 565. *See generally*, M. Perlin, *Mental Disability Law: Civil and Criminal*, Ch. 6 (Kluwer Law Books 1988).

5. 325 *F. Supp.* 781 (M.D. Ala. 1971), 334 *F.Supp.* 1341 (M.D. Ala. 1971), 344 *F.Supp.* 373 (M.D. Ala. 1972), 344 *F.Supp.* 387 (M.D. Ala. 1974), *aff'd sub. nom. Wyatt v. Aderholt*, 503 *F.*2d 1305 (5 Cir. 1974).

6. See, *e.g.*, *Davis v. Watkins*, 384 *F.Supp.* 1196 (N.D. Ohio 1974); *Gary W. v. Louisiana*, 437 *F.Supp.* 1209 (E.D. La. 1976).

7. *Wyatt*, 344 *F.Supp.*, above, at 379.

8. *Schmidt v. Schubert*, 422 *F.Supp.* 57, 58 (E.D. Wis. 1976).

9. *Wyatt*, above.

10. *Gerrard v. Blackman*, 401 *F.Supp.* 1189, 1198 (N.D. Ill. 1975).

11. *Wyatt*, above.

12. *Brown v. Schubert*, 347 *F.Supp.* 1232, 1234 (E.D. Wis. 1972), supplemented 389 *F.Supp.* 281, 283–284 (E.D. Wis. 1975).

13. See, *e.g.*, *Carroll v. Cobb*, 139 *N.J. Supp.* 439, 450, 455, 345 A.2d 355 (App.Div. 1976).

14. *Rennie v. Klein*, 462 *F.Supp.* 1131 (D.N.J. 1978), *suppl.* 476 *F.Supp.* 1294, 1302 (D.N.J. 1979), mod. 653 *F.*2d 836 (3 Cir. 1981), vacated and remanded on other gds. 458 U.S. 1119 (1982), on remand 720 *F.*2d 266 (3 Cir. 1983).

15. See, *e.g.*, *Vecchione v. Wohlgemuth*, 377 *F.Supp.* 1361, 1369 (E.D. Pa. 1974),

further proceedings 426 *F.Supp.* 1297 (E.D. Pa. 1977), aff'd 558 F.2d 150 (3 Cir. 1977), *cert.* den. 434 U.S. 943 (1977).

16. *B.P. v. Martin*, Civil Action No. H-78-104 (D.Conn. 1978) (summarized in "Other Rights," note 3, above, at 1028).

17. See, *e.g., Rutherford v. Pitchess*, 457 *F.Supp.* 104, 115 (C.D. Cal. 1978).

18. See, *e.g., Mitchell v. Untreiner*, 421 *F.Supp.* 886, 898 (N.D. Fla. 1976).

19. See, *e.g., Campbell v. McGruder*, 416 *F.Supp.* 100, 105 (D.D.C. 1976), mod. 580 *F.*2d 521 (D.C. Cir. 1978).

20. *Cf. Vitek v. Jones*, 445 *U.S.* 480 (1980).

21. *Davis v. Watkins*, above.

22. *Davis v. Balson*, 461 *F.Supp.* 842 (N.D. Ohio 1978).

23. *Id.* at 855 (Dr. Clark deposition).

24. *Id.* at 856.

25. *Id.* at 857.

26. *Id.* at 857–876, citing, *inter alia, Meachum v. Feano*, 427 *U.S.* 215, 224 (1976); *Walker v. Hughes*, 558 *F.*2d 1247, 1250–51 (6 Cir. 1971).

27. *Davis*, 461 *F.Supp.*, above, at 877.

28. *Id.*

29. *Id.* at 878, adopting, *in toto*, the standards of *Wolff v. McDonnell*, 418 *U.S.* 539, 563–572 (1974).

30. *Youngberg*, 457 *U.S.* at 326.

31. *Wyatt*, 344 *F.Supp.*, above, at 383.

32. *Davis v. Hubbard*, 506 *F.Supp.* 915 (N.D. Ohio 1980).

33. *Id.* at 921–922.

34. See, *e.g.,* "Other Rights," note 3, above, at 1018–1024; see also, Friedman, "Thirteenth Amendment and Statutory Rights Concerning Work in Mental Institutions," in Ennis and Friedman, eds., *Legal Rights of the Mentally Handicapped* 637 (P.L.I.ed. 1978); Friedman, "The Mentally Handicapped Citizen and Institutional Labor," 87 *Harv. L. Rev.* 567 (1974); Perlin, "The Right to Voluntary, Compensated, Therapeutic Work as Part of the Right to Treatment: A New Theory in the Aftermath of Souder,": 7 *Seton Hall L. Rev.* 298 (1976) (hereinafter "Right to Work"); Kapp, "Residents of State Mental Institutions and Their Money (or, the State Giveth and the State Taketh Away)," 6 *J. Psych. & L.* 287 (1978).

35. See, *e.g., Jobson v. Henne*, 355 *F.*2d 129, 132, n. 3 (2 Cir. 1966); *Downs v. Dep't of Public Welfare*, 368 *F.Supp.* 454, 465 (E.D. Pa. 1973).

36. See, *e.g., Jortberg v. U.S. Dep't of Labor*, Civil No. 13-113 (D.Me. 1974), at 10, cited in "Other Rights," note 3, above, at 1019.

37. 344 *F.Supp.*, above at 381.

38. 29 *U.S.C.A.* §§(r)(1), (s)(4).

39. *Souder v. Brennan*, 367 *F.Supp.* 838, 813 (D.D.C. 1973).

40. *Id.* at 809.

41. "Right to Work," note 34, above, at 300–301.

42. *Id.* at 327, nn. 151–152.

43. *Id.* at 327, n. 150, quoting Kott "Wage Programs for Mentally Retarded Residents of Public Institutions," 1 *Ment. Retard.* 161, 188 (1963).

44. *National League of Cities v. Usery*, 426 *U.S.* 833, 854 (1976).

45. *Kapp*, note 34, above, at 298–299. *National League of Cities* has subsequently been overruled by the U.S. Supreme Court in *Garcia v. San Antonio Metropolitan*

Transit Authority, 469 U.S. 528 (1985); there has as of yet been no litigation attempting to resuscitate the *Souder* methodology in wake of this most recent development. See M. Perlin, note 4, above, §6.16.

46. *Davis*, 461 *F.Supp.*, above, at 854.

47. Docket No. L-41293-75 P.W. (N.J. Super.Ct., Law Div. 1976).

48. The legal theory is based on the arguments in "Right to Work," note 34, above, at 301;p see, for an analysis, *Kapp*, note 34, above, at 300.

49. The full settlement order as to state defendants is reprinted at 5 *Ment. Dis. L. Rptr.* 62 (1981). Subsequently, a virtually identical settlement was reached with defendants representing the county institutions.

50. *Ruffler v. Phelps Memorial Hospital*, 453 *F.Supp.* 1062, 1069–1071 (S.D.N.Y. 1978).

51. *Id.* at 1068.

52. *Id.* at 1070.

53. *Id.* at 1069.

54. *Id.*

55. See, *e.g., Kay v. Benson*, 472 *F.Supp.* 850 (D.N.H. 1979) (private doctor's actions "state action"); *Brown v. Jensen*, 572 *F.Supp.* 193 (D.Colo. 1983) (citing *Ruffler* and *Kay*).

56. Although the entire "state action" concept has been recently seriously abridged by the Supreme Court, see *e.g., Blum v. Yaretsky, 457 U.S.* 991 (1982); *Rendell-Baker v. Kohn*, 457 *U.S.* 830 (1982) [but see *Edmondson v. Lugar*, 457 *U.S.* 922 (1982)], it is likely that the direct state involvement in the civil commitment and admission process, see *Brown v. Jensen*, above, will insulate the *Ruffler* line of cases from attack on these grounds.

57. No. 79-2284 (D.N.J. 1979), cited in "Other Rights," note 3, above, at 1012.

58. N.J.S.A. 30:4-24.1 and 24.2.

59. *Falter v. Veterans' Administration*, No. 79-2284 (D.N.J. 1979), complaint, at Exhibit E.

60. *Id.*, ¶¶126–135.

61. *Id.*, ¶159.

62. *Id.*, ¶153.

63. *Falter v. Veteran's Administration*, 520 *F.Supp.* 1178, 1182 (D.N.J. 1980).

64. *Id.* at 1185.

65. After trial, the defendants' motion to dismiss was granted, the court finding that plaintiffs failed to prove that their constitutional rights were violated. *Falter v. Veterans' Administration*, 632 *F. Supp.* 196 (D.N.J. 1986).

66. *Falter*, 520 *F. Supp.*, above, at 1185.

67. For another approach to the question of *economic* rights, see *Cospito v. Califano*, 89 *F.R.D.* 374 (D.N.J. 1981), on the question of the availability of procedural due process rights to juvenile and elderly patients who lose SSI funds when the Joint Commission on Accreditation of Hospital deaccredits a state hospital. See, for a full analysis, Jost, "The Joint Commission on Accreditation of Hospitals: Private Regulation of Health Care and the Public Interest," 24 *Boston Coll. L. Rev.* 835 (1983). For further proceedings, see *Cospito v. Heckler* 742 *F.* 2d 72 (3 Cir. 1984), *cert.* den. 471 *U.S.* 1131 (1985).

68. *Falter* 520 *F. Supp.*, above, at 1185.

17

The Due Process Rights of the Nondangerous Institutionalized Mentally Handicapped When Placement is Unavailable

Michael L. Perlin

EDITOR'S NOTE

The psychiatric patient who was once committed but is now ineligible for commitment has become a major focus of professional and public concern. In this chapter, the author looks at the legal aspects of the problem—specifically, the rights of such patients to adequate aftercare, and if they must continue to be institutionalized, how their inherent liberties can be preserved and protected.

The New Jersey courts appear to be pacesetters with regard to the rights of psychiatric patients. The New Jersey Supreme Court stated that "Courts have a continuing responsibility to monitor the status of all patients who remain institutionalized in mental facilities, to assure that continuing effort is being made to provide adequate residential placement." The Court also stated that "Although the State does not have the authority to continue legal commitment . . . it is not required to cast [patients] adrift into the community when the individuals are incapable of survival on their own." It called for specific procedures designed to minimize restrictions on the person's freedom, identify the patient's needs, actively investigate suitable aftercare situations, and regularly review each patient's status.

Introduction

As mental health law has developed over the past decade[1] and as courts have begun to grapple with all aspects of both procedural and substantive aspects of patients rights,[2] one overarching problem has remained, appearing virtually insoluble: what can be done in the case of a once-involuntarily committed patient who no longer meets the criteria for commitment or continued institutionalization[3] but for whom there is no suitable and available alternative placement?[4]

While this was one of the first questions raised in the debate over patients' rights issues,[5] it has been one of the last ones to be answered. While virtually every jurisdiction now has some sort of elaborate due process machinery in place to insure that persons are not committed improperly in the first place,[6] there has been almost no litigation on behalf of the thousands of persons hospitalized for extended periods who now, simply, have nowhere else to go.

The decision of the New Jersey Supreme Court—long a national leader in mental disability litigation[7]—in *In re S.L.*[8] has taken on special significance in light of the universality of the problem, the apparent lack of acceptable practical solutions, and the courts' general increased reluctance to grant relief to litigants seeking the declaration of a constitutional right to aftercare services in the community.[9] Although as of early 1988 only one other state has generally followed the S.L. approach,[10] it can be expected that the New Jersey Supreme Court's methodology will be analyzed, incorporated, and adapted by other state courts in the future.[11]

A relatively detailed analysis of pre-*S.L.* developments in New Jersey, the history of the litigation itself, and the wider implications of the court's decision should thus serve as a framework for future consideration of this issue.

For decades in New Jersey, as in most other states, mental patients never had hearings. Commitment applications were merely (and literally) "rubber stamped" in lieu of a judicial hearing.[12] In 1974 and 1975, however, counsel became available to New Jersey patients in danger of commitment as a result of a combination of events:

1. The inclusion of the Division of Mental Health Advocacy[13] in the newly-created Department of the Public Advocate[14] to provide both individual and class action legal services to "indigent mental hospital admittees"[15];

2. The promulgation of a State Supreme Court memorandum, mandating judicial reviews of civil commitments[16];

3. The United States Supreme Court's *O'Connor v. Donaldson*[17] decision;

4. The New Jersey Supreme Court's *State v. Krol*[18] decision; and

5. The New Jersey Supreme Court's wholesale revision of the court rules governing involuntary commitment procedures as part of its decision in *In re Geraghty*,[19] which mandated counsel at all such hearings and at periodic reviews, and established significant procedural due process safeguards[20] for all patients facing commitment.

As a result of these changes in the law, meaningful hearings were held for patients facing involuntary commitment, and these hearings, in fact, did make a difference: more than 70% of all clients represented by the Division of Mental Health Advocacy in its first two years of operation obtained some form of judicial relief.[21] At many of these hearings, though, trial judges began quickly to see that a significant number of patients no longer met the strict commitment criteria — mental illness and resulting dangerousness. Rather, because of years of hospitalization, the patients had lost contact with friends, families, etc., were left with no means of visible community support, and could not survive on their own. In an effort to spur placement of these patients, courts began immediately to enter orders discharging patients "pending placement," or "DPP."[22]

The importance of these placements magnified in 1978, following (1) the court's decision in *State v. Fields*[23] extending periodic review to all patients and elaborating upon the role of the court at such review hearings, and (2) the promulgation of another Supreme Court memo,[24] which specifically mandated review of DPP patients:

PATIENTS AWAITING PLACEMENT

The meetings of the Supreme Court Task Force on Mental Commitments and the Judges Assigned to Hear Mental Commitments have revealed that there is an apparent disparate practice among the various counties concerning those patients who have been determined not to be a danger to self and others but, nonetheless, have remained in the institution because of difficulties in placement. There are presently more than 500 persons in this "limbo" status. The courts have a continuing responsibility to monitor the status of all patients who remain institutionalized in a mental facility. Such patients must be reviewed. The focus of such review is to assure that a continuing effort is being made to provide adequate residential placement; a summary review conducted at least every three months is an acceptable form of follow-up.[25]

It is clear that this memo was written in response to inquiries from trial judges as to what should be done in the cases of the hundreds of patients who no longer met involuntary civil commitment standards but who could not be placed. The memo, however, was responded to in disparate ways. Some trial judges held full-blown placement hearings, others merely asked the hospital's social service director for status reports, still others viewed this memo as purely advisory (and thus not having the force of law).[26] As years passed, it became clear that, unless a case were to be decided by the Supreme Court, the problem would remain unsolved.

That case—*S.L.*—was actually a consolidated appeal of nine individual cases, involving patients who had been institutionalized for periods of time up to 52 years, but who were no longer commitable, "although they remained incapable of carrying on an independent and self-sufficient life."[27] In seven of the cases, a trial judge had classified the patients as "DPP," and scheduled review hearings in accordance with court rules.[28] However, at the review hearing, a second judge refused in each case to recognize the validity of the prior DPP adjudication, characterizing it a "nullity."[29]

The cases appeared to exemplify the confusion that had arisen as to the nature of the DPP status, regardless of whether the patient was considered a "candidate" for a nursing home, a supervised boarding home, an intermediate care facility, a group home, a facility for the mentally retarded, or other alternative.[30] They seemed to illustrate the need for clear judicial recognition of the meaning of DPP status so as to establish clear guidelines for future cases.

These cases ran the gamut on all levels. The patients ranged in age from 36 to 83; their commitments dated back as far as 1931 and as recently as 1980.[31] Their handicaps included epilepsy, mental retardation, and mental illness. One mentally retarded patient had actually been transferred from a state school to a psychiatric facility because it was thought that the mental hospital social work staff would have greater success in finding an appropriate halfway house.[32]

The cases were consolidated before the Appellate Division. That court dismissed the appeals, reasoning that a decision would have "enormous legislative and fiscal ramifications" and should thus be left for either the Supreme Court's rule-making power and/or the legislature's economic judgment.[33] It thus held the issues to be "nonjusticiable," i.e., not a proper matter for the appellate court, and dismissed the cases. The state Supreme Court granted certification almost immediately.[34]

About 14 months later, the court issued a unanimous 38-page ruling, vindicating—in virtually every aspect—the patients' claims. Writing for the court, Justice Handler couched the issue in this matter:

. . . Together these cases require us to determine the legal status of individuals who no longer meet our standards for civil commitment, yet who require some degree of custodial care, and the procedures necessary to ensure protection of their legal rights.[35]

The court began its analysis by specifically rejecting the Appellate Division's theory that the matters were nonjusticiable:

. . . The issues presented are capable of judicial resolution. They require the court to determine the legal status of certain individuals who are currently in mental institutions, the legal procedures necessary to protect their legal rights, and the duties of the State in regard to their care. In numerous situations, procedures ensuring the rights of individuals in the judicial process may be established by rule or by decision. . . . Further, these decisions are within the province of the judiciary even though they have fiscal impact on the State budget. . . . It is clear that courts cannot compel legislative appropriation, . . . but no such action is contemplated or required in this case.[36]

The court noted that plaintiffs asked for formal recognition of the DPP status as an "intermediate stage between involuntary commitment and immediate discharge," as a "logical hybrid status that responds to the legal and human situation of these patients and is consistent with the existing statutory, regulatory and decisional law."[37] Recognition of the category and promulgation of procedural guidelines, plaintiffs argued, would "ensure that the committed persons who are no longer dangerous will be integrated in an expeditious manner into settings less restrictive of their liberty."[38]

Plaintiffs were opposed by the County Counsel (of their county of prehospitalization residence) and by the Attorney General. Both resisted formal recognition of the DPP status and endorsed a report filed by a State Supreme Court Task Force that had recommended expanding the category of commitable patients to include those then in the DPP category.[39]

The court began by reviewing "certain basic principles governing the civil commitment process":[40]

. . . The authority of the State to civilly commit citizens is said to be an exercise of its police power to protect the citizenry and its *parens patriae* authority to act on behalf of those unable to act in their own best interests. . . . However, because commitment effects a greater restraint on individual liberty, this power of the State is constitutionally bounded. . . . In order to comply with due process, the State must adhere to certain procedures when committing individuals. The individual is entitled to a judicial hearing at which the State must establish the grounds for commitment by clear and convincing evidence. . . . The individual who is the subject of the hearing has the right to notice of the hearing, the right to present evidence and the right to be represented by counsel. . . .[41]

The court added that the scope of the commitment power was also "limited," quoting extensively from the United States Supreme Court's *O'Connor v. Donaldson* decision:

A finding of "mental illness" alone cannot justify a State's locking a person up against his will and keeping him indefinitely in simple custodial confinement. Assuming that the term can be given a reasonably precise content and that the "mentally ill" can be defined with reasonable accuracy, there is still no constitutional basis for confining such persons involuntarily if they are dangerous to no one and can live safely in freedom.

May the State confine the mentally ill merely to ensure them a living standard superior to that they enjoy in the private community? That the State has a proper interest in providing care and assistance to the unfortunate goes without saying. But the mere presence of mental illness does not disqualify a person from preferring his home to the comforts of an institution. Moreover, while the State may arguably confine a person to save him from harm, incarceration is rarely if ever a necessary condition for raising living standards of those capable of surviving safely in freedom, on their own or with the help of family or friends.[42]

* * * * * *

In short, a State cannot constitutionally confine without more a nondangerous individual who is capable of surviving safely in freedom by himself or with the help of willing and responsible family members or friends.[43]

The court reiterated its adherence to the *Krol* commitment standards, to *Fields'* insistence on periodic review, and to its court rule providing "for the conditional discharge of institutionalized persons in instances where lesser forms of restraint are sufficient to ensure the public safety and the individual's own well-being."[44]

With this backdrop, the Court specifically rejected the Task Force's request that the *Krol* standards be expanded to cover "an individual who by reason of mental illness is unable to care for himself without some level of aid or supervision."[45] Said the court:

. . . The civil commitment process must be narrowly circumscribed because of the extraordinary degree of state control it exerts over a citizen's autonomy. . . . To widen the net cast by the civil commitment process in the manner suggested by the Task Force is inconsistent with the central purposes of the commitment process. It would permit the State to commit individuals to mental institutions solely to provide custodial care. This authority cannot be justified as a measure to safeguard the citizenry under the police power. Nor is it a proper exercise of the State's parens patriae power because confinement in a mental hospital is not necessary to provide the care needed by individuals who are simply incapable of living independently.[46]

On the other hand, it noted:

Although the state may not commit those persons who are mentally ill but not dangerous, we believe that the State does possess certain authority in regard to these appellants. The appellants have been institutionalized for an average of over 30 years. Although legally entitled to leave the mental hospital, they are incapable of competently exercising that right due, in part, to the effects that prolonged confinement has had on their own personal capacity to survive in the outside world and on their relationships with friends and family who might provide support and assistance. The State cannot simply pull the rug from under these people when they physically deteriorate to a point where they are no longer dangerous. Although the State does not have the authority to continue the legal commitment of the appellants, it is not required to cast them adrift into the community when the individuals are incapable of survival on their own. In a proper exercise of its *parens patriae* authority, it may therefore of necessity continue the confinement of such persons on a provisional or conditional basis to protect their essential well-being, pending efforts to foster the placement of these individuals in proper supportive settings outside the institution.[47]

Under the circumstances, specific procedures must be designed, the court ordered, to "minimize restrictions on the person's liberty."[48] Such restrictions "must be related to the underlying purposes of the confinement — ensuring a safe and orderly transition of the individual into an appropriate setting least restrictive of liberty."[49]

Under these criteria, the Court established the following guidelines:

When a court determines at a commitment review hearing conducted pursuant to R. 4:74-7(f) that an individual is no longer dangerous to self, others or property by reason of mental illness, the individual should be entitled to leave the mental hospital and reenter the community. The court, however, shall make a further inquiry to determine whether the individual is capable of leaving the institution. If the court determines that the individual is not able to survive in the community independently or with the help of family or friends, the court shall direct that the individual remain in the institution, but immediately schedule a placement review hearing to occur within 60 days. At this hearing the court shall inquire into the needs of the individual for custodial and supportive care, the desires of the individual regarding placement, the type of facility that would provide the needed level of care in the least restrictive manner, the availability of such placement, the efforts of the State to locate such placement and any other matters it deems pertinent. In the event that placement can be arranged in a facility able to provide the care needed in a setting not unduly restrictive of liberty, the court shall order such placement. If immediate placement is not possible, the court shall continue the individual's confinement, require that the individual be placed in the environment least restrictive of his or her liberty within the institution, and schedule a subsequent placement review hearing to occur within six months. While the individual remains confined in the institution, all reasonable efforts within available resources shall be made to improve the individual's ability to function in a placement outside the mental hospital.

At subsequent placement review hearings, which shall occur at least every six months, the court shall inquire into the same factors as in the initial placement review as well as into the conditions of the individual's confinement. If placement is not possible, the court must determine whether the State has undertaken all good faith efforts necessary to place the individual in an appropriate setting outside the mental institution and whether in the interim the State has placed the individual in the least restrictive setting in the institution. When an individual is discharged from the institution and placed in an alternative facility, the court may require as a condition of placement that a report be submitted by the parties within a six-month period as to the overall adequacy of the individual's placement. At any time thereafter, any party or the court on its own motion may reinstitute proceedings concerning the continuing care, supervision, placement or commitment of the individual.

The individual shall have the right to counsel in these proceedings. Both the individual and counsel shall be served with notice of the time and place of each placement review hearings no later than ten days prior to the hearing. The patient's counsel shall also be entitled to inspect and copy all records relating to the patient's condition and placement, to introduce evidence and compel testimony and to cross-examine adverse witnesses.

These procedural guidelines will ensure that the continuing confinement of individuals who do not meet standards for commitment and are eligible for discharge but who are unable to survive independently will be in accord with due process. However, we believe that a complete and comprehensive review of these procedural guidelines is necessary to assist the Court in amending R. 4:74-7. We therefore submit these issues to the Supreme Court's Task Force on Mental Commitments for its reconsideration and recommendations for rule revisions that will serve to implement this decision.[50]

Unanswered Questions Affecting DDP Patients

The Court thus remanded the cases in question for immediate placement review hearings in accordance with the opinion, noting that, if at such a hearing the trial judge had reason to believe the patient has again become dangerous as a result of mental illness, a new commitment hearing would have to be scheduled in accordance with the court rules.[51]

Although the opinion was a comprehensive and carefully crafted one, many unanswered questions remained:

1. Who bears the burden of proof at a DPP review hearing? The court merely said that it cannot be allocated "with precision."[52]
2. What is the meaning of the phrase "not unduly restrictive of liberty" in alternative placement cases? Does this differ from the U.S. Supreme Court's limited characterization of the need for "reasonably non-restrictive confinement conditions?" in *Youngberg v. Romeo*?[53]
3. Where such a placement cannot be made, how can it be determined if "all reasonable efforts within available resources" (which must be made to improve the patient's ability to function in an outside placement) have been exerted?
4. How are the state's "good faith efforts" to be assessed?
5. When post-placement proceedings are "reinstituted," what questions will appropriately be before the court?
6. What will the impact of *S.L.* be outside of New Jersey?

A "second generation" of *S.L.* cases is slowly beginning to emerge in New Jersey, indicating that state court trial judges are learning to grapple with the underlying issues in fact-specific contexts.[54] While *S.L.* has not yet had a major impact outside of New Jersey, a recent decision by the New York Court of Appeals (the highest court in that state) reveals a somewhat similar approach.

Subsequent Judicial Rulings

The New York decision, *Klostermann v. Cuomo*,[55] joined appeals of two classes in two separate cases: the *Klostermann* plaintiffs (deinstitutionalized homeless persons) and plaintiffs in *Joanna S. v. Carey*[56] (patients at a New York state hospital who met the discharge criteria but for whom, like the *S.L.* appellant, no adequate aftercare placement was available). As in the *S.L.* case, the intermediate appellate court dismissed, agreeing with the trial court that the matters were "nonjusticiable."[57] As in *S.L.*, the high court reversed, holding that "the appropriate forum to determine the respective rights and obligations of the parties is in the judicial branch."[58]

Klostermann reaffirmed that the "failure to provide suitable and adequate treatment cannot be justified by lack of staff or facilities,"[59] especially where plaintiffs claim "that existing conditions violate an individual's constitutional rights"[60] The court remanded for a full trial to determine whether defendants were satisfying their statutory and constitutional obligations to provide appropriate aftercare placements for the deinstitutionalized and those capable of being deinstitutionalized.[61] That trial has not yet been held.

S.L., then, is the first case to coherently attempt to deal with one of the most significant problems facing mental health professionals, the mentally disabled, patient advocates, and governmental officials. While it has not yet had a major impact on other jurisdictions, such impact appears inevitable, in light of the universality of the problem and the New Jersey court's "track record" as a leader in the area. It is perhaps the first glimmer of light in what all agree has been an exceedingly dark tunnel.

Footnotes

1. Although the Supreme Court first found that the civil commitment process implicated the Due Process Clause of the Fourteenth Amendment in *Jackson v. Indiana*, 406 *U.S.* 715 (1972), the "modern era" of mental health law is usually thought of as beginning with that Court's declaration of a "right to liberty" for the nondangerous mentally ill in *O'Connor v. Donaldson*, 422 *U.S.* 563 (1975). See

generally, for analyses of the major trends in mental health law during this decade (in the areas of involuntary civil commitment, right to treatment, right to refuse treatment, civil rights of institutionalized persons, and the right to aftercare), Perlin, "Mental Health Law and the United States Supreme Court, 1972– 1982," *Directions in Psychiatry, Vol. 3, Lesson 5* (1983); Perlin, "Recent Developments in Mental Health Law," in Sadoff, ed., 6 *Psych. Clinics of North America* 539 (1983); Perlin, "Patients' Rights," in Michels, Cavenar, et al. ed., *Psychiatry*, Ch. 35 (1987); M. Perlin, *Mental Disability Law: Civil and Criminal*, Vol. 1 (Kluwer Law Books 1988).

2. See, *e.g., Addington v. Texas*, 441 *U.S.* 418 (1979) (burden of proof at commitment hearings); *Parham v. J.R.*, 442 *U.S.* 584 (1979) (due process requirements of juvenile commitment hearings); *Vitek v. Jones*, 445 *U.S.* 480 (1980) (due process requirements of prison-hospital transfers); *Youngberg v. Romeo*, 457 *U.S.* 307 (1982) (right of the institutionalized mentally retarded to training); *Mills v. Rogers*, 457 *U.S.* 291, (1982) (right of involuntary mental patients to refuse medication).

3. In most states involuntary commitment must be based on both mental illness and dangerousness (to self, others, or property) as a result of that mental illness. For the classic formulation, see *State v. Krol*, 68 *N.J.* 236, 344 *A.*2d 289 (Sup. Ct. 1975).

4. While this might appear at first blush to be nothing more than a slightly formal way of saying, "Where are we going to put these people?", this formulation reveals the legal and psychological complexity of the question at hand. *See generally*, M. Perlin, note 1, above, §3.56.

5. The plight of patients who could be released from public psychiatric hospitals if there were suitable alternatives available was noted by the courts as early as 1967. See *Lake v. Cameron*, 364 *F.*2d 657, 660 n.9 (D.C. Cir. 1967), and *id.* at 660 (describing the plaintiff: "[she] needs care and kindness," [not] "'constant medical supervision'."

6. See, *e.g., N.J.Ct.R.* 4:74-5; *N.Y. Mental Hygiene L.* § 9.13 *et seq.*; *Ala. Stat. Ann.* § 22.52.1 *et seq.*

7. See, *e.g., State v. Krol, supra; State v. Fields*, 77 *N.J.* 282, 390 *A.*2d 574 (Sup. Ct. 1978); *In re Grady*, 85 *N.J.* 235, 426 *A.*2d 467 (Sup. Ct. 1981).

8. 94 *N.J.* 128, 462 *A.*2d 1252 (Sup. Ct. 1983).

9. See, *e.g., Pennhurst State School and Hospital v. Halderman*, 465 *U.S.* 89 (1984).

10. See *Klostermann v. Cuomo*, 61 *N.Y.* 2d 525, 475 *N.Y.S.* 2d 247 (Ct. App. 1984).

11. The current plight of the homeless has, of course, focused considerable attention on those who have been deinstitutionalized without adequate follow-up or community treatment. See, e.g., Boffrey, "Psychiatrists Call Plight of Homeless Mentally Ill a Tragedy," *New York Times* (Sept. 13, 1984); M. Perlin, note 1, above, Chapter 7.

12. See, for a general description, Van Ness and Perlin, "Mental Health Advocacy — the New Jersey Experience," in Kopolow and Bloom, eds., *Mental Health Advocacy: An Emerging Force in Consumers' Rights* 62 (1977). Practices from other states were similar. See, e.g., Dix, "Acute Psychiatric Hospitalization of the Mentally Ill in the Metropolis: An Empirical Study," (1968) *Wash. U.L.Q.* 485.

13. *N.J.S.A.* 52:27E-21 et seq.

14. *N.J.S.A.* 52:27E-1 et seq.

15. The term is defined in *N.J.S.A.* 52:27E-23.

16. *N.J. Supreme Court Administrative Memoranda #4-74* (Nov. 1974).

17. 422 *U.S.* 563 (1975); see note 1, *supra*.

18. 68 *N.J.* 344 *A*.2d 289 (Sup. Ct. 1975); see note 3, *supra*.

19. 68 *N.J.* 209, 343 *A*.2d 737 (Sup. Ct. 1975).

20. *N.J. Ct.* R. 4:74-7; see generally, Pressler, *Current N.J. Court Rules, Comment to* R. 4:74-7 (1984), at 918:

A general revision of the rule was clearly required in order to correct a long standard history of procedural abuses in the civil commitment process and to insure that no person may be involuntarily committed to a psychiatric institution without having been afforded full procedural due process. The adoption of this rule reflects an increasing national and state-wide concern for the situation of persons suffering from mental illness who have been involuntarily committed on ex parte orders entered without representation of counsel, without adequate notice, without adequate proofs, and generally in violation of the most fundamental concepts of due process.

21. See Van Ness and Perlin, note 12, *supra*, at 67 n. 25. These figures are updated in Perlin, "Mental Patient Advocacy by a Patient Advocate," 54 *Psych. Q.*, 169, 171 (1982). (Through 1980, the percentage remained at 73.)

22. The system is described in *S.L.*, 94 *N.J.* at 131: "These patients, although technically 'discharged,' remain in mental hospitals until appropriate outside placements become available." The first DPP order was entered some two weeks after the court promulgated Administrative Order #4-74; see text accompanying note 16, *supra*. Order on file with the author.

23. 77 *N.J.* 282, 390 *A*.2d 574 (Sup. Ct. 1978).

24. *N.J. Supreme Court Administrative Memorandum on a Regionalized Mental Commitment Program* (July 28, 1978).

25. *Id*. at 2.

26. *In re S.L.*, Docket No. A-1734-80T1 (N.J. App. Div., 1981), brief of appellants at 24 (hereinafter "Appellants' Brief").

27. *S.L.*, 94 *N.J.* at 130.

28. *Id*. at 131–132; see *N.J. Ct. R.* 4:74-7(f).

29. *Id*. at 132. In the two remaining cases (involving patients who had never previously been designated as DPP), the court denied the patients' request for the classification, declaring it did not exist. *Id*.

30. "Appellants' Brief," note 27, *supra*, at 3–20.

31. *S.L.*, 94 *N.J.* at 130 n. 1.

32. "Appellants' Brief," note 26, *supra*, at 20.

33. *S.L.*, 94 *N.J.* at 132.

34. *Id*.

35. *Id*. at 131.

36. *Id*. at 133 n. 5 (citation omitted).

37. *Id*. at 133.

38. *Id*. Plaintiffs, represented by the Public Advocate, suggested the following procedural rules to govern the hearings:

(1) Such hearings shall be full inquiries into the questions of placement into an appropriate

facility which provides the patient with his right to treatment in the least restrictive alternative setting.

(2) Regularly, hospital staff workers, employees of the Bureau of Transportational Services within the Department of Human Services, members of the patient's families and/or friends, and employees of community agencies shall be asked to testify at such hearings as to the nature of the efforts by responsible parties to secure appropriate alternative placements.

(3) Inquiry shall be made of the patient in each case as to his placement desires. If a DPP patient indicates a preference to stay in the hospital as a voluntary patient, the court shall treat this request as if it were brought pursuant to that asspect of *R.* 4:74-7(j)(1) dealing with the summary reviews of voluntary status in juvenile matters. *Cf., In re Williams*, 140 N.J. Super. 495 (Essex Cty. J. & D.R.Ct. 1976).

(4) DPP review hearings shall be scheduled every three months as long as a DPP patient remains hospitalized.

(5) The burden remains on the State and/or county to show by at least clear and convincing evidence (a) what alternatives are available, (b) what alternatives were investigated, and (c) why such investigated alternatives were not suitable.

(6) In weighing each case the court should consider at least the following factors: (a) the patient's clinical condition; (b) the length of the patient's stay in the hospital; (c) the potential of harm to the patient if he spends additional time in the hospital; (d) the type of facility to which release would be appropriate; (e) within the facilities described in (d), the range of available facilities; (f) the restrictions which would be imposed on the patient in each such facility; (g) the extent to which each such facility comports with the patient's expressed desires; and (h) the realistic opportunity the patient will ever have of being fully discharged from the facility in question.

(7) Following a DPP placement, the courts shall retain jurisdiction to review the continued appropriateness of such placement; such review shall be periodic and summary in nature, but, if the patient so requests, a full hearing as outlined in (1) through (6), above, will be held. *Id.* at 133–134 n. 7.

39. *Id.* at 134–135, and *Id.* at 134–137, nn. 7–8.

40. *Id.* at 136.

41. *Id.* at 136–137 (citations omitted).

42. *Id.* at 137.

43. *Id.* at 137–138, quoting *O'Connor*, 422 *U.S.* at 575–576 (citation omitted).

44. *Id.* at 138, citing, in part, N.J. Ct. R. 4:74-7(g).

45. *Id.* at 139.

46. *Id.* (footnote omitted, emphasis added).

47. *Id.* at 139–140 (emphasis added).

48. *Id.* at 140.

49. *Id.*

50. *Id.* at 140–142 (footnote omitted).

51. *Id.* at 143, and n. 11.

52. *Id.* at 141, n. 10.

53. 457 *U.S.* 307, 325 (1982).

54. See, *e.g., Matter of Commitment of B.R.*, 202 *N.J. Super.* 182, 494 *A.*2d 328 (App. Div. 1985) (*S.L.* applies to patients in need of mental retardation services); *Matter of B.H.*, 212 *N.J. Super.* 145, 514 *A.*2d 85 (Law Div. 1986) (summary revocation of conditional discharge violated patient's due process rights); *Matter of Commitment of S.D.*, 212 *N.J. Super.* 211, 514 *A.*2d 844 (App. Div. 1986) (application of *S.L.* to individual case); *In re G.M.*, 217 *N.J. Super.* 629, 526 *A.*2d 744 (Chancery Div. 1987) (court empowered to order judicial review of voluntary patient's status).

55. 61 *N.Y.*2d 525, 475 *N.Y.S.*2d 247 (Ct. App. 1984).

56. *Id.*

57. *Id.*, 475 *N.Y.S.* 2d at 251.

58. *Id.* at 253.

59. *Id.*, quoting *Matter of Kesselbrenner v. Anonymous, 33 N.Y.*2d 161, 168, 350 *N.Y.S.*2d 889 (Ct. App. 1973).

60. *Klostermann, supra.*

61. *Id.*, 475 *N.Y.S.* 2d at 255.

Index